Praise f
previously published as
FOCUSED AND FEARLESS

"*The Jhānas* is a wonderful book. Shaila Catherine describes the paths of deep concentration and transforming insight in a way that both inspires and enriches our practice. Her prose and her understanding are exceptionally lucid. This book is a treat to read."
—JOSEPH GOLDSTEIN, author of *One Dharma: The Emerging Western Buddhism*

"Shaila Catherine represents a new generation of Dharma practitioners in the West, with in-depth experience studying with some of the greatest masters of both the Theravadan and Tibetan Buddhist traditions. Her commitment to intensive practice has been matched by her dedication to study, and her exploration of the practice of concentration and jhānas reflects both these strengths."
—SHARON SALZBERG, Insight Meditation Society cofounder and author of *Lovingkindness: The Revolutionary Art of Happiness*

"I love Shaila's book. Her descriptions of deep jhānic states are imbued with her own experience. As you read, you know she would never stretch the truth in order to be impressive, but there's some impressiveness that comes through almost in spite of itself. As a bonus, the connections she makes to the suttas make the Buddha's time seem much closer to our own, lit up with relevance and interest."
—LILA KATE WHEELER, Dharma teacher and author of *When Mountains Walked*

"This is the best jhāna book I've come across in English. *The Jhānas* is inspiring, practically detailed, systematic, and well-grounded in the Pali sources."
—SANTIKARO, editor of *Heartwood of the Bodhi Tree*

"Among the many how-to books about Buddhist meditation, this book stands out for its deep commitment to the frames of reference developed in the Pāli Canon, specifically the role of concentration (both 'momentary concentration' in the insight path and the jhāna path) and its relationship to insight. With these frames, Catherine creates exercises and steps that develop calm meditative states and lead to liberating insight."
—MU SOENG, author of *The Heart of the Universe*

"Shaila Catherine penetrates the mysterious world of jhāna practice with rigorous investigation and lucid explanations. Her book's strength lies in that she knows the territory intimately and teaches from her own experience. The author has deeply devoted her life to awakening through meditation, and her confidence and wisdom ring true throughout the whole book."
—DIANA WINSTON, author of *The Little Book of Being* and Director of Mindfulness Education at UCLA

"This book is both scholarly and personal. It describes the terrain of intensely concentrated mental states and the dedication required for their cultivation in language that is so alluring and thorough that readers will, I am certain, be inspired to redouble their zeal for practice."
—SYLVIA BOORSTEIN, author of *Pay Attention, for Goodness' Sake: The Buddhist Path of Kindness*

"Developing a stable and undistracted mind is essential to most forms of meditation. This book will be of interest to anyone, regardless of their style of practice, wishing to incorporate the deeper stages of concentration of jhāna into their meditation."
—*Inquiring Mind*

THE JHĀNAS

A Practical Guide to Deep Meditative States

SHAILA CATHERINE

Wisdom Publications
132 Perry Street
New York, NY 10014 USA
wisdomexperience.org

First published in 2008 as *Focused and Fearless: A Meditator's Guide to States of Deep Joy, Calm, and Clarity*.

Library of Congress Cataloging-in-Publication Data for the first edition is as follows:
Catherine, Shaila.
  Focused and fearless : a meditator's guide to states of deep joy, calm, and clarity / Shaila Catherine.
    p. cm.
Includes bibliographical references and index.
ISBN 0-86171-560-8 (pbk. : alk. Paper)
1. Meditation—Buddhism. I. Title.
BQ5612.C38 2008
294.3'4435—dc22
            2008002694

ISBN 978-1-61429-946-2   ebook ISBN 978-1-61429-970-7

27 26 25 24
5 4 3 2 1

Cover design by Jess Morphew. Interior design by Tony Lulek.
Set in DGP 12.25/15.5.

Wisdom Publications' books are printed on acid-free paper and meet the guidelines for permanence and durability of the Production Guidelines for Book Longevity of the Council on Library Resources.

Printed in the United States of America.

MIX
Paper from
responsible sources
FSC
www.fsc.org   FSC® C005010

Please visit fscus.org.

Contents

INTRODUCTION

From Focused Concentration to Fearless Awakening

ESTING UNDER THE SHADE of a rose apple tree, the young Siddhartha Gotama (whom we would later come to know as the Buddha) spontaneously entered a state of deep concentration, satisfaction, and ease.[1] Much later, after he had studied intensively with two meditation masters and practiced extreme asceticism, he recalled that quiet moment in his youth and decided to cultivate those naturally pleasant states as the means to awakening. In so doing, he harnessed the potency of the unified mind and transformed a conventional practice of concentration into a catalyst for awakening, for enlightenment. Austere practices of self-mortification understandably lost favor as he taught his disciples to unlock the power of a happy mind.[2]

The development of intense concentration that leads to sublime states of mental absorption, known as *jhāna*, predated the Buddha—but because he was able to use it as a foundation for his enlightenment, it became a critical feature of his teachings. The practice of using jhāna as a basis for insight has been preserved to this day. In the discourses of the Pāli Canon, an early record of the Buddha's teaching, "concentration" appears repeatedly and is taught as a pivotal method for inner transformation.

In Pāli, *jhāna* literally means "to think" or "to meditate." Consequently, the term is open to a wide variety of uses and interpretations and there has been much debate about its precise meaning. In this book, *jhāna* practice refers to a traditional sequence of specific states of absorption in which the mind is secluded from sensory impingement and deeply unified with a chosen object. Attention is neither distracted by stray thoughts nor affected by the flutter of moods. Even physical sensations and sounds eventually fade as the mind becomes entirely immersed in a single coherent focus.

Jhānas are states of happiness that can radically transform the heart, reshape the mind, imbue consciousness with enduring joy and ease, and provide an inner resource of tranquility that surpasses any conceivable sensory pleasure. Jhānas are states of deep rest, healing rejuvenation, and profound comfort that create a stable platform for transformative insight. In this approach to jhāna, we use the calming aspects of concentration to support the investigative aspects of insight meditation. The fruit of concentration is freedom of heart and mind.

This book will teach you about and guide you through the traditional sequence of eight levels of meditative absorption that constitute jhāna practice—though it will focus in detail on only four. While jhāna is a powerful practice not intended for the dilettante, diligent beginners will benefit from the stability and strength afforded by deep concentration, and seasoned meditators will find in jhāna practice a potent method for intensifying insight.

Although the notion of mastering sequential stages of deep concentration may appear daunting at first, the jhāna system is easy to follow and surprisingly simple. Traditionally this practice was not reserved for special people, nor was it restricted to the monastic order. In the Buddha's time, lay disciples and busy merchants would, from time to time, enjoy the benefits and joys of abiding in jhāna.[3] These eight levels of concentration remain accessible to contemporary practitioners who can dedicate sufficient time for retreat, remain ethically clear, and apply balanced effort. Although I've included many teachings useful to beginners, a working knowledge of one's own mind and some facility with mindfulness practices are assumed as prerequisites to the serious undertaking of jhāna practice. Nonetheless, I will review mindfulness practice and how it is used to avoid common pitfalls in jhāna practice.

This book emerged from my experiences during a ten-month silent retreat focused on the cultivation of jhāna as the basis for insight. Although I had more than twenty years of meditation experience, until this retreat I had not systematically used these refined levels of consciousness to develop insight. The methodical techniques of establishing access to jhāna, strengthening and sustaining each level of absorption, and then applying the concentrated mind for insight had a powerful effect on my consciousness: it opened me to an experience of unremitting happiness, dramatically reduced the lure of sensual pleasures, and strengthened confidence and equanimity. When I emerged from retreat and shared some of my experiences with friends, I realized that the attainments and insights gleaned from this retreat described a clear path of concentration and wisdom. I want to offer serious practitioners this method for developing the mind and attaining unwavering clarity.

Through reading this book, some seasoned meditators will discover that they have already experienced some jhāna factors (rapture, happiness, and equanimity, for instance) while engaged in other meditation practices. Indeed, states of extreme happiness characteristic of jhāna naturally arise during many intensive meditation experiences. However, cultivating and harnessing them as the basis for insight is a technique unto itself, quite beyond the random "slipping into jhāna" that long-term meditators often describe. *The Jhānas* can serve as a manual for contemporary practitioners who are prepared to cultivate jhāna as an expression of the stable mind and use that concentration to deepen insight.

When the Buddha was asked, "Why are some people liberated and others not?" he did not say that the most concentrated meditators attain liberation. He replied, "Whosoever clings to the objects perceived by the senses cannot gain liberation. Whosoever stops clinging will be liberated."[4] Liberation through non-clinging is the core of the Buddha's teaching. The human propensity to cling is the problem; meditation is designed to solve it. Working in tandem, the twin practices of concentration and insight create conditions remarkably conducive to awakening.

Some readers may find variances in method and emphasis from teachings received from other teachers. Many approaches have developed over the centuries, each based on an individual teacher's understanding of the ancient texts and how those understandings manifest through his or her own meditation practice. If you would like to authentically experience jhāna, you will probably need time in silent retreat under the guidance of teachers. A book can provide a map of the terrain, describe the required skills, and indicate signposts along the path, but there is no substitute for diligent practice and the guidance of skilled teachers.

This book is an introductory guide, not a definitive or exhaustive study. Many exercises and reflections are interspersed throughout. Please try them, even if they slow the pace of your reading. Merely reading exercises will neither develop meditation skills nor produce the profound experience of concentration. I encourage you to, at times, set the book down, close your eyes, and collect the mind in silence. If you do, these practices will contribute to a living ease and an undistracted presence—with or without the attainment of jhāna levels of absorption. But do bear in mind that the cultivation of serenity and wisdom can't be rushed. Please give it the time to work. Don't grow impatient if you don't understand it completely at first. Certain principles are repeated throughout the book and are refined as the practice progresses.

This book systematically explores the framework of eight classical states of unified consciousness: the four primary jhānas and the four formless realms. It gives instruction on accessing these states, discerning their qualities, and using each as the basis for wisdom. While its thrust is cultivating the deep concentration of jhāna, the development of right concentration in the Buddhist tradition must always be intertwined with wisdom. Undertaking jhāna practice without the framework of wisdom would be pointless at best—and also contains the danger of reinforcing attachment to the pleasures of jhāna. Accordingly, I have included wisdom teachings on developing mindfulness, practicing non-clinging, applying skillful effort, setting intentions, overcoming habitual thoughts, recognizing emotions, learning to let go, and understanding the aim of the spiritual life. These wisdom teachings will anchor the reader's cultivation of concentration to a liberating path.

Additionally, practitioners should be aware that ethical conduct is a necessary condition for developing right concentration. Although this book does not explore in detail the cultivation of morality and right action, practitioners who aspire to attain jhāna should first develop a high degree of purity in ordinary activities.

Mental stability is essential for this training. The use of mind-altering drugs, including legal plant-based hallucinogenic substances, is antithetical to the development of jhāna. A healthy mind is a rare and precious thing in this world—do not take casual risks with the stability of your mind. If you are serious about undertaking the practice of jhāna, it is critical to cease the use of mind-altering substances and develop skills in renunciation, right effort, right intention, and right concentration that will support the refinement of the higher mind.

Some people are attracted to jhāna practice as a route to dramatic blissful spiritual experiences, and wrongly confuse meditative attainments with drug experiences. They do not know what an actual jhāna state is and therefore conflate meditative altered states of consciousness with drug induced psychedelic trips, out-of-body experiences produced by extreme physical or breath exercises, or unity experiences that occur through orgasmic sexual encounters. Please understand that physical and drug-induced activities do not lead to jhāna. Inducing altered-state experiences through the use of chemical or organic substances, intense physical exercises, or ritual ceremonies is incompatible with this path of meditative training.

If you are still enchanted with the possibility that drugs might open the door to spiritual experiences more quickly than traditional practices, please be aware of some characteristics of jhāna that would strongly distinguish it from psychedelic states:

1. profound inner calmness and the absence of craving for tantalizing experiences;
2. continuous mindfulness of one's meditation object;
3. balanced effort, discipline, and an inclination toward renunciation;
4. clear attention that is maintained without mental wandering or associative mental activity;
5. fitness and flexibility of mind that responds to intention and sustains focus without being influenced by sounds, distracting thoughts, or sensual stimuli;
6. sustained absence of unwholesome states such as fear, anger, remorse, sensual desire, stories of self, memories, images, thoughts, narratives, dullness, agitation, restlessness, and all hindrances and unwholesome states;
7. conscious control over the meditative perception that remains stable throughout the absorption; and
8. the ability and skill to enter and exit the states of jhāna at will.

These abilities and experiences develop naturally with the practices of concentration that are taught in this book and will serve the meditator long after the meditative session has ended.

⁓

This book contains five sections. The first, "The Joy of the Focused Mind," positions the practice of jhāna as training in relinquishment and an exploration of happiness. The second, "Preparing the Mind for Absorption," addresses themes necessary for preparing the mind to enter jhāna. The third, "How to Establish Meditative Absorption," contains instructions for the four primary levels of jhāna. The fourth, "Doing the Work of Insight," explores the wisdom that arises when using jhāna as the basis for insight. The fifth, "Experiencing the Formless Dimensions," examines the four formless realms as an experiential investigation of emptiness. The Epilogue discusses the significant role jhāna can play in living a fearless, awakened life.

> May readers discover deep peace within their hearts
> and bring lasting peace into our world.
> May this book contribute
> to the liberation of all beings.

PART I

THE JOY OF THE FOCUSED MIND

CHAPTER 1

Cultivating the Focused Mind

As a stone mountain, one solid mass, is not stirred by the wind, so no
forms and tastes, sounds, odors, and tactile objects, and phenomena
desirable or undesirable stir the stable one's mind. His mind is steady
and freed, and he observes its vanishing.
—Aṅguttara Nikāya 6:55

CONCENTRATION IS a central feature of a contemplative life. It can be cultivated through formal meditation practice as well as seemingly mundane daily activities. Concentration brings with it a natural joy that arises as the mind settles and is free from distraction. A surgeon may love surgery not because the operating room is a pleasant place to be but because the task demands such complete attention that the mind is filled with the delight associated with concentration. Kayakers are often enveloped in rapture even though their bodies are cramped in little boats and splashed by frigid water. A concentrated mind is focused, unified, and stable, regardless of whether the conditions are uncomfortable or luxurious.

In the Pāli language of the early Buddhist scriptures, *samādhi* is the term that has most often been translated into English as "concentration," yet samādhi describes something more than the narrow focus implied by "concentration." It is a calm unification that occurs when the mind is profoundly undistracted. Samādhi is the beautiful state of an undistracted mind, described in the Pāli texts as "peaceful and sublime, gained by full tranquilization, and attained to unification."[5] These four qualities indicate that samādhi is not merely focused on a single object. It is a state of profound serenity that encompasses a balanced, joyful composure, expressing the natural settledness of undistracted awareness.

The Buddhist tradition discusses three levels of samādhi:

- the samādhi of momentary concentration
- the samādhi that grants access to the jhānas
- the samādhi of absorption into the jhānas

Each of these levels is a deeply undistracted state of consciousness, and any of the three can be the support for liberating wisdom. The momentum of clear and sustained attention brings calm to the mind as that continuity of attention simultaneously restricts energy that might nourish unwholesome or distracting mental states.

Don't worry if, right now, you feel far away from these beautiful calm states. Most people need to bolster their intention and practice diligently to develop the inner conditions for samādhi. All of this can come with time and practice, and this book is the first step to helping you cultivate them.

THE SAMĀDHI OF MOMENTARY CONCENTRATION

Buddhist disciplines distinguish between the quality of samādhi developed through a continuity of mindfulness of changing perceptions and the quality of samādhi developed with a fixed focus.

When the breath is used to develop mindfulness, emphasis is placed on clear perception of changing sensations through the full duration of an inhale and exhale. With tremendous precision, the meditator experiences a multitude of fleeting sensations: tingles, vibrations, pressure, heat, for instance. Pressure may increase or decrease. Pulsing may vary in rhythm. The intensity of heat or cold may fluctuate. This meticulous sensitivity to physical variations brings the mind to a state of exquisite clarity that allows you to see the impermanent and empty nature of phenomena and witness the relationship between the mind and body. You can observe how sights and smells can trigger vivid memories, how intentions affect physical movements, and how emotions manifest in the body.

As the momentum of mindfulness increases, concentration correspondingly strengthens. The concentration that develops through a continuity of mindfulness with changing objects is called "momentary concentration." The mind momentarily collects, but then it disperses as the flow of sensory experiences ebbs and alters. Thinking can arise, but the thoughts do not diminish the concentrated state. Mindfulness inhibits proliferations of thought because it immediately meets the experience of thinking. The content of thought relates only to the phenomena at hand.

Before samādhi is established, thoughts may multiply through cognitive associations. A personal story is fabricated out of simple sensory triggers. For example, what begins as the simple sight of a stain on my shirt could proliferate into a rapid train of thoughts: plans for how to wash it, reflections on the last meal that might have caused the stain, embarrassed recollections of who I encountered since my last meal, speculations about what those people might think of me, fabrication of excuses for the stain, and on and on.

In contrast to this proliferating tendency, when mindfulness is present we apprehend the thought quickly. For example, I arrived on my last retreat quite tired and slept through the early morning meditation on the first day. As I sipped some tea after breakfast, my mind was active: sustaining the story of how tired I was, creating the identity of a busy person, justifying my extra hour of sleep because of all the important things I was doing in the previous days.

Between sips of tea I became aware that this story was activating restlessness. I reviewed my physical condition and noticed that I was not actually tired. The only thing that seemed to be sustaining tiredness was a perverse identification with the story of exhaustion. As I became aware of the experience of thinking, the story of being tired dissolved. Attention settled easily in the present-moment experience of feeling the cup in my hand, hearing the sounds of activity that surrounded me, and sensing my body and breath.

Ajahn Chah, a master in the Thai Forest Tradition, compared momentary concentration to taking a walk, resting, walking, and resting. The journey is periodically interrupted with the arising of a thought, yet undisturbed, because in a short time the journey is continued. Developed through a continuity of mindfulness, momentary concentration can grow very strong and bring the mind through stages of intense happiness that culminate in wisdom. Although momentary samādhi is not the focus of this book, it is a valid expression of concentration worthy of respect—and extraordinarily useful for insight.

I assume most readers who have done mindfulness practice are familiar with this quality of concentration or can learn about it through the ample literature available on mindfulness practices. Therefore, I have narrowed the scope of this book to the sequential development of samādhi with a fixed object for attention, as demonstrated in the next two types of samādhi. The purity of mind produced at the threshold to absorption is called "access to jhāna" and complete absorption is called "jhāna."

ACCESS TO JHĀNA

To attain the stage of access to jhāna, you won't highlight the changing nature of experience. The basic *occurrence of breath* will be the object for attention rather than the dynamic flow of changing sensations. As concentration develops, the physicality of changing sensations becomes less dominant, and the breath becomes known as a mental object. For some practitioners, the mental sign of breath manifests as the occurrence of bright light in awareness or as a distinctive stability of awareness. Each practitioner will discover how this shift in consciousness is perceived, and experiences will vary. As samādhi deepens, the mind gradually withdraws from its orientation to the sensory world.

Sensory orientation is, of course, a deeply ingrained aspect of the healthy functioning of perception. It plays a valuable role in the survival of animals, the development of children, and the structure of social organizations—to name but a few broad areas. However, the critical refinement that sets the stage for the possibility of absorption into jhāna and marks these states of concentration as "altered states" occurs as consciousness withdraws its dependence on sensory perception.

Ajahn Chah compared *access to jhāna* to wandering about inside your own home. Consciousness is at ease within the confines of a comfortable arena of perceptions. Attention does not move away from the meditation object. Thinking may still arise, but it circles closely around the meditative experience. Light and wispy thoughts might arise, perhaps as reflections on the meditation process, yet this mental activity does not disturb a calm tranquility that pervades the mind. A strong and fundamental purity has been achieved, yet there is still a subtle restlessness that inhibits the depth of stillness required for absorption.

Although there is nothing wrong with thoughts that regulate the meditation experience—such as the desire to calm obsessive thinking and the intention to return to the breath—greater rest and concentration can be attained by cultivating further stillness. As attention continues to settle, an opportunity for absorption (entering the next level of samādhi) may arise.

ABSORPTION INTO JHĀNA STATES

When the mind abandons its contact with the senses, including dis-cursive thinking, the concentrated absorption of jhāna begins. The mind is utterly still and focused on its object. The specific object of focus becomes progressively refined in the development of concen-tration. Coarse physical sensations that are the consequence of the movement of breathing give way to a mental sign of breath. This mental sign is often perceived as luminosity in the mind. Rapture, pleasure, and equanimity may accompany the bright, radiant mind, while attention is continually directed toward the place where the breath is known. As these perceptions grow increasingly subtle, attention remains connected, and the subtle perception of breath is recognized as a perception of stable brightness in the mind.

In jhāna, attention is virtually merged into its object, creating an impression of complete unification. Even if sounds happen nearby or if pressure impinges on the meditator's body, the mind remains completely unmoved. Sensory contact—even strong pain or loud noise—does not disturb the tranquility or affect the unification of the mind with its object of concentration. It is as though you don't hear anything, yet the capacity of hearing is not impaired. It is as if you don't feel physical sensations, yet the bodily processes are func-tioning. Because the mind is so still that even pain will not disrupt the attention, jhāna can be sustained for very long periods of time. Although this depth of detachment is often challenging to attain, once seclusion is established the sequential development through the stages of jhāna unfolds rather effortlessly.

The standard formula repeatedly presented in the discourses of the Buddha describes concentration through the development of four primary levels of jhāna:

> And what, bhikkhus, is the faculty of concentration? Here, bhikkhus, the noble disciple gains concentration,

gains one-pointedness of mind, having made release the object. Secluded from sensual pleasures, secluded from unwholesome states, he enters and dwells in the first jhāna, which is accompanied by thought and examination, with rapture and happiness born of seclusion. With the subsiding of thought and examination, he enters and dwells in the second jhāna, which has internal confidence and unification of mind, is without thought and examination, and has rapture and happiness born of concentration. With the fading away as well of rapture, he dwells equanimous and, mindful and clearly comprehending, he experiences happiness with the body; he enters and dwells in the third jhāna of which the noble ones declare: "He is equanimous, mindful, one who dwells happily." With the abandoning of pleasure and pain, and with the previous passing away of joy and displeasure, he enters and dwells in the fourth jhāna, which is neither painful nor pleasant and includes the purification of mindfulness by equanimity. This is called the faculty of concentration.[6]

Developing this faculty requires appreciation both of the power of seclusion and of forms of happiness that go beyond sensory gratification. The next two chapters explore these elements that are so vital to bringing about jhāna.

ᕗ *The Foundational Practice: Developing Access Concentration*

This initial approach to concentration meditation forms the basis of jhāna practice. Though deceptively simple, it leads to profound focus and transformative insight when practiced daily. The many exercises and reflections interspersed throughout this book build upon the primary technique of developing concentration through careful attention to the breath.

For concentration meditation, we establish a very simple task: we choose one object and maintain concentration on that. The method I teach uses the breath as the focus for attention. We give ourselves the initial task of observing the breath as it enters and exits at the nostrils. Narrowing the focus to a single object discards many of the stray thoughts that occupy and divert precious mental energy. The simple practice of repeatedly bringing attention to the breath and letting it rest there forms the basis of this meditation. Here are some basic instructions:

Sit in a comfortable posture. Feel how the body is sitting. Feel the contact with the chair. Gently bring attention to the breath. First feel the whole breath and notice how the chest and abdomen expand and contract. Then direct attention to the sensation of the contact with breath in the area of the nostrils or upper lip. It can be useful to begin by observing the sensations of breathing and practice letting the body breathe naturally. Do not alter or manipulate the breath. Simply become mindful of the experience of breathing as it happens now. Observe continuously from the very beginning of the inhalation, through the middle, and to the end of each in-breath and each out-breath.

To establish mindfulness with breathing you may initially perceive sensations with each inhalation and exhalation. Observing the physical expression of the breath at the beginning of the meditation can help you to direct attention to breath and dispel distractions. Do not, however, enhance the physical qualities or engage in a detailed examination of changing sensations. Your meditation object will be a refined recognition of the basic occurrence of breath, not the flow of tangible sensations.

At some point in the meditation, you may stop feeling physical sensations—this is fine. You may discover that you can direct attention to breath without the coarse support of sensation. Steadily direct attention to where breath occurs, in the general area of the nostrils. If your mind remains dependent on sensations even after most hindrances have faded away, then try directing your attention to breath just off the body; aim your attention a couple of inches in front of the nostrils. Without relying on tangible qualities, collect and settle attention in this place where breath occurs.

If your attention drifts off into thoughts, bring it gently back to the breath. The mind will probably stray many times. When the mind is lost in thought and mindfulness is weak or absent, the conditions are not present to choose alertness. When you wake up to the bare fact that thinking has subsumed the attention, you can redirect your attention to breath in the area of the nostrils or upper lip. Without judging your capacity to meditate, without criticizing how you breathe, return to the perception of breath as simply and directly as possible. Attention is not strengthened by harshly riveting attention to the breath with super glue or hammering it into the nostrils with nails. Attention becomes unwavering by the consistent willingness to gently begin again.

With this exercise you are cultivating your capacity to let go of distractions and strengthening your ability to direct attention. It diminishes habits of distraction and cultivates a peaceful and calm awareness. As your mindfulness develops, the perception of the breath will become increasingly subtle. Your meditation object may gradually transform from coarse physical sensations related to breathing to a simple and steady mental knowing of breath.

Please set some time aside each day to do this fundamental meditation exercise. I recommend twenty to sixty minutes a day as the general guideline for a committed daily practice; however, it is fine to adjust the time as your lifestyle and interest allow. A daily practice of any length can bring great fruits in concentration and wisdom.

⟿ *Counting the Breath*

Counting breaths is a simple technique for sustaining focused attention on the breath. As you direct your attention to the experience of breath at the nostrils, add a count in the pause between breaths. Breathe in, breathe out, count 1; breathe in, breathe out, count 2; breathe in, breathe out, count 3. Count the breaths from one to ten, then from ten to one, then from one to ten. Limiting the number to ten reduces the tendency to try to accomplish something. Several rounds can help focus the attention on the simple activity of breathing.

This exercise strengthens your ability to direct and sustain attention. Keep the focus of attention on the breath; do not give excessive attention to the conceptual number. The number should be soft, like a gentle whisper in the mind; the breath remains your primary interest. If mindfulness weakens, you might experience a dull state while continuing to automatically count and find yourself counting to 11, 12, or 13. You can work to counteract this weakness by sustaining a vivid interest in each individual breath.

ᖇ Additional Tools

Mindful Movement: Gentle stretching, mindful walking, or mindful movement can enhance the calmness and composure of mind. Physical expressions of composure through posture and movement support inner unification. Although gross movements can certainly be performed mindlessly—as many people walk daily from their cars to their offices without conscious awareness of their surroundings, footsteps, or breath—the discipline of mindful movement cultivates concentrated attention by coordinating gestures of the body with the awareness of the inhale and exhale; the flow of feeling, energy, and balance; and sometimes visualizations. Different people tend to prefer different styles of mindful movement, so rather than recommend a single approach I suggest incorporating some movement imbued with awareness into your daily practice. It could be a structured discipline like yoga, tai chi, qi gong, line dance, or swimming. It could also be something less structured, such as walking your dog with the intention of being fully aware. The key is to feel yourself moving in space and to remain composed and mindful during the course of an activity. Bring calm attention to the sensations of the dynamic body.

Count Your Steps: If you want more structure for cultivating concentration while you take a walk, you can count
your steps. Count from 1–10, then 1–9, 1–8, and so forth,
until you get to 1–1. Then, repeat the process in ascending order: 1–1, 1–2, 1–3, 1–4 . . . 1–10. There is no value in
attaining a big number. No one really cares how many steps
it takes to walk around your block. But the counting gives
the mind something to do, keeping it out of trouble, supporting the spirit of concentration. You can try counting
for some time and then let the numbers go and rest with
direct awareness of walking. Counting focuses attention,
but if we obsessively or continuously count then the added
numerical concepts can eventually distract us from the viv-
idness of present-moment awareness.

CHAPTER 2
The Joy of Seclusion

He resorts to a secluded lodging: the forest, the root of a tree,
a mountain, a ravine, a hillside cave, a charnel ground,
a jungle thicket, an open space, a heap of straw.
—Aṅguttara Nikāya 10:99

THE BUDDHA DESCRIBED the transition from ordinary consciousness to the altered state of jhāna thus: "Secluded from sensory pleasures, secluded from unwholesome states, one enters and abides in the first jhāna."[7] This chapter explores the search for seclusion through removing distractions and training the mind. It also considers the deeper implication of solitude as an awakening beyond separation.

First let it be said that "seclusion" does not imply repression or denial; it is not a state of alienation, loneliness, or division. The seclusion that supports a meditation practice is rooted in wisdom and clarity. Knowing what leads to suffering, you wisely choose a path that leads to happiness. The Buddha addressed this point quite simply:

If, by giving up a lesser happiness,
One could experience greater happiness,

A wise person would renounce the lesser
To behold the greater.[8]

Sparked by this basic instinct toward happiness, we follow the trajectory of training that will eventually carry us beyond conceivable delights.

The Buddhist teachings describe three kinds of seclusion: (1) physical aloneness that is experienced as we remove ourselves from complex social dynamics; (2) mental seclusion that describes the aloofness of the mind while it is absorbed in jhāna, marking a separation from unwholesome states and sensory pleasures; and (3) liberation as detachment from the root causes of suffering. The combination of these three types of seclusion calms the mind and suspends conceptual proliferations.[9]

THE SECLUSION OF BEING ALONE

Physical solitude creates a temporary separation from the distractions and activities that fill daily life. The Buddha suggested, "A bhikkhu resorts to a secluded resting place: the forest, the root of a tree, a mountain, a ravine, a hillside cave, a charnel ground, a jungle thicket, an open space, a heap of straw."[10] We could expand that list to include the modern options of formal retreat centers or a quiet corner in your home that you use for daily meditation practice.

At the rudimentary level, this detachment may be likened to a spiritual vacation. A retreat may be for any length of time, from a single day of silence to many years. It can be a relief to take time away from the exaggerated responsibilities of your routine. Most people need some degree of periodic solitude to learn to calm the anxious heart and quiet the distracted mind. Alternating time for retreat with time fully engaged with career, family, and social concerns makes for a balanced approach to the lay lifestyle. Silence supports depth in meditation, but it is through our social interactions that our understanding matures and is tested. The Buddha's life is an exemplary model for balancing seclusion with compassionate engagement with society. There were periods in his ministry when he remained aloof from his disciples and periods when he taught, led, and served the community.

I have a deep love for silence. It has been an indispensable asset on my own path of inner discovery. At the age of sixty, I have spent approximately nine years in silence. Not everyone will need to or have the opportunity to undertake extended retreats, and concentration can still be developed in active social settings—but spiritual satisfaction is something you must discover alone. You might stay in a monastery, reserve a room at a retreat center, go camping in the mountains, sit in a city park, or abide comfortably in a quiet room in your own home. The place does not matter, although retreat centers offer the advantage of skilled teachers and safe conditions for settling the mind.

Unable to imagine the exquisite joy that arises from a quiet mind, many people presume a silent retreat would be boring, but when you enter retreat you leave behind your array of projects, distractions, and entertainments. You can allow the mind to unwind in a secluded shelter without the need to defend your safety or maintain your social roles. When you can arrange for a spiritual retreat, it is important to make the most of it by putting your worldly affairs in order before entering the silence. Don't bring entertainments with you. Give your mind a real vacation from your daily life routines. Let silence reveal a depth of knowledge that is usually unseen in the rapid swirl of daily personal achievements.

Concentration states benefit from the protected conditions of a retreat. Even in ideal circumstances, however, these states are, like all things, impermanent—and they dissipate after the retreat. Even so, insights stemming from the purity of concentration remain accessible long after the retreat has ended. Concentration does not need to be permanent to be important.[11] In the transition back to your ordinary routine, worldly activities may seem to be moving ridiculously fast. This period of adjustment poses no serious threat. As you ease back into your routine responsibilities, you may find that your ability to be steady and present with daily events has improved and that the wisdom gleaned through your meditation practice informs your life.

⌒ *For Reflection*

How do you fill the space in your life? Do you preserve space for solitude, or is it squeezed out by compulsive busyness, obsession with email and text messages, or trivial errands? Is it easy or difficult to be alone with yourself? Do you go from one relationship to the next, or is there space between relationships when you are content alone? How densely have you organized your life? If you were to describe how you spend your days, would your life sound like a schedule or a life you are happy to live?

Inspired by some early experiences in my meditation practice, I actively sought physical seclusion. At a small forest monastery in Chonburi Province, Thailand, I spent one retreat on a platform made of wooden planks. It had no walls, but was partially covered by a grass roof. My intention was, simply, to meditate there, alone. I did not leave the platform except briefly for the single daily meal, toilet, and a bath at a nearby stream. I wanted to allow the meditation practice to flow unrestricted by schedules and social conventions. I quickly discovered that I was never actually alone. I shared that simple platform with two snakes, the wind, birds, bugs, and the universe. The moon visited at night, the rain freely blew through, and the air was filled with flying and floating creatures. I lived among a natural community of friends.

Young and not yet understanding the deeper meanings of solitude, I sought greater seclusion in a cave in Krabi District, Thailand. The only entrance was through a tunnel that bent in such a way that no light penetrated. But even underground, in the total darkness of that cavern, life abounded. Bats cluttered the ceiling and a large white snake periodically appeared to feed on the bats. Sometimes local villagers entered with flashlights scavenging for bat droppings that are used as garden fertilizer. Even underground, I was not alone.

We may search for a quiet place to meditate, but complete physical seclusion is not necessary. Profound solitude involves more than renunciation of material possessions and withdrawal from sounds and society. It is a process that divests the heart of the habits and roles upon which personality relies. I have come to understand solitude as an experience of relationship, specifically our relationship to reality. Lovers of solitude value this relationship and give it attention. We devote time to meditate, time to listen to silence, time to breathe in the vastness of space that surrounds us, time to make friends with ourselves.

In a dialogue on solitude with a monk named Migajāla, the Buddha elaborated on the attributes of two types of meditators, one described as "a lone dweller," the other as "one dwelling with a partner." The Buddha explains:

> There are, Migajāla, forms cognizable by the eye that are desirable, lovely, agreeable, pleasing, sensually enticing, tantalizing. If a bhikkhu seeks delight in them, welcomes them, and remains holding to them, delight arises. When there is delight, there is infatuation. When there is infatuation, there is bondage. Bound by the fetter of delight, Migajāla, a bhikkhu is called one dwelling with a partner. . . .

Migajāla, even though a bhikkhu who dwells thus
resorts to forests and groves, to remote lodgings where
there are few sounds and little noise, desolate, hidden
from people, appropriate for seclusion, he is still called
one dwelling with a partner. For what reason? Because
craving is his partner, and he has not abandoned it; therefore he is called one dwelling with a partner.[12]

⌒ Is Craving Your Partner?

When you feel moved to go somewhere, get something, or
do something, ask yourself, "Is craving affecting my decision?" Craving may take the form of sensual desire that
moves toward the agreeable, or it may take the form of
aversion that moves away from the disagreeable.

When involved with repetitive thinking patterns, notice
how the mental stories are fueled by craving and attachment. Planning, hoping, dreaming, longing, and expecting
often involve craving. Notice craving whenever it appears.
Greet it—"Hello, craving!"—and consider if you want to
entertain craving as your partner.

The "lone dweller" is not the one who has found physical seclusion but rather is the one who has abandoned craving. Experiences
can be pleasing and agreeable. If you seek gratification through that
contact, infatuation will entrap consciousness and craving will be
your companion. From a meditative perspective, solitude is not
concerned with how many people populate your residence. Solitude is a contemplation of the question: What companions are we
housing within our minds? Solitude does not demand that other

people go away; rather, in solitude we consider what states we are entertaining within our own minds. Is craving the company we wish to keep? Physical solitude minimizes the complexities of social life. It is, however, only a first step.

THE SOLITUDE OF A QUIET MIND

You take your mind with you whether you are at the beach, on a hike in the forest, in a formal meditation retreat, or spending a quiet day in the garden. You may be sitting in a quiet place, but if your mind is agitated by judgmental thoughts, future plans, restlessness, or fantasy, you are not yet secluded for meditation. When I lived in India serving my teacher, H. W. L. Poonja, one student requested a private meeting with Poonjaji. The student said, "I want to see you alone before I leave." Poonjaji replied, "You are invited to see me alone. You come alone to me. Don't bring anyone with you, not your clothes, not your body, not your mind. Then you can see me alone."[13] He was not suggesting the student meet him without a shirt and pants but asking for a deeper level of relinquishment—a stripping away of the personality masks, social ranks, and self-image that habitually accompany us.

Do you ever stand that exposed, emptied of the facades of identity, without your roles, without identification with social status, utterly empty of concepts, not preoccupied with who you are and how you are perceived?

Inner solitude invites us to empty our minds of thoughts, reactions, and obstructive mental states like lust, aversion, restlessness, and doubt. Although the basic level of instruction for jhāna practice is to simply set distractions and hindrances aside, mindfulness and understanding are needed to set them aside skillfully. Frantically batting thoughts and difficult mental states away as unwelcome intrusions while trying to rush into jhāna won't work. If thoughts are pushed away without the support of wisdom, the mind may become agitated or be unprepared to respond wisely if similar thoughts reoccur. You need to investigate thoughts until their nature is unmistakably obvious. Then you will be able to sweep them aside easily, without denial or confusion.

It is imperative for the sincere meditator to unwaveringly witness the functions of desire, aversion, restlessness, and doubt, witness these forces arising—but without acting them out, without buying into them. See them arise as empty thoughts and see them pass just as quickly. If they are not seen clearly, these mental states can obstruct progress in concentration. Doubt can assail the mind with indecision, worry, or chronic judgment. Unabated, the momentum of uncertainty can paralyze spiritual progress. Yet doubt is nothing more than a thought. Through examining the experience of doubt, you will come to understand doubt, rather than be consumed by it. Doubt is a category of thought that you can definitively set aside. The very instant you realize that you are thinking, you have an opportunity to affect the patterns of mind. Thoughts of self can clutter attention with a plethora of diversified tales—preventing composure, stillness, and unification. Concentration abandons this diffusing activity. When you clearly perceive a thought, natural disinterest replaces identification with the stories. As the mind calms, mental seclusion is established.

In contrast to concentration practice, the strategy for insight meditation is to meet difficult mental states head-on and illuminate them with wisdom. In this way vipassanā practices are described as "practicing near suffering." By escorting the attention to meet the often painful conditions of body and mind, insight develops. On the other hand, when strengthening samādhi, disengage from obstructive energies quickly. Set the hindrances aside. Let them go. Clear a space in the mind. Don't give much attention to the hindrances, but instead preserve your energy for purifying the mind within the realm of happy wholesome states. Allow the joy that arises in the absence of hindrances to suffuse your mind. In this way jhāna practice is said to be "near to happiness." With the repeated dismissal of distractions, the mind settles, and the hindrances lose their charge until they eventually stop arising.

The secluded mind is separated from unwholesome states. This sets the stage for absorption. Hindrances are not permanently uprooted, but they are very remote. At this point you must be firm in your resolve. Intrusions on the seclusion could shatter the tenuous foundation of concentration. The gross struggles with obstructions that habitually siphon off our energy have been overcome. Now energy is recaptured and accumulated for samādhi. These conditions are prerequisites for jhāna.

⤳ Setting Thoughts Aside

It can be useful to develop a variety of methods for setting thoughts aside, like a meditator's tool kit.

One method is to "sweep thoughts into trash bins." One by one, observe each thought, and then imagine you can toss it into a bin, clearing the space of mind from the clutter of mental proliferation. Take a moment to look at the thought, know it, but then toss it aside.

Or imagine thoughts flying at you like baseballs. You catch each one and throw it back. Don't pocket it. Just look at it, know what it is, consider it for a moment, and toss it away. And if it comes back, do it again.

ULTIMATE SOLITUDE

The culmination of seclusion goes far beyond a quiet state of mind. The Buddha described true seclusion as an experience that is free from attachment. In a discussion with a monk named Elder, he said, "And how, Elder, is dwelling alone fulfilled in detail? Here, Elder, what lies in the past has been abandoned, what lies in the future has been relinquished, and desire and lust for present forms of individual existence has been thoroughly removed. It is in such a way, Elder, that dwelling alone is fulfilled in detail."[14] Thus, inner seclusion is a way of being that is freed from attachment to past, future, and even present perceptions. Consciousness ceases to take its stand on forms, feelings, perceptions, or thoughts. Nothing is taken up as a basis upon which to construct personal identity. This realization of the unfabricated nature of things brings the uncluttered mind to perfection. We don't just clear away physical and mental rubbish and then rest in that neat and tidy mental space. The very constituents of personality are exposed as utterly empty. There is nothing there to hold, and no one to do the holding. Nothing exists that would structure a relationship between assumed constructs of I and you, this and that, there and here, past and future.

Awakening is a realization that is utterly unshakable. What's more, it occurs to no one, requires no confirmation, and attains nothing. Such knowledge will transform your fundamental orientation in life. With no place to stop, ease is limitless, happiness is unbounded, and freedom is realized. In a famous verse, the Buddha says,

> Where water, earth, fire and wind have no footing,
> there the stars do not shine,
> the sun is not visible,
> the moon does not appear,
> darkness is not found.

> And when a sage, a worthy one, through wisdom
> has known this for himself,
> then from form and name,
> from pleasure and pain,
> he is freed.[15]

⬟ *Becoming Comfortable Alone*

Do you enjoy spending time alone? Can you calmly sit for a few hours in your own home or yard without pursuing entertaining distractions? Some people find that fear, anxiety, boredom, rumination, and sensual craving arise more strongly when alone. Try heightening your awareness of your own states of mind during normal solitary activities.

- Eat a meal alone in a public place without occupying yourself with reading or texting. Just eat alone and notice your experience. Does being alone trigger agitation, restlessness, or emotional discomfort? Are you enjoying being alone with yourself?
- Spend a day by yourself. What are you drawn to do? How does it feel to do each thing you decide to do? Try doing an extended task, such as gardening or housework by yourself, with no distractions from music, radio, or TV. And also spend some time simply resting back in a comfortable chair, quiet and watchful. What is your experience of being alone, both when you are active and when you are at rest? What kind of thoughts arise in your mind?
- You might enjoy one morning each month as a screen-free solitary period. From the time you wake up in the morning until mid-day, practice sitting and walking meditation, and engage in activities that do not involve phones, computers, TVs, other people, or pets. For example, repair a fence, bake a pie, wax your car, launder clothes, scrub stains out of a carpet. Watch your mind while you are doing ordinary activities.

Ultimately, solitude is the separation from suffering—not sensations, feelings, or perceptions. Physical and mental seclusion creates conditions conducive to deep investigation. The seclusion of jhāna is like learning to ride a bicycle with training wheels. The concentration states help you to stay balanced while you practice. Through the practice you let go in so many ways, until finally you ride without the crutch of those conditioned states. The Buddha described realization beyond the support of jhāna:

> There is that sphere of being where there is no earth, no water, no fire nor wind; no experience of infinity of space, of infinity of consciousness, of nothingness or even of neither-perception-nor-non-perception; there is there neither this world nor another world, neither moon nor sun; this sphere of being I call neither a coming nor a going nor a staying still, neither a dying nor a reappearance; it has no basis, no evolution and no support. It is the end of suffering.[16]

CHAPTER 3
Happiness

Whatever happiness is found in sensual pleasures,
And whatever there is of heavenly bliss—
These are not worth one sixteenth-part
Of the happiness that comes with craving's end.
—Udāna 2:2

EVERYONE WANTS TO BE happy and not suffer. We strive for pleasing and successful experiences. We avoid what is uncomfortable or unpleasant. Wanting to be happy in and of itself is not a problem. Problems arise when we limit happiness to the narrow scope of sensuality and personal comfort. The spiritual life introduces the possibility of deep joy independent of sensory pleasure.

At the heart of Buddhist teachings is the recognition of the four noble truths: to understand the fact of suffering; to abandon the craving that causes suffering; to realize the end of suffering; to cultivate the way leading to the end of suffering.

These teachings can make Buddhism appear to be a philosophy that emphasizes suffering. However, the Buddha realized these truths after he saturated his consciousness in the sublime happiness of jhāna. Happiness is the essential context for a liberating insight into the basic facts of discontent.

This chapter provides an overview of jhāna from the perspective of pleasure. Pleasure includes the common happiness of pleasant mental and physical experiences and also the sublime happiness associated with the subtle state of equanimity. Later chapters will give step-by-step instructions on how to attain each level of absorption with the unique qualities of pleasure inherent in each jhāna.

Images and stories of the Buddha portray him as a happy man who lived the simple life of a renunciate, delighted in the calm clarity of meditation practice, and led a thriving community of seekers toward awakening. He appears to have lived content and carefree, responding to his disciples with compassion that was sometimes tender and at other times sharp. The Buddha had a remarkable wit and on occasion taught profound subjects through humorous anecdotes and puns. Speaking in the common dialect, the Buddha stayed close to the hearts and humor of the people. The ancient discourses are riddled with jokes (often explained in the translator's notes, since wordplay is one of the primary modes in which the Buddha's humor is preserved).

As I teach from the discourses of the Buddha today, my students sometimes burst out laughing at the odd twists, brazen instructions, and amusing similes that permeate these ancient teachings. Interspersed with profound insights into the nature of suffering, the Buddha made jokes about such things as the name of the questioner. He displayed surprising humor regarding human foibles. He teased the disciple Malunkyaputta, who asked endless skeptical questions. He consoled the despairing Venerable Soṇa with similes of music.[17] He comforted the dullard Cula Panthaka when that monk stood weeping outside the monastery.[18] He tricked Nanda, who was struggling with lust, promising five hundred pink-footed nymphs.[19] He gladdened the hearts of merchants, soldiers, potters, farmers, kings, queens, and prostitutes alike. The Buddha urged, instructed, and cajoled his followers to awaken to the liberating truth of things. He was not, in any way at all, dour.

The community of disciples who practiced with the Buddha were also happy and cheerful. The association of Buddhism with suffering can make you think the disciples must have been a grim order of alienated renunciates, disaffected and discontent, who selfishly pursued extreme withdrawal from society for personal satisfaction. This was not at all the case. The ancient records of the Buddha's ministry describe a community that was amiable, dedicated, humorous, and happy. On one occasion, King Pasenadi of Kosala visited the Buddha. Seeing the joy and delight that pervaded the community, he praised the monastic sangha. The king observed, "Here I see bhikkhus smiling and cheerful, sincerely joyful, plainly delighting, their faculties fresh, living at ease, unruffled, subsisting on what others give, abiding with mind [as aloof] as a wild deer's."[20] The king attributed the cheerfulness of the monastics not only to a congenial social order but also to the depths of inner happiness available to those skilled in the attainments of jhāna.

When the Buddha recounted his own practice, he described joy independent of physical comfort and unshaken by the hardships of famine, illness, and verbal abuse—and beyond what can be experienced through the senses.[21] "There are two kinds of happiness: the kind to be pursued and the kind to be avoided," the Buddha said. "When I observed that in the pursuit of such happiness, unwholesome factors increased and wholesome factors decreased, then that happiness was to be avoided. When I observed that in the pursuit of such happiness, unwholesome factors decreased and wholesome ones increased, then that happiness was to be sought after."[22] The Buddha asks us: What pursuits lead to wholesome forces developing? And what pursuits lead to unwholesome forces thriving? The Buddha was a proponent of an efficient, long-term, sustainable approach to happiness, never settling for resigned acceptance of limited conventional comforts.

⤳ Dwelling with Joy

Choose a virtuous cause for joy that you experience some-
what regularly. It might be the discipline required to keep
the precepts, ordinary acts of compassion, a good deed, a
meditative attainment, a generous response, or a moment
of mindfulness or concentration. When joy arises based
on these virtues, allow your mind to dwell with that joy.
Let the experience of wholesome joy permeate your consciousness for some minutes. Then, later in the day, recall
the experience again, and if joy arises with the thought of
that virtuous deed, dwell with that joy for some minutes,
aware of wholesome joy. Reflecting on virtues, we allow the
mind to experience the power of beneficial pleasures that
will deepen our practice.

HIERARCHY OF HAPPINESS

The Buddha described a threefold hierarchy of happiness, classically
designated as *carnal happiness*, *spiritual happiness*, and *happiness that
is more spiritual than spiritual happiness*. Carnal happiness is based
upon the sensual pleasures derived from sights, sounds, odors, tastes,
touches, and even thoughts that are "desirable, lovely, agreeable, pleasing, sensually enticing, tantalizing."[23] Many of us live our lives knowing no other kind of happiness, but there is an even greater delight
than what the senses can offer. This higher pleasure is reflected in
states of rapture, joy, and equanimity, developed through concentration and clarified in jhāna. In the language of the discourses:

> There are these five cords of sensual pleasure. What five?
> Forms cognizable by the eye that are desirable, lovely,

agreeable, pleasing, sensually enticing, tantalizing. Sounds
cognizable by the ear . . . odors cognizable by the nose . . .
tastes cognizable by the tongue . . . tactile objects cognizable by the body that are desirable, lovely, agreeable,
pleasing, sensually enticing, tantalizing. These are the five
cords of sensual pleasure. The pleasure and joy that arise
in dependence on these five cords of sensual pleasure; this
is called sensual pleasure.

Though some may say, "This is the supreme pleasure
and joy that beings experience," I would not concede this
to them. Why is that? Because there is another kind of
happiness more excellent and sublime than that happiness. And what is that other kind of happiness? Here,
secluded from sensual pleasures, secluded from unwholesome states, one enters and dwells in the first jhāna.[24]

Jhāna offers an alternative for those willing to turn away from
the familiar obsession with sensory pleasure. Each level of jhāna is
characterized by sequentially more refined qualities of pleasure. A
direct experience of the higher happiness in jhāna states creates a
corresponding dispassion toward coarser pleasures. Instead of resist-
ing attraction to pleasure, the Buddha skillfully invoked the mind's
natural interest in happiness to realize a more stable happiness than
what sensual delights can offer. When something better is discovered, coarser pleasures lose appeal. My teacher, H. W. L. Poonja,
often said that once you know the taste of bees' fine honey, you will
not crave coarse brown sugar.

The Buddha did not stop his exploration of happiness with
the "spiritual happiness" of concentration states. His discovery
of happiness encompassed the joy that is intrinsic to awakening.
This unexcelled happiness manifests from the liberated mind that
is freed from attachment, attended by insight, and not restricted
to the temporary boundaries of concentrated states. The Buddha

➤ Mindful Presence to Taste

Try to be totally and precisely mindful of the experience of eating a brownie, a cookie, or something you really like. Resist the temptation to just wolf it down or, on the other hand, to savor it with indulgence.

Instead see what you might notice by eating it with complete awareness.

Take note of the changing qualities of pleasure, when it intensifies or diminishes. Observe the distinctions between a physical sensation of pleasant feeling, a thought of craving, or a commentary on the delights.

In the rush of daily life, we often miss the details of pleasure. Entranced by the conceptual notion of a "good" taste, we may not notice contrasts in color of the food against the backdrop of the ceramic plate, a slightly salty flavor stimulating the tongue, or the changing textures of crispy, crunchy, smooth, or gooey as the morsel turns over in our mouths.

To develop appreciation of pleasure with daily sensory experiences, extract the conceptual assumptions from the physical knowledge of pleasure.

Notice the interactions of mind and body in this intimate experience of a favorite taste. See what there is to learn.

described this unwavering happiness as being "more spiritual than the spiritual," more sublime than the temporary pleasures of either sensual pursuits or concentrated meditative attainments.

SENSUAL PLEASURE

The Buddha said of pleasures that "the happiness here is slight, giving little gratification; the suffering here is more; this is a hook."[25] Sensual pleasures are inherently brief, but they are not necessarily bad or immoral. Desire for sensual pleasure is simply not an effective strategy to find lasting happiness. Wherever there is attachment to sensual pleasures, there follows fear of unavoidable change.

It is important to explore your relationship to pleasurable activities. I often hear people say that they "love" doing something. Hiking, for example, may be a generally pleasant activity, but like any activity, it is not a reliable source of happiness. Is a walk on a forest path entirely pleasant? Will it remain pleasant if you continued to walk for nine hours or fourteen hours, in summer and winter, by day and by night? Some aspects are pleasant and some unpleasant.

Sexuality and love may be exquisitely pleasurable, but the intensity of sexual contact can shift rapidly between pleasure and pain. Sexual pleasure is not permanent. Every sensory experience is limited, conditional, and unreliable as a basis for happiness. To unhook the attachment to these fragile pleasures, bring mindfulness to your experience of pleasant events throughout your day. What occurs that sparks pleasure? How do you respond to it? Open yourself to pleasure, but resist adding the attachment that wants it to last.

THE HAPPINESS OF A CONCENTRATED MIND

We must stop searching for gratification through sensory experiences if we wish to attain the first jhāna. Most people have been conditioned since birth to look toward successful work, home life, and relationships as the strategy for attaining well-being and lasting happiness. Most people have also discovered that it has never actually worked to do that! Whatever success we have attained can quickly be lost. An achievement such as winning in an election, a

> ## ⌇ *Pleasure Seeking*
>
> Choose one or two activities in your daily life through which you often seek happiness. Notice the following:
>
> - How long does the pleasant feeling last?
> - What is the quality of the pleasure or happiness that you experience during the activity?
> - Does it lead to physical or mental pleasure?
> - Would you categorize it as worldly or spiritual happiness?
> - Is it based on virtue or defilement?
> - Does it lead to satisfaction, dissatisfaction, more craving, or loftier states of joy?
> - What is the cost or downside to the activity?
> - What are the limitations of this pleasure?
> - Is it a reliable basis for happiness?

tournament, or a competition brings only temporary success. At another time a different competitor will take the prize. The possessions we value can be lost. A cherished home can be destroyed by fire. Our lifestyle can be disrupted by war, famine, or violence. A tidy retirement fund can be eroded by medical costs. Anyone can die at any time. Seeing the vulnerability in this familiar cycle of craving, accumulation, change, and loss, a wise person looks elsewhere for happiness. It does *not* matter at this point whether you believe that there is a happiness higher than material success. It is enough to know what has not worked in the past. Take the risk of trying another way. Detach from what you already know will not bring you lasting happiness; this release sets the stage for deep concentration.

The Buddha instructed his disciples to not merely recognize a present-moment feeling, but to discern the genesis of the feeling.[26] For the deepening of concentration, it is useful to distinguish sensually based feelings from feelings that arise through spiritual practice. These would include the delight of non-remorse associated with virtue, the rapture that arises with concentration, the happiness that comes with wholesome states such as love and compassion, the contentment that comes with simplicity and renunciation, the equanimity of tranquil states, and the bliss of release. These feelings are not conditioned by lust, hate, or delusion; they are vital supports for the cultivation of concentration and insight. Invoking these states propels the spiritual journey beyond the conventional confines of sensual experiences.

Awareness practices usually develop mindfulness by giving attention to present-moment sensory experiences. The cultivation of jhāna takes a different approach. Mindfulness is required, but the locus of attention soon shifts from sensory phenomena to a refined mental object. The first stage of concentrating the mind involves turning attention away from the coarse stimulation of sense pleasures that can easily agitate and diffuse consciousness. This is the critical shift of orientation that makes access to the "pleasant abidings" of jhāna possible.

The Buddha described five qualitatively distinct feelings of happiness found within the progression of jhānas: happiness born of seclusion, happiness born of concentration, happiness associated with mindfulness and equanimity, the feeling of equanimity that is neither pleasant nor unpleasant, and the "peaceful abidings" characteristic of the formless spheres.

As absorption deepens, the mind is saturated with increasingly sublime delights. These satiate the mind as it lets go of gradually more subtle fixations. Detaching from the habitual allure of the domain of sensory pleasures prepares attention to find a deeper resource for happiness. Each jhāna state has certain characteristic features that distinguish the particular absorption, but the nuances of each are subjectively experienced by the individual practitioner. The intimate pleasures of jhāna present a risk of attachment that could stall a meditator's progress. Becoming overly impressed with a relatively minor degree of sublime rapture is the beginner's pitfall. When the mind is freed from the restrictions of physical pleasures and jhāna is attained, the potential for joy is virtually limitness.

HAPPINESS IN THE FOUR JHĀNAS

Absorption in the first jhāna frees the mind from unwholesome states and the impingement of sensuality. Just as there comes a time when continuing to chew a bite of brownie no longer is pleasant, there comes a point when you are no longer delighted to dwell in the happiness born of seclusion. You are ready to "swallow" the brownie and move on. It is no longer intriguing. Conviction will begin to grow that conditioned states, even pleasant jhāna states, are not reliable sources for happiness. Empowered by this understanding, the mind naturally withdraws from the pleasures distinctive of the first jhāna, curious to discover an abiding that is more subtle.

As consciousness unifies in the second jhāna, it is filled with joy, rapture, pleasure, and delight. The rapt interest of the second jhāna is described as "happiness that is born of concentration." Here, one's entire experience is drenched, filled, and infused with the ecstatic experience of joyous rapture. One can remain completely absorbed in the second jhāna, suffused with this delight, for as long as conducive conditions sustain it. Rapture may initially be felt as exciting, but infatuation with rapture will settle as the experience of concentration becomes calm and subtle. A concentrated mind will prefer quieter, less agitated states of pleasure. As dispassion toward rapture grows, the rapture characteristic of the second jhāna naturally fades. There is no need to rush through the experience or reject rapture and joy. Experience this delight with clarity; allow it to refresh attention. Let the joy support your concentration without becoming infatuated with it. At some point you will emerge from the second jhāna and then prepare to enter and abide in the third jhāna.

The third jhāna is characterized by happiness yet divested of delight. It possesses a sublime quality of happiness that is associated with mindfulness and equanimity. It is a calm and deep sense of contentment and peace suggested by the half smile that artists render on Buddha images. Those half smiles imply full acceptance and deep happiness, regardless of conditions. This third absorption provides a smooth resting place for the heart. One feels content with a mind that is unified with the meditation object (breath). In that absorption one does not seek thrills through the experience. In jhāna states, sensory experiences are not the focus; attention is thoroughly absorbed in the experience of knowing the meditation object. This produces a quality of happiness characteristic of the third jhāna: happiness due to mindfulness and equanimity.

Third jhāna can feel so sweet that you might wonder if you would ever honestly grow disenchanted by it. During one long retreat I was instructed to remain with the third jhāna until the sign of the fourth jhāna naturally arose—to endure as much pleasure and joy as the mind could tolerate until it naturally and genuinely threw off engagement with pleasure. I had no idea how long that would take!

The texture of consciousness was smooth, with contentment saturating not only the meditations but also the meals, walking, sleeping, showering, working, and so forth. One week passed, then two. I glided along on a creamy cloud of quiet joy, wondering if I could ever tire of this fantastic state. Sustained through the momentum of concentration and the protected conditions of retreat, absorption required virtually no effort to maintain. It was utter bliss. To my surprise, by the end of the third week there arose a clear sense that "this is enough."

Even this most sublime and peaceful joy was ultimately unsatisfactory. Genuine dispassion arose naturally, without the harsh imposition of renunciation tactics. Gentle saturation and natural relinquishment brought forth deep faith in the liberating force of concentration. In the wake of this realization the mind willingly released its engagement with the pleasure characteristic of the third jhāna. No longer enchanted, I found that pleasure fades to reveal the more peaceful neutral feeling of the fourth jhāna. This is an important transition. This recognition of the limitations of pleasure allows the mind to shed engagement with the whole spectrum of pleasure and pain.

The fourth jhāna is characterized by a deep stillness, complete focus, and equipoise. The shift can occur only when we are willing to let go of pleasure. This release is not disappointing. In the absence of obvious pleasure, there is nothing unpleasant. The mind settles and stops swinging between worldly dualities: from happiness to sadness, excitement to dullness. Still and quiet, consciousness abides undisturbed, beyond the range of pleasure and pain. The fourth jhāna has an exquisitely pervasive neutral feeling, but without a trace of blandness, described as the feeling of equanimity. Though it is an accentuated state of evenness, it is without the slightest implication of mediocrity.

Resting with equanimity, we have shed yet another layer of agitation. This is a deeply stable state, praised by the Buddha as a powerful platform for insight, spiritual powers, or absorption in the "peaceful abidings" of the formless perceptions.[27] With deep equanimity there is no agitation pulling consciousness toward one thing or away from another, no struggle, no resistance. The mind rests in a complete state of ease, cooled out, unperturbed, equanimous. The quality of equanimity is so profound and important that I will discuss it in more detail in the next chapter.

THE HAPPINESS OF A LIBERATED MIND

The Buddha took a broad approach to pleasure. His discussion of happiness often began with the common pursuits of sensual experiences. It developed through meditative concentration that includes jhānas imbued with rapture, happiness, and equanimity, and extended to the peaceful abidings of the formless perceptions. He also described a pleasure beyond the realm of conditioned experience: the happiness of a liberated mind. The Buddha declares that when he speaks of pleasure he "describes pleasure not only with reference to pleasant feeling; rather, friends, the Tathāgata describes as pleasure any kind of pleasure whenever and in whatever way it is found."[28] At each level of this development of happiness we abandon the gross for the subtle. This process of cultivating the finer happiness and letting go of the coarser pleasures gradually purifies the potentially seductive relationship with pleasure until finally we experience the release of true detachment. This final release is what the Buddha referred to as bliss that is "more spiritual than the spiritual."

The happiness of freedom is not conditioned by pleasant or unpleasant feelings. It does not require comforts, ease, wealth, health, solitude, or society. The happiness of a liberated mind is not limited to the protected conditions of meditative absorptions. The peace of liberation goes beyond the temporal states of rapture, joy, and even equanimity. Enlightenment brings a complete release from all constrictions. It is the happiness that describes the end of suffering, a happiness that is "more spiritual than the spiritual."

ᗝ *The Happiness of Non-Attachment*

What is true happiness?

To begin to explore this, notice the mind that grasps at perceptions, and notice when there is no grasping in the mind. When you feel the mind without grasping, even for a moment, let yourself fully experience that quality of ease, from head to toe. There is happiness in the expression of non-attachment. Can you find it? Rest into the state of ease beyond attraction and repulsion. Try it in fairly neutral encounters, with physical pleasure, or in the face of pain.

The joy of pure detachment is discovered whenever you are not struggling against the fact of things.

ᗝ

With the daily meditation and the counting exercise introduced in chapter 1, you have been focusing attention at the point of contact where the breath meets the nostrils. With some practice, you may notice that your attention gradually becomes steady and is not so easily scattered by stray thoughts or the barrage of passing sights, sounds, and sensations. The mind is beginning to compose itself in present-moment awareness. As you begin to recognize this gathering of mental energies, notice any lightness or happiness that might arise. Notice the ease and even relief that comes from ceasing to roam through the fields of sensory stimuli. Notice these qualities accompanying your mindfulness of breath; do not divert attention from breath to chase after lightness or pleasure. Pleasure and happiness accompany the knowing of breath, but do not replace the breath as your meditation object.

Let your experience of breath be saturated with joy and happiness born of seclusion. This happiness is entirely wholesome. It is a healing and joyful energy, intrinsic to the concentrated mind. This happiness is not based in craving; it does not depend on nor condition states of greed, hatred, or delusion. It should not distract you from the consistent focus on breath. There is nothing to fear from the pleasure that accompanies absorption. As your mind approaches absorption, I encourage you to experience non-sensual happiness fully and completely, while maintaining your focus on breath. Let the mind that is knowing the breath be drenched in joy and pleasure. Allow the experience of spiritual happiness to deepen. Open to wisely experiencing the immense depths of spiritual happiness, and observe how joy and pleasure serve as supports for concentration.

CHAPTER 4
Equanimity

Such it is.
—Saṃyutta Nikāya 35:130

Happy is one who dwells with equanimity and mindfulness.
—Dīgha Nikāya 2:79

EQUANIMITY IS ONE OF the highest kinds of happiness. Superior to delight and joy, equanimity remains undisturbed as events change from hot to cold, from bitter to sweet, from easy to difficult.

Equanimity will enable you to remain balanced through the vicissitudes of life, equally close to the things you may like and the things you do not like. Observe when the tendency to move away from what you do not like ends and the tendency to hold on to what you like is equally absent. Personal preference no longer dictates the direction of attention. Equanimity implies the complete willingness to behold the pleasant and the painful events of life equally. It points to a deep balance in which you are not pushed and pulled between the coercive energies of desire and aversion. When your mind is equanimous, you will have the capacity to embrace extremes without getting thrown off balance. Equanimity excludes the aversive states of indifference, boredom, coldness, or hesitation. It is an expression of calm, radiant balance that takes whatever comes in stride.

The taste of a favorite meal, perhaps eggplant parmesan, may be exquisitely clear: the sweetness of cooked tomatoes, the aroma of basil, the soft texture of the eggplant that melts on the tongue, the saltiness of the parmesan cheese. Each taste may be discerned with acute precision and clarity. They are also enjoyed as a unique blend and appreciated for their combined qualities. When equanimity is dominant, the experience of craving another morsel is absent. That eggplant parmesan will instead be fully experienced with equanimity rather than delight. For many people such balance around taste would be a unique moment.

Some of my beginning students have told me, "But I don't want that kind of happiness. I enjoy the *gusto* of delight. I relish a passionate involvement with my life. I love the excitement of experience." I understand. As a concept, equanimity may appear unappealing, but students nonetheless discover, quite to their surprise, that the exquisite peace of balanced states has a taste of happiness beyond pleasure and beyond pain. Every experience of liking something has as its counterpart disliking something else. The fickleness of personal preference agitates consciousness. The deeply balanced state of equanimity makes a sustained investigation of things possible. Out of this combination of concentrated stability, penetrative investigation, and mindful awareness, consciousness may awaken to a remarkable and subtle quality of happiness.

Spiritual practitioners thrive in unpredictable conditions, testing and refining the inner qualities of heart and mind. Every situation becomes an opportunity to abandon judgment and opinions and to simply give complete attention to what is. Situations of inconvenience are terrific areas to discover, test, or develop your equanimity. How gracefully can you compromise in a negotiation? Does your mind remain balanced when you have to drive around the block three times to find a parking space? Are you at ease waiting for a flight that is six hours late? These inconveniences are opportunities to develop equanimity. Rather than shift the blame onto an institution, system, or person, one can develop the capacity to opt to rest within the experience of inconvenience.

Equanimity matures when you deal with what is difficult without being thrown off balance by it. It is in the difficult or even tragic moments, when we receive a diagnosis of cancer, or learn of the death of a friend, or are suddenly disabled in an automobile accident, that our mettle is tested. Understanding that things occur due to causes and conditions, we don't struggle with the fact that the event occurred; we let the body be a body. It is the nature of physical form to decay and die. No wish will change this natural law. The concentrated mind then rests composed, even as the body is affected by accident, illness, and death.

In 1996, in the midst of several years of living and practicing meditation in Asia, I returned to California to visit my family. It was scheduled as a three-week holiday. During this visit, when some friends and I were traveling to a trailhead to take a day hike, we were involved in a head-on collision. My life instantly changed. Although I was able to walk away from the accident, my injuries caused intense pain that dominated my experience for years. Returning to Asia was simply impossible. During the years I was occupied by medical treatments and physical therapies, I met many fellow accident victims. We were all struggling to regain some ability to function, to have a life that we valued and enjoyed.

In my case, I used meditation skills to protect the mind. Any time my mind drifted into thoughts of things I could no longer do, how my life had been ruined, or the beginnings of a mental story that bemoaned my situation, I quickly brought my attention back to mindful clarity. This clarity repeatedly allowed me to distinguish between the physical and the mental qualities of suffering. It was a practice that required diligence. Observing the interactions of thought, emotion, and sensation had to be continuous throughout the day and night. It became a practice that guided my mind toward the deep peace of equanimity even in the face of physical pain and an uncertain future. I did not have to struggle against the pain or grapple toward pleasure. In the absence of desire and aversion, there is the quiet happiness of equanimity. This kind of happiness is steady and strong; it pervades the mind even when the body is racked by searing physical pain.

I have on occasion suggested that some students actually enter challenging situations in order to refine equanimity. I recommend avoiding car accidents, but I favor foreign travel as one excellent way to develop equanimity off the meditation cushion. I lived in India during my late twenties and early thirties. The initial experience was a confusion of incomprehensible events. I did not even recognize the street sounds. The cuisine was unfamiliar and more spicy than my digestive system was accustomed to. Many customs appeared strange. Having known only a suburban-California lifestyle, I found India unpredictable, uncontrollable, and confusing.

We may not realize to what extent we impose our expectations on things until those expectations are left unmet. I had always expected post offices to have stamps, banks to have cash, drugstores to sell aspirin, and international airports to have money-changing services, until I traveled. On a trip to China, I arrived midmorning at an international airport. The airport money changers were all closed until late afternoon. Without local currency I just had to sit in the airport for six hours until the exchange counters reopened. If we live protected by our routines, we grow to expect our days to go the way we plan them, and for the most part in California it works. Traveling encourages us to rest a bit more and enjoy being where we are, with all its beauty and frustration. I may have on my to-do list to buy stamps today, but that does not guarantee that the post office will have stamps for sale today. Traveling asks us to demand less and accept things as they are, to remain balanced and equanimous whether or not things go according to plan.

When I practiced in Thailand, I joined a large group of monks, nuns, and laypeople who were walking in the jungle in a remote region for several weeks. It was a practice called *tudong* that develops equanimity through having us renounce luxury and work intentionally with austere conditions. For us, these conditions included a virtual absence of possessions and comforts, sleeping on the ground covered only by a mosquito net or a black plastic trash bag on cold nights, bathing on riverbanks, making do with the very simple food we could carry (rice and chili paste) or gather in the forest (bamboo shoots and bitter leaves). Some days water was scarce. We walked all day, sometimes long into the night, usually barefoot.

This was no high-tech backpacking trip. It was a practice of renunciation, acceptance, and equanimity that brought tremendous happiness. I was quite surprised to find myself sitting down to rest, exhausted, aching, and hungry yet very definitely happy. Equanimity has a quality of deep peaceful bliss. When we are not insulated by highly structured routines or pampered by luxurious comforts, equipoise develops by resting in the presence of the things we cannot control, predict, or even comprehend.

In India, my teacher was not interested in experiences confined to a formal meditation session. Insight must be lived. When Poonjaji saw me enter very quiet, rapturous states while sitting still, he would send me to the bazaar, to the kitchen, or to run an errand. He insisted that no distinction be made between the tranquility of the sitting meditation and the busy haggling of the Indian bazaar. A peace that was worth attaining must remain utterly undisturbed and undistracted in the chaotic moments as well as the still moments, equally present to an experience of comfort or pain, equally balanced when things work out conveniently or inconveniently. Equanimous, we cease imposing our personal preferences and demands on life.

Two of my grandparents lost their short-term memory as they aged. Visiting them was challenging. Conversations were repeated over and over and over again. Sentences repeated, questions were re-asked, worries were restated. This became an important place for my practice. It is too easy to reject, avoid, or resent the frustrating dimension of interactions like these. I noticed that with my grandparents the content of the conversation was not important. The words were simply a means of connection or reassurance, expressions of loneliness, fear, love, or appreciation—all very basic interactions. If I focused on the content in communicating an idea, exploring a philosophy, or sharing a story, there was no reason to talk with them at all. But if I focused on the connection and the love, then the lack of variation in the words and subject matter didn't matter. I could happily answer the same question over and over again. We could discover the same flower nine times in four minutes. When we accept the difficult things in our lives, they become supports for developing equanimity, happiness, and peace.

A student recently told me about attending a church service that included a point when parishioners greet each other with a handshake or hug as a sign of peace. The young woman sitting to her left leaned over and full of joy told her, "I'm pregnant." The man sitting to her right greeted her next with the question, "Did you know my wife died?" Equanimity asks us to remain balanced and present with both the pain and the joy—no matter how extreme each may be.

Intense or profound moments can draw out a pure quality of presence without conscious effort. I sat with my grandmother in the hospital, her hand in mine, as she died. It felt connected, peaceful, and somehow harmonious. There was deep acceptance and an awesome wonder of the incomprehensibility of life and death. The profundity of her peace superseded all struggle and brought forth a state of serenity and wonder in my heart. What would it be like to bring the same quality of stable presence, deep release, attention, and wonder to mundane daily interactions with our family members?

Equanimity is not limited to the painful areas of life. Equanimity also protects us from being swept away by praise, flattery, and success. Careless excitement in response to praise can cloud good judgment. A friend recently showed me a new dress that she could barely afford. She purchased it when the salesperson said that it made her look ten years younger. On the other side of the spectrum, self-hatred or anger can fester when we are blamed, are criticized, or find our faults exposed. We live in a world where we may be barraged by both praise and blame. As a teacher who gives public lectures, I have many opportunities to experience these vicissitudes. Students often approach me after my lectures. Some people are deeply moved and offer me high praise. Other people who sat in the same room and heard the same talk may react with anger, boredom, or annoyance.

How equanimous are you when people express their views of liking or not liking what you do? Do you take it personally or understand they are simply expressing their own bias? Does praise or blame disturb your balance?

During the time of the Buddha there was a lay disciple who repeatedly approached the monks asking for teachings. The first talk he heard was comprehensive and detailed. This layman walked away complaining that the monk was long-winded. The next time he came to the monastery, he approached a silent monk; this time he left complaining because there were no teachings. The third time this layman requested teachings, Ānanda, who was aware of the previous two visits, offered a talk of medium length, neither too long nor too short. But this man again complained that the talk was mediocre, neither detailed nor succinct. When all this was reported to the Buddha, the Buddha simply observed that there is always blame in this world.[29] Praise and blame, gain and loss, pleasure and pain are inevitable facets of human existence. Meditation practice invites us to expand the range of happiness to include the full spectrum, so that we remain joyful, balanced, and happy in the face of change.

ᴖ *Clarifying Equanimity*

Daily activities outside the formal meditative experience are a useful training ground to explore this refined quality of the happiness of equanimity. Mindfulness of simple daily events such as buttering toast, eating bland food, washing dishes, commuting with traffic, drinking water, or folding clean clothes can clarify the characteristic of equanimity.

Notice the feelings and behaviors associated with equanimity during your engagements at home and work.

Notice when the mind is free from the tension of judging and craving, when you meet the present moment intimately and fully without being pulled by desire or aversion.

You don't need to wait until the fourth jhāna to cultivate this critically balanced factor!

~ *Restoring Balance in the Midst of Change*

To strengthen equanimity in daily life, notice your responses to pleasant and unpleasant events and incline your mind toward a mindful, accepting, balanced response to the feeling. If you find your mind refusing to accept the unpleasantness of a feeling, reacting against an opinion that is different from your own, or becoming angry when things you like change, note the resistance and agitation that is in your mind. Experiment with ways of restoring equanimity and balance in the midst of the changing events of daily living.

You might remind yourself that "things are as they are" and that you have the capacity to be mindful of both pleasure and pain. You might take a mindful breath, feel your feet on the ground, or reflect that peace is more important than having things your way. Experiment with strategies for restoring balance to the mind in daily life until you find ways to quickly regain your equilibrium.

You might also notice if there are times when equanimity naturally arises. Explore what conditions support the arising of equanimity. Become familiar with the sense of equanimity, with how it feels in the body.

PART II

PREPARING THE MIND FOR ABSORPTION

CHAPTER 5
The Wisdom of Letting Go

"Remove greed for sensual pleasures,
(Jatukaṇṇī," said the Blessed One),
"having seen renunciation as security.
Do not take up or reject anything:
let neither of these exist for you."
—Sutta Nipāta, verse 1098

THE WISE UNDERSTAND the importance of letting go—even letting go of the things we strive for and attain. Developing wisdom demands that we courageously relinquish anything harmful and diligently cultivate wholesome states. Development and relinquishment together carry one systematically through the jhānas, strengthening the wholesome forces and leading to release. At each level of absorption new perceptions are discovered as others are abandoned. We use the deep happiness of jhāna to encourage our practice of letting go. As we release control over body and mind to absorb into the peace of jhāna, we let go into the cradle of blissful jhāna states.

Meditative training is more about letting go than it is about attaining levels of absorption. Spiritual life invites you to relinquish all that binds you, whether that is your cherished fantasies, roles, beliefs, and ideals or your destructive attitudes, assumptions, and views. The guiding principle of jhāna practice is relinquishment, and release is both the method and aim of concentration. "If you don't want to suffer, don't cling" could summarize the main thrust of all the Buddha's instructions. But if you can't follow that simple instruction completely and need more detailed approaches to help you along or keep you busy until you finally tire of clinging, an extensive array of meditation tools have been devised by generations of Buddhist practitioners. And yet, if at any point you are unsure what to do in this practice, just let go.

As meditation teacher Joseph Goldstein advises, "You can't go wrong with not clinging."[30]

Meditation is designed to solve a specific problem: attachment. Awakening is not the experience of spiritual ecstasy accompanied by rainbows and fireworks. Awakening is the experience of a profound relinquishment of clinging, of abandoning the cause of suffering. By understanding that the problem lies in the clinging, we learn to let go.

The Buddha boldly declared, "Nothing is worth adhering to."[31] In a vital discourse, the Buddha instructs Sakka, the ruler of the gods, on this topic. The dialogue begins with Sakka asking, "How is one liberated by the destruction of craving?" In reply, the Buddha says that by learning that "nothing is worth adhering to" one gains an understanding that is applicable to all things. From the perspective of this wise understanding, you can experience whatever feelings may arise—pleasant, painful, or neutral—with wisdom, recognize the impermanence of feeling, and not cling. Not clinging, the wise person is not agitated and abides in peace.

Satisfied, Sakka asked no further questions and returned to his home, resuming his heavenly business and becoming preoccupied with the various affairs of the daily life of the gods. He was an important god of his time. With many godly responsibilities and duties to perform, many entertainments to pursue, places to go, and people to

✏ *For Reflection*

Look into the stories, fantasies, fabrications, desires, aversions, reactions, and doubts that periodically occupy your thoughts. Notice what your mind conjures up in the first moments after waking up in the morning—that period between waking and breakfast is a fascinating window into your habitual thought patterns. Where does your mind go when you sit down for a few moments to rest without the distractions of radio or TV?

Take ten minutes now and lie down on your bed watching the mind without falling asleep.

What patterns of thought dominate? Where does your mind wander when it is not directed by the structure of a task? Can you identify your habitual thinking pattern? Is it blame? Memory? Fantasies of success? Complaining? Worry? Insecurities about finances, relationships, opinions, self-image? Are you planning your next activity?

see, Sakka's meditation practice became quite lax. He made excuses for neglecting it, complaining, "We are so busy; we have so much to do."[32] Something always seemed to be more important or more compelling.

Perhaps your situation is not so different. You may read a spiritual book, hear a lecture, or attend a meditation retreat. You may learn that nothing is worth clinging to and become aware that many daily activities do not support concentration. You appreciate these teachings, value them, perhaps feel inspired, but still may be preoccupied with the various affairs of your life. You might check your email, respond to text messages on your phone, become absorbed in the frenzy of daily news, turn on the TV in the evening when you're tired. You have good intentions, but your commitment to daily sitting meditation could start to wane.

Only you can clear the craving from your mind. Only you can prepare your mind to delve into the depths of concentration. So you make some changes: you may commit to checking email only once or twice each day, or decide to limit your intake of news to one period of the day. You might develop a variety of evening activities that will not dull your mind, such as reading a book, walking around the block after dinner with friends, exploring a hobby, taking an evening class, or attending a meditation group. You make time for meditation even when your schedule is full and your life is active. You take care of your mind in the evening so that you wake up refreshed and can enjoy a clear meditation session in the morning.

Many practices cultivate the skill of letting go through renunciation, contemplating death, and perceiving impermanence. Letting go does not require strenuous effort. It is not necessarily one more task to perform. It is, simply, what occurs when you are not clinging: a direct expression of wisdom arising in a moment of experience. Simple wisdom tells us, "When you are being dragged, let go of the leash." When you feel the pain of grasping and understand the holding on as the cause of your suffering, the solution becomes obvious.

The Buddha illustrated his teaching on relinquishment with the simile of a quail tethered by a thin rotting vine. It is a trifling bond, but for the frail bird it is a strong fetter. For an elephant, however, a rotting vine is no tether at all.[33] The thing that binds may be feeble or strong; the measure is not in the fetter itself, but rather in the ability to abandon or in the tendency to be bound. Thus, to escape the fetter of clinging we develop the facility to abandon, and we cultivate a direct and vivid knowledge of the unfettered mind.

◇ *Observing Clinging and Not-Clinging*

When the mind is well-settled in your meditation, you might be able to recognize the subtle ways that the mind craves for or clings to experience. Perhaps you might recognize craving or clinging manifesting as a subtle tightening, a familiar pressure, a sense of leaning forward, a quality of insecurity, a sense of becoming someone in the experience, a sense of positioning of self.

What signs help you recognize when your mind is clinging? And what are the signs that indicate that the mind is not presently craving or clinging? For some minutes in each meditation session, try to notice the movements of clinging and not-clinging, craving and not-craving, as they occur.

FOUR WAYS OF ABANDONING TROUBLESOME THOUGHTS

You may sit down to meditate with the best of intentions but find yourself inundated with uncontrollable memories, intense desires, complex plans, or insidious doubts, fears, or hopes. You may *aspire* to let go but find it difficult to do.

The things that obsess one person may not attract another person. Power is not inherent in the thing to which one feels bound. Through meditation, we discern our relationship to our thoughts: What are our patterns, and what is sustaining the attachment? In the Discourse on the Simile of the Quail, the Buddha observed four ways of meeting the thoughts of attachment that may beset the earnest meditator.

The first approach is to indulge distracting thoughts. A person taking this approach is considered *fettered, bound, not free.* The second approach is to reject, deny, avoid, or react against repetitive thoughts. Although this practice may remove the thoughts temporarily, aversion becomes a binding force and the thoughts may well return. The third approach is to quickly abandon and remove memories and thoughts during meditation. Mindful, the meditator is free of indulgence and aversion. Interestingly, the Buddha described the practitioner of this approach, like the first two, as fettered, bound, not free. The mindful person recognizes when the mind gets obsessed by thoughts and skillfully returns to an awareness of the present moment by letting go of the habitual thought patterns. This person practices admirably, but still is not fully free. Wisdom has not yet uprooted the cause of obsessive thoughts. Thus, this practitioner knows how to let go of distractions that arise, but has not penetrated the process deeply enough to prevent further distractions from occurring. This practitioner is caught in an alternating sequence of distraction, mindfulness, and letting go.

Only the fourth way is liberating. The Buddha described the fourth way, saying, "Some person, having understood that attachment is the root of suffering, divests himself of attachment, and is liberated with the destruction of attachment. Such a person I call *unfettered, not fettered.*"[34] Wisdom has penetrated to the root of the problem for this meditator and extracted the fundamental cause of obsessive thinking.

In this system of four approaches, the first two ways, indulgence and rejection, describe the two extremes of reactivity. The third way is practice: developing mindfulness and cultivating the ability to let go. The fourth approach achieves another level altogether: liberating wisdom. With this understanding well established, the Buddha continues the discourse with instructions on establishing the sequence of jhāna.[35]

⌒ *Patterns of Attachment*

The Simile of the Quail discourse[35] includes a description of four kinds of people:

1. one who tolerates attachments and indulges them
2. one who abandons attachments whenever they arise
3. one who experiences attachments in the periods when mindfulness lapses but then abandons those attachments when mindfulness arises again
4. one who has understood that attachment is the cause of suffering and has freed the mind from all attachments

For the sake of the exercise, rather than think of these as four descriptions of static individuals, consider the possibility that you might experience all four at different times. Notice how you deal with attachment and consider if one or more of these modes is a repeating tendency.

The wisdom that understands attachment as the root of suffering reveals the possibility of a transformation that doesn't require us to abandon one obsessive thought pattern after another. This transformative wisdom clears away the distractions that inhibit concentration, and it directly liberates the mind from all forms of clinging. It manifests in the moment of contact with any sensory experience, in any moment of feeling or thinking. The experience of wisdom is not just letting one particular problem pass; the Buddha taught that nothing whatsoever should be clung to. When you know this so clearly that clinging loses its power, you possess the wisdom that liberates.

ABANDON ONLY WHAT IS NOT YOURS

Some people fear that letting go could diminish the quality of their lives, health, abilities, achievements, or personal property. To this the Buddha said, "Whatever is not yours, abandon it; when you have abandoned it, that will lead to your welfare and happiness for a long time."[36] This invites a profound reflection on impermanence and what we can authentically claim as our own. As we discern the fleeting, conditioned character of all material and mental processes, we eliminate perceptions, sensory experience, and material things as fields for possession. On the surface, it seems like we are being asked to give up everything. But we quickly realize that we possess nothing. Everything is impermanent: there is nothing to be given up. The great abandonment is to let go of the concept of ownership.

Letting go in meditation is the relinquishment that involves no loss. Recognizing impermanence leads to the realization of the pure and ungraspable nature of things. Knowing this basic fact about the world, we have nothing to fear. And the extraordinary delight that arises with realization surpasses all temporary pleasures, softening any residual fear that may want to grasp again what can never actually be possessed.

UNDERSTANDING FEELING

For a person with an untrained mind, attention can become entangled with grasping as it moves toward pleasant encounters and avoids unpleasant ones. Notice how you respond when you don't get what you want. Also, observe how you respond when you succeed and do get exactly what you want.

The Buddha's following poetic instruction on feelings refers to the basic quality of a feeling being pleasant, unpleasant, or neither-pleasant-nor-unpleasant.

⟶ *For Reflection*

Have you had any recent experiences of clearly letting go? They happen all the time, although we rarely investigate the experience. You make a plan in the morning, but a flat tire demands that you let go of your agenda for the day. You might like milk in your tea, but when you don't find any in the refrigerator you release the desire rather than suffer irritation. A friend might be emotionally distraught, and you realize there is nothing you can do to make her happy; although you care about her and listen, you don't hastily jump in to "fix" her feelings. You might want to be recognized and appreciated by a colleague, and you only discover relief when you release the desire for that acknowledgment.

Notice moments of letting go throughout your day.

What feelings occurred with the experience of that release?

What burdens would you be happier living without?

Just as many diverse winds
Blow back and forth across the sky
Easterly winds and westerly winds,
Northerly winds and southerly winds,
Dusty winds and dustless winds,
Sometimes cool, sometimes hot,
Those that are strong and others mild—
Winds of many kinds that blow;
So in this very body here
Various kinds of feelings arise,
Pleasant ones and painful ones,

And those neither painful nor pleasant.
But when a bhikkhu who is ardent
Does not neglect clear comprehension,
Then that wise man fully understands
Feelings in their entirety.[37]

Throughout the development of concentration, one must be mindful of these qualities—pleasant, unpleasant, and neither-pleasant-nor-unpleasant—because when one does not see the *feeling-tone*, habits of desire and aversion are reinforced.

Feel the undercurrent of the affective tone distinct from any conceptual assumptions about what you like or dislike. Discover what is actually pleasant, unpleasant, or neutral right now. It may not be obvious. A favorite meal might be pleasant generally, but also might include bits of unpleasant chewing, disturbing textures and sounds, and sudden changes in flavor. A pain in the body might include aspects that are pleasant, such as warmth, tingling, and softness. Let your attention drop below the level of concept and personal history to directly experience the quality of feeling.

For the spiritual aspirant committed to uprooting lust, aversion, and delusion, mindfulness of feeling-tone is an indispensable skill. Unless we clearly recognize how feeling affects perception, the three poisons of lust, aversion, and delusion will be reinforced. For example, an unmindful connection with a pleasurable experience can activate the underlying tendency to lust, generating a stronger conditioning toward desire. An unmindful experience of something painful can ignite the underlying tendency to aversion, further conditioning resistance, hatred, or fear. And an unmindful encounter with a neutral experience may trigger the underlying tendency to delusion. Subtle neutrality often goes unnoticed. In the absence of clear attention, preconceived ideas easily distort perception, perpetuating ignorance.[38] Feeling is a crucial link to observe, a strategic point for release. Consistent awareness of the present-moment feeling, wedged just between simple contact with a sensory stimulus and the grasping reaction, can not only cool the agitated mind but also uproot the source from which suffering springs.

I step outside on this early spring day and stand for a few moments basking in the late-morning sun. Although the sun warms my face and my right side, a crisp coolness in the air chills my left hand, which is shaded. My habit of mind is that warmth is pleasant and cold is unpleasant. Rather than instinctively shoving my hand into my pocket at this moment, I look into the feeling. I notice that cold is not a static feeling. It is composed of many changing sensations. The icy coldness is at first an unpleasantly sharp sting. Then come moments of pleasant tingles and warm pulses that intensify into unpleasant throbbing. Soon these sensations soften into a basically pleasant vibration. Within the area where I had felt the initial coldness, many changing sensations quickly arise and pass—some pleasant, some unpleasant, and some indistinguishable.

Try this yourself. Rather than act according to the assumption that something is entirely pleasant or unpleasant, attune your attention to the flow of feeling. Let the attention rest in the current of feeling as the framework for mindfulness; experience the dynamic flow of feelings. What is directly felt as pleasant, unpleasant, and neutral can be surprising.

To illustrate this point, I shall use the example of chocolate cake. I like chocolate cake—and one time I had a piece of homemade chocolate cake for dessert and a scoop of rice left on my plate from the meal. It was plain white rice, nothing special. As I ate these two, bite by bite, my attention focused on the *quality* of feeling. I let the process slow down, exploring in meticulous detail the actual experience of a bite of rice and then a bite of chocolate cake. What were the tastes, and how did they evolve throughout the process of eating? I settled into the experience of texture and temperature as the two foods moved from the plate to be consumed through contact with my tongue and teeth. I noticed what occurred when my eye landed on the cake or the rice, observing the initial desire, preference, interest, and craving. Without rushing, I took the time to explore my consumption of these morsels of food.

In this experience, I learned something that amazed me. During that entire examination, I could find nothing about the cake that had a more pleasant feeling than the rice. It was the opposite actually; the chocolate had a roughness and bitterness that periodically flared into an abruptly unpleasant sensation. When the craving subsided and attention rested on the stream of changing feeling, the actual experience of cake did not confirm my habitual view of cake. I can no longer assume that I like cake better than rice.

Liking and not-liking are triggered by an unmindful relationship to feelings. By maintaining focused awareness on the stream of changing feelings, one can break the link to craving early enough to suspend habitual reactions.

Exploring Feeling-Tones

Although many insight meditation students can be mindful of what is arising, they nevertheless find themselves reacting to particular pains and discomforts. Students may diligently notice the details of the burning, stabbing, searing, pricking sensations that compose pain, but are frustrated because their minds resist the basic fact of pain. In a situation such as this, it may not help to force yourself to meticulously notice more nuances in painful sensations. Instead, shift your attention to the unpleasant feeling-tone accompanying the pain. It doesn't matter if it is a bitter taste, caustic music, indigestion, or searing shoulder pain; all are accompanied by an unpleasant feeling-tone. If you shift your attention to become mindful of the subtle feeling-tone, the specific perceptions and personal narratives that trigger unpleasant feeling become relatively inconsequential. Know it as unpleasant; accept it as it is.

The Subtle in the Mundane

This exercise explores how the three kinds of feeling may trigger reactions of craving, aversion, and dullness, or be tools for cultivating equanimity. Choose three food items: one that you generally like, one that you distinctly dislike, and one that you feel fairly neutral about.

Place enough of each item on your plate to permit several bites of each.

Slowly and mindfully eat each item, bite by bite, noticing the qualities of pleasantness, unpleasantness, and neutrality in the experience.

Carefully notice the impulses, textures, temperatures, stimulation, affects, and opinions related to each perception.

Observe not only the experience of tasting but also the experiences of seeing, smelling, touching, thinking, and comparing. Notice the extent to which your perceptions are influenced by expectations, preferences, or the presence of emotions.

Is there a desire to increase contact with the food you like or to avoid contact with the food you dislike?

As you move back and forth between slow, mindful bites of each item, allow a harmonious investigation and balanced equanimity to pervade the experience of the bare fact of each perception.

Take at least twenty minutes to mindfully explore this exercise. Slowing down will permit you to notice subtle aspects of an otherwise mundane experience of eating.

When hearing an unwanted sound during meditation, some people may get irritated and angry, search for earplugs, and yell, "Stop that racket!"—thinking the sound is disturbing their meditation. The sound might not have disturbed the meditation if it was known with mindfulness, but we often react to assumptions about what sounds are acceptable during meditation, and then agitation ensues. This often occurs at retreat centers located near freeways. The volume and quality of the sound produced by wind blowing through trees may not be so different from traffic noise, but meditators will usually complain about traffic sounds and not the rustle of leaves. Our assumptions and ideas, not the mere presence of sounds, trigger the reaction.

Imagine yourself eating a piece of berry pie. Even before finishing the serving, you begin to think about a second helping. It may not be more pie you want; in fact, a second piece might bring unpleasant feelings of bloatedness. The desire may not be to have more pie but, rather, to sustain the pleasant feeling-tone. Craving for pleasure stimulates greed for more pleasant sensations. Unaware of the dynamic of feeling, we reinforce the assumption that more pleasure will come through more experiences—if one piece of pie was good, more is better. This habitual drive for *more* strengthens the pattern of greed.

You can save yourself a lot of anguish by investigating your response to the fundamental qualities of pleasure and pain. If you are unmindful of a pleasant feeling, the underlying tendency to greed gets activated. If you are unmindful of an unpleasant feeling, the underlying tendency to aversion gets activated. If you are unmindful of a neutral feeling, the underlying tendency to delusion gets activated.[39] People commonly try to increase the pleasant, react against the unpleasant, and are dulled, confused, or inattentive to the neutral feelings. A skillful meditator will develop the flexibility to direct awareness to these subtler layers of experience and will investigate the interaction of pleasure and greed, pain and aversion, neutrality and delusion.

The Freedom of Release

Wherever clinging is perceived, that is the place for release. As your equanimity grows, it becomes easier to let go. Wisdom will begin to infiltrate your days, sometimes consciously, often subtly. Wisdom may manifest as the ability to keep your mouth shut when you feel the impulse to come back with that witty retort that would only increase the conflict.

More profoundly, wisdom gives us greater courage to face the grief of a loss, to understand loss not simply as a personal tragedy but also as a manifestation of the broader dynamic of life's suffering. It leads us to discover a deeper appreciation of life and inspires us to live aligned with our highest aspirations. Most people notice improvement in the quality of their lives through the cultivation of this training; this brings confidence that the practice is working. Students who have practiced awhile say, "I may not be enlightened yet, but I am at least a bit more patient," or "I don't feel very different, but my family says I am easier to live with." The benefits of developing patience, kindness, equanimity, calmness, compassion, and the ability to bear the pain in life must not be underestimated. They are the benefits of learning to let go.

CHAPTER 6
Dynamics of Emotion

Feelings are understood as they arise, understood as they remain present, understood as they pass away. Thoughts are understood as they arise, understood as they remain present, understood as they pass away. Perceptions are understood as they arise, understood as they remain present, understood as they pass away.
—Saṃyutta Nikāya 47:35

THE POPULAR CARICATURE of the meditator is someone in full lotus posture—totally cool, even-tempered, utterly unemotional, sitting perfectly still and peaceful like a statue. But in actual experience, meditation is neither static nor stoic. As sentient beings, we feel the full range of emotions and feelings. Some will be difficult, others delightful. Calmness and peacefulness are so subtle you may not even notice them. Rage, grief, sorrow, and terror are so intense that you can sometimes notice little else. A mindful engagement with sensory and emotional life intimately informs meditation. Steadfast mindfulness is an essential precondition for creating a strong foundation for jhāna, but mindfulness does not require the withdrawal characteristic of jhāna. It develops in the midst of sensory contact.

MINDFULNESS IS YOUR GUARDIAN

The Buddha urged, "One bent on his own welfare should practice heedfulness, mindfulness, and guarding of the mind thus."[40] Mindfulness protects concentration from the impulsive intrusion of lust, hate, confusion, and infatuation. Mindfulness balances the mind and dispels the extremes of restlessness and sleepiness, agitation and dullness, wanting and not-wanting, doubt and unwise faith. If your mind is left unguarded and a pleasant thought occurs to you and you are unaware that it has arisen, the mind might begin to go wild. Images proliferate; fantasies of pleasure emerge; rippling responses run through the body; tension builds; concepts of "me and mine" are reinforced. In an unguarded, unrestrained mind, attention is lost in fantasy. Although the initial contact may be pleasant, the associative sequence can create a wake of mental agitation; suffering results. The problem is *not* that a pleasant thought arises; the problem is that the mind is unprotected. When mindfulness is absent or muddled, clinging finds an opportunity, and identification with the experience ensues.

You don't need to shut your eyes and ears or practice in a sensory deprivation chamber. Mindfulness is alert, screening for obstructions and reactions. It does not prevent perception; it only restrains the tendency to grasp at the contact. Experience shines freshly as unique moments that come and go in a relaxed and clear mind. The habit of attachment is inhibited.

The Buddha taught:

> Here, having seen a form with the eye . . . heard a sound
> with the ear . . . smelled an odor with the nose . . . tasted
> a taste with the tongue . . . felt a tactile object with the
> body . . . cognized a mental phenomenon with the mind,
> a bhikkhu does not grasp its marks and features. Since, if
> he left the mind faculty unrestrained, bad unwholesome

states of longing and dejection might invade him, he
practices restraint over it; he guards the mind faculty, he
undertakes the restraint of the mind faculty.[41]

Mindful awareness is the guard we post at the door of each sense.
For example, if you experience an unpleasant tactile sensation,
such as cold on your arm, you might begin to complain about the
weather. Although there has never been a time when the weather
changed in response to human complaints, we still make them. Stories circulate in the mind about not having enough warm clothes;
judgments reinforce the view that this climate is unfit for human
habitation; criticisms are aimed at companions who we feel are
being cheapskates by keeping the heat too low. Hatred grows and
the heart closes. Feeling alienated and separated, we become irri-
table, callous, easily annoyed.

In this kind of scenario, self-condemning thoughts proliferate:
"I'm not good enough. I'm not worthy to get enlightened. How
can I become enlightened if I don't even wear the right clothes for
the season?" Such an unguarded mind suffers. The suffering is not
caused by the sensation of cold on the arm. Lack of mindfulness is
the problem. Mindful attention to the initial contact will prevent
suffering from entering. The sooner mindfulness meets the mental
embellishments that arise, the easier it will be to interrupt the cycle
of suffering. A moment of discontent becomes nothing more trou-
blesome than a fleeting perception of discontent. A lyrical teaching
of the Buddha states:

> Having seen a form with mindfulness muddled,
> Attending to the pleasing sign,
> One experiences it with infatuated mind
> And remains tightly holding to it.
> Many feelings flourish within,
> Originating from the visible form,

Covetousness and annoyance as well
By which one's mind becomes disturbed.
For one who accumulates suffering thus
Nibbāna is said to be far away.
When, firmly mindful, one sees a form,
One is not inflamed by lust for forms;
One experiences it with dispassionate mind
And does not remain holding it tightly.
One fares mindfully in such a way
That even as one sees the form,
And while one undergoes a feeling,
[Suffering] is exhausted, not built up.
For one dismantling suffering thus,
Nibbāna is said to be close by.[42]

WHEN WE HURT

Living with a human body with physical needs for food, sleep, and warmth, vulnerable to illness and injury, you will experience pain. If you can distinguish between physical suffering and mental suffering, pain will not impede concentration. I have practiced with traditional Asian masters who encourage using pain as a strong object for concentration. Because attention is easily drawn to intense pain, focus remains undistracted. In this book, however, I recommend using the breath as a more neutral object of concentration, since for jhāna, neutral or pleasant states are preferred.

Yet, given the nature of the body, pain will inevitably arise. We can't avoid it. If mindfulness is weak when we feel pain, an undercurrent of aversion could fester, creating a mental dimension of suffering intertwined with the physical pain. The traditional Buddhist teachings illustrate this through the story of a man who is stabbed by a dart and immediately stabbed by a second dart.[43] The Buddha explains that the first dart represents bodily feelings—the simple pain that comes with having a body. This first dart might arise from an illness, accident, mosquito bite, or from hunger, thirst, or cold. The second dart—mental feelings—we inflict on ourselves with reactions of desire, aversion, craving, and ignorance.

The Buddha concludes the teaching with the instruction:

> If he feels a pleasant feeling, he feels it detached. If he feels a painful feeling, he feels it detached. If he feels a neither-painful-nor-pleasant feeling, he feels it detached. This, bhikkhus, is called a noble disciple who is detached from birth, aging, and death; who is detached from sorrow, lamentation, pain, displeasure, and despair; who is detached from suffering, I say.[44]

No one can completely control physical life. We may exercise, eat well, and live healthy lives, but our bodies are subject to illness, injury, and decay. We cannot end feeling, but we can train our minds to experience feelings with a balanced awareness free from aversion. We respect our physical vulnerability by not forcing ourselves beyond reasonable limitations and by not fearing aging, judging wrinkles as bad, or believing that our joints should not ache as we age.

As you practice bringing mindfulness to pain and become aware of the sensations themselves—distinct from thoughts and interpretations about them—you narrow the range of possible obstruction. Although physical pain may fatigue the body, it need not spark the parallel mental suffering of frustration, agitation, or annoyance. Practice experiencing pain as only a single dart; free yourself from the extra suffering of stabbing yourself with the second dart of aversion. You might still have pain, but you will be peaceful and happy nonetheless.

At one retreat a student appeared particularly restless. He struggled to maintain the silence, writing notes to the coordinators,

➢ Relating to Pain

Consider: Bodily pain and difficult emotions are an inescapable fact of embodied life. Sometimes pain is so intense that it commands all our attention; sometimes it is so subtle that it colors our experience without notice; often it fluctuates somewhere between those two degrees of intensity.

We cannot ignore the real needs of the body or deny painful states of mind. We must learn to work skillfully with the conditions at hand, whether it is a throbbing migraine, an aching back, a painful degenerative disease, or grief from the loss of someone we love.

Identify: During your daily activities this week, make a point of noticing when you are touched by pain. Identify whether you feel the pain physically, mentally, or both. Consider if the pain was primarily caused by physical or mental conditions.

When physical pain or difficult emotions are present, notice the quality and focus of your attention. Are you willing to feel the pain? If thoughts and interpretations are predominant, can you interrupt the stream of thoughts and reconnect with sensations in the body? If resistance arises, can you soften your attitude to be present with discomfort?

Notice: Notice the moment that preceded awareness of the pain. For example, were you distracted, mindful, joyful, angry, rushed, anxious, grateful, tired, excited, or calm just prior to becoming aware of pain? By observing daily instances of mental or physical discomfort we collect information about our own feelings, conditioned patterns, and the way that we respond to those feelings.

You may respond differently when you are tired versus when you are energetic. You may make different choices when you feel rushed versus when you feel calm. The intensity of the pain may feel different when mindfulness is weak versus strong.

Reflect: What have you learned about your relationship with physical and emotional pain?

conversing during work periods, requesting personal items he'd forgotten, and perusing books to identify plants, animal tracks, and local bird species. On the second day of the retreat, he urgently requested buckets and rags to wash his car. By the third day, he was collaborating with the cook to produce a recipe book. When I met with him, it was apparent something was agitating him deeply; these distractions were manifestations of an inner state. Clearly it wasn't the car that needed attention.

In our conversation he nonchalantly mentioned the recent death of his wife and told me he was supporting a daughter with cancer. In the telling he felt his pain; intense grief bubbled to the surface. With a courageous heart and a box of tissues nearby, he gently opened to his anguish. A deep calmness settled over his experience. He experienced it as painful, yes, but he also saw it as the truth of his life. When he felt the authenticity of his feelings, he knew that his heart was big enough to experience the intensity of both grief and love.

Restlessness, a common obstacle to concentration, is often a cover for painful states that hide below the surface of busy, agitated energies. Pain may be calling for your attention. Is there loneliness, fear,

⤳ *Meeting Perceptions*

While sitting comfortably, notice how your attention meets perceptions of sounds, sights, thoughts, sensations, and emotions.

Observe phenomena from the stability of your restful seated posture.

Each time the attention pounces on a thought, a sight, or a sound, rest back again.

Imagine a comfortable armchair positioned in a room with large picture windows opening out to a vast view. Imagine yourself sitting in the chair observing the expansive view. You don't need to chase thoughts or follow after feelings to be aware of them.

Simply observe how each thought or perception arises and passes like a bird flying across the sky.

Remain comfortable and steady in your grand and royal seat, observing all things with mindful attention.

grief, or sadness you are staying too active to feel? Gently ask yourself if you can open to this pain. You don't need to rip your heart open all at once, but see if you can touch some of your pain—it may give you strength.

The seclusion of jhāna is supported by the clarity that comes with mindfulness, not by dullness or aversion. This essential point may be overlooked if one tries to rush the attempt to gain meditative attainments. Avoid the temptation to concoct a feeling of being separated from sensory experience by blunting your perceptions or by diffusing your perceptions through a "spaced-out" state. There is nothing whatsoever dull about jhāna. The serene mind is not sleepy, diffused, or inert; it is without the slightest trace of uncertainty.

Each jhāna state incorporates mindfulness and a bright attention. You need to trust mindfulness as your mind's guard. With mindfulness as protection, vividly encounter any experience of body, mind, or the world as it unfolds.

ENLIGHTENING PLEASURE

At times, positive emotions will arise. You may see an injured bird as you walk through the forest and recognize genuine compassion as your natural response. You may step out of your home into the cool morning air and realize you are infused with a spontaneous appreciation of life. In watching a spider build a web, you may discover the commitment necessary to repair a troubled relationship. While struggling with illness, you might be filled with unlimited love. While sitting in meditation, you may discover a great peace pervading your heart.

In the meditative process you will encounter a variety of qualities related to happiness and peace. Pleasure arises quite spontaneously as the mind settles. Allow yourself to fully experience the wholesome and healing states that arise with concentration, whether their expression is intense or subtle. Open to those positive feelings; allow their healing character to infuse you with energy. You do not need to push away the pleasures of jhāna by thinking you should work harder to overcome your personal problems or out of fear of potential attachment. Allow the pleasant feelings to support your concentration. Sometimes we might endure rapture so intense that it feels as though our bones could break from the ecstasy or burst from the flood of joyful bliss; other times pleasure is so subtle we barely recognize it. The pleasure known through jhāna is described as a subtle accompaniment to the state; it is fuller and calmer than the ecstatic intensity felt in the early stages before absorption. Like all phenomena, the happiness and peace that develops through meditation will eventually fade and pass away.

In the introduction, I referred to some of the events leading up to the Buddha's enlightenment. Already quite experienced in the systematic attainment of jhāna, he remembered a moment in his youth when the pleasures of jhāna spontaneously arose as he rested in the shade of a rose apple tree. This recollection led to a pivotal shift in his relationship to pleasure. Recalling this spontaneous experience of happiness, the emaciated recluse wondered, "Could that be the path to enlightenment?" And he came to think that it might be so. Then the thought arose, "Why am I afraid of that pleasure that has nothing to do with sensual pleasures and unwholesome states?"[45] His examination of pleasurable feeling continued. He noticed there was nothing to fear from pleasure that arose in a steady mind, and he ceased the severe austerities of fasting. His concentration deepened, and his mind grew ripe for awakening. As he sat under the Bodhi tree with the resolve to awaken, he traversed the jhānas and, using jhāna as the basis for insight, realized enlightenment.[46]

Tremendous strength resides in feelings of peace and happiness. The Buddha instructed his disciples to liberally allow the jhāna factors of delight, interest, happiness, joy, and equanimity to so pervade, suffuse, irradiate, and saturate their bodies and minds that no part is left untouched.[47] We can actively harness the potency of these feelings to fortify our concentration.

The Buddha illustrated the process of completely immersing oneself in the field of wholesome pleasure with four similes, each linked to the experience of a level of jhāna: (1) soap powder sprinkled and thoroughly blended with water as it is kneaded into a ball; (2) a lake fed by a cool spring that permeates unimpeded every area of that lake; (3) a lotus that lives entirely immersed in a cool lake, drinking of the water, never rising out of the water, completely enveloped in the coolness of the water; and (4) a man completely covered by a clean white cloth so that no part of his head or body is exposed.

These similes recommend a complete saturation of mind and body with the beautiful qualities of these wholesome states. The images suggest a total immersion in jhāna states. When the state recedes, however, you don't need to conjure up ways to make it stay, because it was known, honored, valued, and fully met as it appeared. It is equally recognized when it fades, changes, or dissipates. The Buddha noted that profound pleasure arises through concentrated states, but even these sublime pleasant feelings do not "invade the mind and remain."[48]

Confronting Difficult Emotions

During the absorption of jhāna, wholesome states dominate the mind. But prior to absorption and after emerging from jhāna, the mind may in fact feel all sorts of things. Mental states are not trading cards you can exchange, swapping unpleasant ones for preferred feelings. You don't need to be trampled by difficult feelings or repress them, but you do need to know them in the clear light of mindfulness.

Trust the capacity of the heart to be spacious enough to feel not only the things you like but also mental states that are difficult. The challenge of difficult emotions is the impulse to avoid confronting them. Denial is ultimately ineffective, however. Often when we try to remove ourselves from the feeling, however slightly, we discover that we are dwelling on the story of the emotion. The story creates a slight separation from the direct feeling of the painful state. For example, you might remember something hurtful that a friend said and rehearse various defensive responses during your meditation session. Thinking removes your attention from what anger, disappointment, and betrayal actually feel like in this moment right now. When you experience a repeating memory, it's your opportunity to explore the feelings that underlie the story.

In a situation of highly charged emotions, you'll find it helpful to gather the support of stillness. Bring awareness to the posture. If you are sitting, take a deep breath and stay sitting. If you are standing,

⤺ *Working with Difficult Thoughts*

For this exercise, intentionally bring to mind a thought that will trigger some emotion. It may be a memory that sparks annoyance, anger, or sadness. It might be an expectation that causes envy, fear, or shame.

As you give rise to the difficult thoughts, be conscious that they form stories in your mind.

Feel the impact of these emotionally charged thoughts in the body.

Is there tightness in your chest, shoulders, and face? Are there sensations in the belly or limbs?

Notice how those physical sensations manifest and evolve.

Notice how the emotional quality shifts, perhaps from anger to fear, pity, sadness, shame, worry, love, melancholy, or desire.

Emotions are dynamic processes that are in a state of flux. If you don't refuel them through obsessive thinking, they will change and fade.

We learn to be present to the full range of emotions by feeling their changing energetic expressions in the mind and body.

For example, anger might bring heated, agitated, explosive feelings radiating from the chest; sadness might carry a sinking vulnerable quality in the belly; fear might create an unstable quivering sensation in the knees or throat. Attending to the physical manifestations of emotions keeps attention focused on the process long enough for you to learn directly about how these difficult states impact your mind.

When the mind is obsessed by a difficult emotion, it may construct repetitive stories about who did what and why. Caught in the storyline, you might dwell on painful narratives and not discover how to free the mind from the painful thoughts. Let go of the story and investigate the emotion directly. When you allow feelings to evolve through their natural changes, the emotional landscape clears, like clouds passing on a stormy or windy day.

take a deep breath and keep standing. Feel your feet on the floor. Sense the stability of your body. Scan your body and know the sensations you are feeling. Physical sensations serve as a tangible guide to the felt sense of the mental state. Are you experiencing contraction? Are specific areas of tension, quivering, shaking, pulling, or throbbing dominant? Locate the feeling in the body and let the attention rest in the embodied experience of the emotion. Emotions are never static. Notice how they flow and change: intensifying, dissipating, or fluctuating within a cluster of related sensations. Every time the mind reengages the storyline, disentangle yourself from the concepts and return to the felt sense of the feeling.

I recall a painful conversation during which I was informed that I had been rejected for a position that I had earnestly sought. This was the culmination of a long process of qualifying for the position, and an equally long exploration of my desire to attain it. After the decision was finally announced and all hope was exhausted, waves of sadness and loneliness flowed through me. Needing some space to attend to these feelings, I went for a walk. Each time I noticed that my mind was retelling the story, I intentionally dropped the story and settled into the bare feeling, opening to the sadness and disappointment. Although my feelings repeated through much of the walk, they were neither constant nor overwhelming. I saw a bulldozer pushing a pile of dirt around and for a few moments stood fascinated. A friend walked past me on the path, and I felt tender appreciation fill my heart. When a rabbit hopped by, I felt joyful delight. When my attention moved freely between these various responses, disappointment did not burden my mind. After several waves of feeling, it passed, leaving a residue of lightness, acceptance, and confidence in its wake.

Noticing change and observing the spaces between feelings can bring a balanced perspective to emotion. Emotions are an expression of empty phenomena that arise in response to stimuli, are experienced, and cease.

The Buddha described a human being as a guesthouse; many kinds of feelings come, stay for a while, and then travel on.[49] Try greeting all emotions as visitors or guests. Allow them to visit, accept that they arise due to conditions, but don't adopt them as permanent residents.

CHAPTER 7
Effort, Ease, and Intention

All wholesome qualities are rooted in heedfulness and converge upon
heedfulness and heedfulness is declared foremost among them.
—Aṅguttara Nikāya 10:15

I N THE HONESTY OF silence you will encounter your own mind without pretense. You may sit still and yet discover that your mind is anything but still. At times it may feel as though you have sat down with a monster. A great challenge lies before you. How can you embrace this companion who is sometimes monstrous, insulting, and raucous? How can you develop a deep friendship with your own mind, so deep that your mind becomes your trusted ally?

No matter how restless and uncooperative your mind might appear, concentration improves with practice—yet stillness cannot be imposed by strenuously wrestling down distractions. Concentration grows through the willingness to encounter, understand, and eventually remove all that agitates the mind. Recognizing the messy aspects of the mind will support spiritual development and help you meet challenges with clarity and skill.

Effort is an integral aspect of the Buddha's teaching. Just moments before his death, the Buddha urged his disciples, "Strive on untiringly!"[50] This injunction crystallized a teaching of diligent effort that pervaded the Buddha's forty-five-year ministry. Skillful application of effort is fundamental to the art of meditation: you must apply yourself completely, yet without the caustic energies of force. You need both the utmost fortitude and the gentlest touch— applying just the right amount of energy to be fully present to whatever is actually happening in your life and spiritual practice.

As you begin the concentration practice, you may notice tension caused by overexertion. It is common to blame the effort for the unpleasant feeling of tension and then rebel against discipline. But if you incline toward the other extreme, of making no effort, you may never gather the strength to progress. Self-doubt, withdrawal, laziness, resistance, uncertainty, or holding the view that non-effort is superior can weaken resolve and stall the development of concentration.

Please don't throw the baby out with the bath water.

The problem is not effort per se, but how to adjust it. Usually only a slight modification is required. Explore effort and ease dynamically. Continue to notice how you are applying attention to meet the present object of meditation.

How Little Is Enough?

The art of meditation explores how attention meets its meditation subject. Meditative attention shines like a light beam, illuminating the subject but not interfering with its natural process of change. What is the quality of effort that meets its object without excessive aggression? Overly intense observation might bash right through your focus. Stiff control might cause you to lose alignment with the graceful unfolding of things. Excessively zealous energy may backfire into an inner rebellion of self-judgment, tension, and doubt.

Try doing less rather than more. Half the effort might be sufficient to bring composure and balance to attention. You may not even be aware you are doing too much until you stop. Tension in the face and eyes may indicate excessive striving. Aim for the attitude of zeal that does not impose itself onto its object but softly rests into the meditation subject. Then explore it. Meditators describe this connection as "dropping back to observe," "dropping into experience," "settling into the experience," or "merging with the perception."

Efforts that don't support the task at hand can creep unnoticed into meditation. Reduce any unnecessary muscular effort in your jaw, eyes, facial muscles, chest, or hands. When I lead retreats, I sit in the front of the room, facing my students. We usually meditate with eyes closed, but I peek. Sometimes I see indications of excessive striving—faces puckered, mouths scrunched, foreheads wrinkled, postures rigid, chins jutting forward as if to reach for the breath. Such exaggerated physical effort interferes with the clarity of concentrated attention.

Relax! Breathe! Enjoy! Don't force the practice. Gather the dispersed energies of mind in a loving and consistent way. Loving diligence is stronger than the tense shell of striving. A composed, coordinated, gentle attention is usually enough to meet the rapidly changing perceptions that unfold.

Guard Your Mind as a Cowherd Guards the Cows

In the early stages of concentration, most people need strong resolve to abandon distractions and unwholesome tendencies of mind. To illustrate the need for timely energetic attention, the Buddha used a simile of a cowherd working in the autumn when the crops thicken. The cowherd knows that he could be punished, fined, or blamed if he allows his cows to stray into the crops. During this season the cowherd guards his cows by poking them, to check them and curb them. The Buddha said, "So too I saw in unwholesome states danger, degradation, and defilement."[51] Mindful of how unwholesome thoughts lead to affliction, a wise meditator actively removes harmful thoughts and hindrances. Obstacles must be met with resolute dedication.

⌇ *Adjusting Your Engagement*

During your meditation session, notice the quantity and quality of energy that you apply to observation. Is there interest or dullness, precision or diffusion, intensity or passivity?

Notice the conditions in which greater energy is available, such as when interest is piqued. And notice when there is less energy, such as when attention is dulled by fantasy.

Sense your ability to adjust the quality and quantity of energy and effort during a meditation session.

How much effort is required initially to direct the attention to the breath?

Try it again, and see whether the same quality and quantity of effort are needed.

Try again when there is noise in the room, or pain in the body, or you feel a little sleepy.

Notice the varied modulations of effort that are needed to precisely meet each of these changing conditions.

Effort becomes gentler as concentration deepens. As the mind moves from coarser toward more refined states of consciousness, harmful agitating thoughts cease to arise; thoughts of kindness, compassion, letting go, and peace dominate. The Buddha, continuing with the simile of the cowherd, taught that activity of mind is more spacious when the contents are wholesome: "Just as in the last month of the hot season, when all the crops have been brought inside the village, a cowherd would guard his cows while staying at the root of a tree or out in the open, since he needs only to be mindful that the cows are there; so too, there was need for me only to be mindful that those states were there."[52]

> *⁀ For Reflection*
>
> Consider the following questions during work, recreation, or home activities.
>
> Under what circumstances do you find that more vigorous energetic effort is required?
>
> When is equanimous relaxation more appropriate?
>
> Notice tasks at home or work during which alert attention and relaxation are both present and in balance.

TUNING A MUSICAL INSTRUMENT

During the Buddha's days, many eager young monastics were deeply intent on awakening. Having left their homes to undertake the holy life of a recluse, some were excessively energetic in their meditative pursuits. Young Soṇa, desperate to become enlightened, was one such monk. He was not yet mature in his practice; the impact of his overexertion caused genuine inspiration to sour into discouragement:

> Then, while the Venerable Soṇa was alone in seclusion, the following course of thought arose in his mind: "I am one of the Blessed One's most energetic disciples, yet my mind has not been liberated from the taints by non-clinging."

Dear Soṇa was deep in doubt, discouraged, and ready to quit. Fortunately, the Blessed One appeared before him and gave these instructions on effort:

"Now Soṇa, before, when you were a house dweller, were you skilled at playing the lute?"

"Yes, Lord."

"And when the strings of your lute were too taut, was your lute in tune and easy to play?"

"No, Lord."

"And when the strings of your lute were too loose, was your lute in tune and easy to play?"

"No, Lord."

"But when the strings of your lute were neither too taut nor too loose, but adjusted to an even pitch, was your lute then well tuned and easy to play?"

"Yes, Lord."

"Similarly, Soṇa, if energy is applied too forcefully it will lead to restlessness, and if energy is too lax it will lead to lassitude. Therefore, Soṇa, keep your energy in balance, . . . and there seize your object."[53]

There is no single correct setting for our effort that will apply to all situations. Tuning the instrument of effort occurs continuously, with each inhale and exhale, in each moment of connecting and sustaining the attention. We adjust our energies moment by moment. We automatically employ different qualities of effort when we lift an empty tea cup and when we lift a full pot of soup. As we encounter the phenomenal world we adjust the vigor with which we interact with things. Through meditation we learn to refine this capacity so that we apply our minds wholeheartedly to perception. Just as a child intuitively determines the variations in strength needed to push a toy car or shove the living room sofa, so too we learn how vigorously to relate to a lustful fantasy and how to soften our vigor when encountering a subtle perception of joy.

The Buddha taught a multifaceted approach to effort. He did not merely demand that students just keep trying harder. Skillful effort requires the wisdom to bring forth the quality and quantity of energy that keeps the attention balanced, stable, and aware.

INTENTION: THE POWER OF THOUGHT

A disciple once asked the Buddha how he realized the end of suffering: "How did you cross the flood?" The Buddha replied, "By not halting, and by not straining, I crossed the flood."[54] The power of intention guides the unfolding of the meditative path, enabling smooth progress without strain. Our intentions establish the direction for what we will cultivate. Once an intention is set, the mind and body instantly orient toward that perception. Before you are consciously aware of a physical movement or personal decision, intention has mobilized and established the inclination. This interaction of mind and body occurs in all activities—the familiar impulse to reach for the doorknob on a closed gate, the movement of a hand brushing hair off the face, the decision to drink when we are thirsty.

Actions don't happen only in the body; they result from an intricate interrelationship of body and mind. Momentary impulses, springing from your contact with the myriad perceptions you encounter, shape the countless choices you make every day.[55] Being mindful of intentions presents an opportunity to explore how this mind-body process works and how a thought leads to an action.

Intention is the basis of all deliberate action. Intentions, sometimes referred to as "volitions," are subtle forms of thought that link a mental impulse to physical action. As the Buddha said, "It is volition, bhikkhus, that I call kamma. For having willed, one acts by body, speech, or mind."[56] Some intentions will lead to happiness; others will generate suffering. Intention is a potent force, powerful enough to either reinforce or interrupt conditioned patterns.

Although largely unnoticed, intentions permeate virtually all actions and choices. An intention will impel the movement from the sitting posture to standing or will move you from the living

❧ Noticing Intention

As you prepare to end your next meditation session, notice what moves you from sitting to standing. How is that shift organized? What initiates the change in postures? Observe the arising of intention as a moment of being "about to" do something.

Practice playing with intention during meditation when you're experiencing subtle pain, perhaps an itch. The impulse arises to scratch. Don't move. Keenly observe that mental impulse to move. Observe the intention to scratch arise and keep watching until you observe the intention to scratch pass. You may notice that the tingling itchy sensation is distinct from the mental impulse to scratch.

What happens if you inhibit the intention to move and just stay still, awake and aware, attuned to the whole realm of mind-body phenomena?

Explore the links between body and mind, between sensation and intention, and between stimulus and response.

Notice what forces come together to mobilize a mindful movement. How does a decision occur?

room to the office. Intentions generated by the mind manifest in speech. Intention will also move you from one level of jhāna to the next jhāna. And intention will be the impetus for emerging from the absorption state at the proper time.

Intentions often lie hidden, obscured by the complex and rapidly changing activities we busy ourselves with. Buddhist practice shows the way to achieve liberation from all greed, all hate, and all delusion and confusion, which involves more than simply becoming a good person. Most people attracted to meditation already live with a decent standard of morality and ethics. Awakening, however, has

---

🖛 *For Reflection*

Out of the many intentions you may notice, which ones do you select to act on?

What intentions do you regret having acted on? Remember some times that you chose restraint and were glad.

---

the potential to completely uproot even our slightest negative tendencies. Most people do not want to think of themselves as cruel or filled with ill will, but little nasty thoughts may have infected the mind and become intertwined with complaints, gossip, criticisms, or a chronically judgmental attitude. Whether the judgments are directed at ourselves or others makes little difference; both poison the heart with ill will. The aim of this practice is to refine intention so that only the purest impulses—those that support awakening—interest the mind.

I have learned to see my pattern of justification as a signal to stop and reflect. When I notice a residue of justification in my mind—a train of thought, usually repetitive, that explains why I did something, that holds on to past actions and defends my strategies—I stop what I am doing to consider: What were my intentions that brought forth the action I am obsessing about? Since my mind became so unsettled and agitated, since restless justification manifested, perhaps my action was rooted in an impure intention. By reflecting, we create the opportunity to choose which intentions to support and which to withdraw our energy from.

Inevitably, we all make mistakes. Focusing on purity of intention more than on perfection of action allows us to accept our imperfections and personal limitations. When we trust our intentions, we learn without dwelling on mistakes and condemning ourselves. We cannot control the results of our actions, but we can have tremendous influence over the intentions from which our actions spring.

∽ Composing Your Intention

It can be helpful to write out your intentions for practice.

What is your highest purpose? Focus on your deepest aspirations for yourself and all beings. Reflecting on your highest purpose might inspire you when progress appears slow. Knowing your intentions can keep you going even when you are tired, bored, or busy. Try to use language that resonates for you personally; write it to inspire yourself, and then use it to remind yourself of your deepest aspirations.

I wrote out my intention at the start of one personal retreat. When the meditation became difficult, when my body throbbed with aches and pains, when I wanted to take a nap, lose myself in fantasy, or distract myself with books, I would recite it, encouraging myself to realign with my deeper values. Since I am greatly inspired by the early discourses of the Buddha, I included some lines that refer to his teachings. I share it as an example, but please compose one that is meaningful to you.

> Today I have a fortunate opportunity,
> not easily come by,
> supported by the sacrifice, trust, and generosity
> of many benefactors.

> Let me not waste this precious chance
> to free the mind from habitual obstructions,
> to unclog the conditioned tendencies of judging,
>   selfing, craving, and distraction.

> May my practice this day be energetic and bright, earnest,
> steadfast in the face of any difficulty,
> concentrated, focused, unwavering.
>
> Happily, I apply myself with vigor
> until this mind is utterly freed,
> beyond the range of grasping,
> having willingly done
> what needs to be done.

INTENTION AND THE STILLNESS OF ABSORPTION

As concentration deepens, the activities of mind are sequentially stilled; unwholesome thoughts are set aside until the thoughts that arise are of an entirely wholesome flavor and sparked only by immediate experience. When you review such a mind, you'll find nothing to fear. As the Buddha discovered, "If I think and ponder upon this thought even for a night, even for a day, even for a night and day, I see nothing to fear from it."[57] It is essential to examine the purified mind, to know that you can trust yourself. Recognizing the beauty of a purified mind frees you from the struggle against disruptive tendencies. Enjoy the mind that has no ill will, cruelty, or greed present. Know when it is safe to relax.

When the Buddha found his mind entirely free of unwholesome states, he recognized that the very presence of thinking disturbs tranquility. He noticed, "with excessive thinking and pondering I might tire my body, and when the body is tired, the mind becomes disturbed, and when the mind is disturbed, it is far from concentration. So I steadied my mind internally, quieted it, brought it to singleness, and concentrated it. Why is that? So that my mind should not

ᴥ *Start Your Meditation with an Intentional Routine*

You might establish the habit of reflecting on your intentions at the beginning of each meditation sitting. After establishing a relaxed and upright posture, and grounding attention in the body, briefly consider three levels of intention:

- First, recollect your highest spiritual aspiration, perhaps one of the intentions that you identified in the exercise above. For example: "May this practice be a contributing cause for the ending of greed, hatred, and delusion."
- Second, bring to mind a compassionate or altruistic intention that aligns with your values and motivates your growth. For example: "May my practice be for the benefit of all beings."
- Third, articulate a practical aim or immediate objective for this particular sitting period. For example: "May I attend wholeheartedly to each in-breath and out-breath."

While it is not necessary to articulate elaborate intentions every time you sit down to meditate, you may find that routinely affirming clear and practical aims reduces distraction and strengthens your sense of purpose. When the mind forgets its intention and becomes dull or lost in thought, remembering your intentions will quickly restore mindfulness, enthusiasm, and concentration on your chosen meditation object.

be disturbed."[58] After energetically removing everything unwholesome, after reflection that confirms only wholesome thoughts are present, you may wish to consider the possibility of going beyond good and bad thoughts. This is a pertinent step for progressing in concentration practice: here one enters the domain of jhāna.

☞ *For Reflection*

What is the purpose of your efforts?

What is beyond the immediate reach of even your best effort?

What is accomplished through effort and what is effortless?

Breaking Out from the Shell

The Buddha likened developing a mature practice to incubating eggs:

> Suppose there were a hen with eight, ten, or twelve eggs, which she had covered, incubated, and nurtured properly. Even though she did not wish: "Oh, that my chicks might pierce their shells with the points of their claws and beaks and hatch out safely!" yet the chicks are capable of piercing their shells with the points of their claws and beaks and hatching out safely. So too, a bhikkhu who thus develops various wholesome faculties supportive of wisdom and concentration is capable of breaking out, capable of enlightenment, capable of attaining the supreme security from bondage.[59]

You can cultivate many things through dedicated interest: patience, generosity, joy, and understanding. You can develop conditions that are conducive to concentration and supportive of wisdom. You can "sit on your eggs" by diligently nurturing the meditative explorations. Giving yourself to the spiritual life is like sitting in the nest. But the actual rate of maturation is not under your control. It would be senseless to wish, "May I attain the fourth jhāna today," and expect that wish to be fulfilled without any practice. You can diligently nurture your practice, but maturation occurs due to the ripening of conditions, not from how fervent your wishes are.

No one will make you meditate, no one requires you to cultivate deep spiritual happiness, and no one can insist that you become aware. Meditation practice is not a prescription, obligation, or punishment. In the absence of authoritarian requirements, we must each discover for ourselves the tender discipline that sustains us. Spiritual discipline is a precious resource for maintaining a practice, even when it feels dry, tedious, and difficult. We need effort to progress on this path. Only after all need for effort ceases are we entitled to make the ancient declaration of enlightenment: "What had to be done has been done."[60]

CHAPTER 8
Calming the Restless Mind

Whatever one frequently thinks and ponders upon,
that will become the inclination of his mind.
—Majjhima Nikāya 19:6

To ATTAIN THE JHĀNAS, we need both concentration and wisdom. The basic instruction for concentration training is marvelously simple: let all distractions go and steadily focus on your meditation subject. Yet wisdom training requires us to be sensitive to what is being let go. Both concentration and wisdom practices require a composed and clear mind that is neither stuck nor distracted. Since distraction can take many forms, it is helpful to have a toolkit of practices that allow us to work with various modes of distraction. This chapter offers the reader several helpful approaches for investigating and dealing with distraction that emphasize both *letting go* and *clear understanding*, a combination vital for developing wise concentration.

Once a student decides in principle to let go of distracting thoughts, a common question arises: "How?" In the early days of my meditation practice I employed a rather unsophisticated technique that I now call the Caveman Approach. In *The Flintstones* cartoon, Barney Rubble's son Bamm-Bamm wielded a favorite club and pursued a single theme in all his actions. Whatever he encountered, he clobbered with his club. When an errant thought arose during meditation, my mind would bash it immediately with a walloping *bamm-bamm!* This is a very coarse technique, and not one I recommend.

Instead, when practicing letting go, notice how your mind tends to respond to unwanted thoughts. Does it respond by clobbering them with judgment? If a painful feeling arises, do you wham that away too? Certainly thoughts and feelings that lead to harm must be wisely abandoned, but the single-minded aggression of Bamm-Bamm tends to increase self-judgment, fear, and aversion, exhausting the zealous meditator rather than providing the understanding that can support deep release.

And yet we need determination to avoid entertaining unwholesome thoughts. The Buddha teaches:

> Here, a bhikkhu does not tolerate an arisen sensual thought; he abandons it, dispels it, terminates it, and obliterates it. He does not tolerate an arisen thought of ill will . . . an arisen thought of harming . . . bad unwholesome states whenever they arise; he abandons them, dispels them, terminates them, and obliterates them. This is called the perception of abandoning.[61]

In addition to this determined approach, we also need a more precise tool, the "sword of wisdom," which represents the power of sharp decisiveness. You must identify where the problem lies and cut directly through that attachment. There is no use bashing sensations, thoughts, or perceptions. Effective removal is more surgical: cutting the link of craving. This can take the form of a stern but clear "No, thank you!" That cuts the energy off at the root—not because you're angry, but because you don't choose to go where those thoughts will lead. You don't need to maintain habits that lead you

ᕲ *Working with Restless Thinking*

In the first ten minutes of one of your meditation sessions, notice your thinking rather than the sensations of breath. Without judging yourself for the presence of thought during meditation, count each thought.

Observe closely, so you can count each discrete thought. Each thought begins and ends. When each thought ends, let the mind relax quietly until the next thought arises and is counted.

Count each subtle thought about the meditation and judgments of how the process is developing, in addition to the coarser thoughts about past events and future plans.

It isn't necessarily better to get a higher or a lower "score"—but to perform this exercise, you need to distinguish between the occurrence of thought and the content of thought. De-emphasize the content of the story and focus simply on the energetic occurrence of thinking.

into agitated distraction or mental obsessions. Tell unruly, undisciplined thoughts to go away—and mean it. As your concentration strengthens, you will find this approach increasingly effective.

Distraught at the persistence of their thoughts, students ask, "How can I quiet my mind? How can I get rid of thoughts? How can I stop my mind from wandering?" If we are to free the mind from the influence of restless thinking, we must understand the forces that push and pull at the mind, jerking it along the trail of associative thought.

You do not need to get rid of thoughts, just cease to believe them. If you are not seduced by the stories that they represent, the thoughts will not disturb your mind. Tenzin Palmo, a nun in the Tibetan tradition, wrote:

> There is the thought, and then there is the knowing of the thought. And the difference between being aware of the thought and just thinking is immense. Normally we are so identified with our thoughts and emotions, that we are them. We are the happiness, we are the anger, we are the fear. We have to learn to step back and know our thoughts and emotions are just thoughts and emotions. They're just mental states. They're not solid, they're transparent.[62]

A well-settled mind is not devoid of thought, but at the same time it is not seduced by the stories. You needn't buy into the story-line just because you thought it. Instead of believing your thoughts, inquire: Can I actually know this? Is this sure? Work directly with the energy of thinking, unseduced by the content of the thought. When you connect with a thought as just a thought, there is no distraction. It is just what it is, nothing more and nothing less.

AS THOUGHTS PROLIFERATE

Many meditators find that certain thoughts proliferate—thoughts about the past and future may preoccupy our minds during meditation. You might feel disappointed about an event that you witnessed, but the event is long past. It has already changed and gone. Or you might feel insecure about an activity you have to perform in the near future and hope for reassurance and support. The event, however, has not even occurred. The grasping—and consequently the place for letting go—is in the presently arising desire for recognition. Here is where the illusion of self is fabricated; here is where it can be abandoned. By momentarily ceasing to construct self-concepts through daily experiences, you simplify and clarify your relationship with all things.

⤳ *Catching Thoughts*

This exercise encourages the observation of the arising and passing of thoughts.

Try to catch each thought at its inception—as soon as a thought arises, try to catch it. Ask yourself, "What is a thought? What can I catch?" Give your full attention to the observation of mental objects, not breath. How fast can you observe the arising of thoughts? See the moment thought begins and disappears. Between each thought, rest back into the quiet mind, until the next thought appears out of nothing.

Rest between thoughts. Stay alert. Be ready to catch the next thought.

As you practice mindfulness and concentration, you learn to rest in the first moment of contact at any sense door, before it evolves into a chain of discursive thinking.

One student described a series of thoughts to me: She had lost her hair clip that day; she knew she had to go buy a new one. She felt annoyed that she had to go shopping; the thought arose that she was stupid to lose it; how could she lose it? Now she has to spend more money; her job is not paying well; she never has enough money; she will never have enough; deep feelings of worthlessness and failure dominated her mind; she decided she had better get a new job, but wondered what else she could do. Over lunch, she read through the want ads in the newspaper. She felt trapped, angry, afraid, and depressed. Finally, she remembered she could observe her own mind. All this anguish was nothing more than a proliferation of thought sparked by an absent hair clip. If she had brought mindfulness to the first thought "I lost my hair clip," noticing that it was a thought rather than identifying wholly with the elaborate

➣ *Talking Back to Your Mind*

If while you are cultivating concentration you discover that your mind is preoccupied with thoughts of people, relations, work, reputation, activities, roles, past events, future plans—talk back to it! Send those thoughts away. Talk back in a tone of voice that is clear but not abusive. Tell the thought, gently but firmly:

> *That is not my concern.*
> *There is nothing to be done right now.*
> *This is not the time for this subject.*
> *That is uncertain, unknown, not sure.*
> *That may not be true; I just can't know whether it is really true.*
> *That is long past; it is over and done with; too late now.*

Arguably, some topics merit reflection and responsible attention. However, most thoughts merely reflect habitual tendencies and can be seen clearly, then abandoned, without pulling attention away from the meditation object of the breath. If certain thoughts persist, you may need to temporarily set aside the practice of concentration to mindfully explore the process of thinking, glean insight through investigation, and then later return to concentrate on breathing. At times, it may be wise to explore how and why your mind is distracted by thoughts, but meditative investigation should be kept very brief. Just a couple of minutes of mindful curiosity is usually sufficient to expose the conditioned patterns, assumptions, fears, and emotions that feed habitual thoughts. Time spent reflecting on thought implies a corresponding absence of attention to the breath, thereby weakening concentration. You can gently dismiss the many kinds of distracting thoughts that do not require deep reflection.

story, the suffering would have ended there, eliminating the chain of distorting associations.

This may seem like a trivial example, but our days can be filled with such low-grade distress. Misperception blows event after event out of proportion. Although unrestrained associative thinking is a deeply ingrained habit, you do not need to entertain it. You can train yourself to mindfully rest in the direct recognition of any sensory experience, without the entanglements of the scattered and restless mind. Look into your own vivid experience of seeing, hearing, smelling, tasting, touching, and thinking.

Personal history makes each of us vulnerable to our own set of chronic thoughts. Be heartened: these patterns are arising in order to be released. When a familiar scenario recurs, one you have set aside dozens of times before, you may need to investigate it more precisely and understand it more thoroughly before you can abandon it completely. The next time you find repeating thoughts dominating your meditation, try using the exercise below.

UNDISTRACTED COMPASSION

The problem of distraction doesn't exist "out there," in the objects. You don't need to remove objects, prevent perceptions, or control your external environment to abide without distraction. It's in the thick of life's activities where you will learn to discern the difference between a distraction and a genuine, free, wise, and compassionate response to life.

Several years ago I was in Nepal with a group of friends receiving a series of teachings from a Tibetan lama. This teacher lived in a monastery at the top of a hill. Each day we would ascend the hill by a trail that passed a few little village shops near the base, then wove back and forth in switchbacks until it reached the monastery perched at its summit. One day we were hurrying up the trail. I turned to notice that two friends had fallen behind. They had stopped at the outskirts of the tiny village and were standing near a sobbing young girl. She had been sent to the shop to purchase two eggs but had accidentally broken one and was afraid to go home for fear her mother would beat her. My friends had stopped and talked with her, and they had sent a boy with two rupees to buy another egg.

By the time my friends and I finally ascended the hill that day, the room was full and the doors were closed. We sat outside, perched against the building near an open window, catching only a smattering of words. Yes, we missed the formal teachings that morning. We had traveled halfway around the planet to receive these teachings from a renowned senior lama, but I did not consider this a distraction from our spiritual quest. It was the practice—a compassionate response to immediate needs.

When Consciousness Is Not Distracted or Diffused

As we have noted, a common way to overcome distraction is by concentrating on an object such as the breath. This is an effective way to dissolve the tendency to feel scattered, but it may introduce a subtle fixation. The Buddha taught:

> A practitioner should so investigate that, as she investigates, her consciousness is not distracted and diffused

---

⤺ *Laughing at Thoughts*

Be clearly aware that a thought is occurring. Notice the theme of the story. Disentangle the energy of thinking from the content or storyline the thought is narrating.

For example, you may find yourself repeatedly planning what you will say in next week's staff meeting. Give the story a title or name such as "Presenting Me," "Endless Dramas," "Great Catastrophes," "Grand Plans," "My Witty Retort." Give the repeating thoughts funny names: "The Story of My Life," "The Tragedy at Dinner." These repetitive stories are like songs we sing over and over again.

Humorous names can depersonalize the thought patterns, minimizing their power over the mind. A playful or humorous name makes it easier to deflate any charged energy in the thoughts and recognize them simply as thoughts.

---

externally, and internally is not fixed, and by not grasping anything she should remain undisturbed. If her consciousness is not distracted and diffused externally, and internally is not fixed, and by not grasping anything she remains undisturbed, then there is no . . . suffering in the future.[63]

In today's world, people often experience being distracted by external conditions. Yet, it is possible for a multitude of discordant experiences to occur without scattering attention. Imagine walking through a crowded train station during your daily commute, but not veering off your path. Discordant images—people, noises, smells, and announcements—just occur; they do not disturb your route. In other situations, a variety of experiences could distract your attention. Perhaps music is playing, the telephone is ringing, a child is calling for attention, and your hands are wet from washing a salad; you feel pulled in many directions at once. What, then, turns an experience into a distraction rather than just another complex moment of sensory encounters in the fabric of daily life?

The Buddha explained that consciousness becomes scattered when it "is tied and shackled by gratification."[64] This occurs when the mind revels in the gratification of sensory contact—attention follows after sights, sounds, tastes, sensations, and thoughts. Sensory experience does not in and of itself distract us; the mind is not inevitably fettered by contact. The problem resides in the movement of desire. We are bound by seeking gratification through sensory perceptions and then using those perceptions to construct a personal identity. Therefore, the Buddha cautioned that the meditator should not be "stuck internally" or "internally fixed." In the effort to establish the jhānas, one should not become stuck internally through attachment to the rapture and happiness.

Whether the bondage is to internal states or to external objects, the principles regarding the cause of suffering are the same. The rapture, joy, and bliss of jhāna are not in and of themselves problematic, nor is the pleasure that naturally arises in a concentrated mind—unless there is clinging. If consciousness follows after the signs of rapture, joy, contentment, equanimity, or any subtle meditative attainment, then it could be establishing a relationship to inner experience that is "fettered by the fetter of gratification."[65]

After dwelling in each jhāna, it will be important to reflect upon your relationship to the dominant jhāna factors and to rest into the absorption with detachment. Allow the mind to become unified, not indulgent. Explore your relationship to pleasure by examining the subtle and intense delights of concentration. As the concentration practice develops, you must maintain a parallel contemplation on fixation and inquire, "What is the stillness of a unified mind, and how does that differ from the static fixation of clinging?" You must know when the mind is stuck and when it is simply at rest.

As your observation skills develop, you might discover that attention remains vibrant during the space between breaths and that a clear awareness pervades the space between thoughts. Those spaces are opportunities for deep rest as things fluidly arise and pass in awareness. Sounds, sensations, or thoughts appear and disappear, as temporary as a bird flying through the sky-like space of mind; they leave no trace, no markers, no wake. From this well-settled sense of spaciousness, you can notice when the mind seems to contract around a perception. Often something we either desire or are averse to triggers our more noticeable reactions. If you can discern this contraction, instantly let it go and rest back into spacious awareness. You will experience the ephemeral nature of experience as it flows and changes, and feel the mind narrow and expand, undistracted in the moments of contraction and release.

You cannot control the experiences of living. There will always be unpleasant sensations, challenging thoughts, and abrasive sounds. Difficult events happen: illness, death, betrayal, cruelty. These are part of our world. You cannot avoid them, but you can cultivate such a vast quality of awareness that your mind remains undistracted. If you mix a teaspoon of salt in a glass, its impact is strong. If you mix a teaspoon of salt in a lake, the impact is much more tempered.[66] Meditation will not eliminate abrasive conditions from your life, but it can temper their impact and enhance your ability to remain balanced in the face of life's challenges.

UNDISTURBED TRANQUILITY

Jhāna practice introduces the mind to the stability of mental unification; it drenches the heart with tranquility. Free of desire or aversion, thoughts remain quite simple. A concentrated mind is essentially undisturbed. A mind influenced by jhāna is so coherent, almost crystalline, that it reenters the world of sensory contact without binding itself to the various perceptions that habitually preoccupy unconcentrated attention.

After emerging from a deep absorption, the mind is pliable, concentrated, and ready to investigate. You can use this steadiness to explore the nuances of the objects that you perceive or turn your attention from external sensory objects and become aware of knowing itself. Exploring the process of perception is a subtle inquiry. We do not reject things; we simply are no longer fascinated with them. We look into the process of perceiving rather than the content of our perceptions.

One of the great contributions of the modern art movement was the production of nonrepresentational art. Art works were created from an interest in the varied uses of materials—canvas, paint, wood, metal, paper, and so forth—rather than from a wish to represent a person, still-life, or landscape. A line was just a line; it did not always represent the contour of a visible or imaginary object. These innovations challenged the viewer to see without indulging in stories, to view the canvas as canvas, the paint as paint, a stroke of the brush as a stroke of the brush. Art broke through the conventional expectations that limited it to representing historic events, portraying wealthy patrons, or recording social, natural, or fictitious scenes. Similarly, meditation challenges us to experience a thought as a thought, a feeling as a feeling, a sight as a sight, without embellishing each encounter with a personal story of representational significance.

If you keep examining—not until you find something, but until you realize seeing without grasping, inquiring without fixating, exploring without expecting, knowing without controlling, living without suffering—you will discover a purity of happiness that is unbounded. It is a happiness beyond anything contrived by concentration: the deep joy of release.

⤳ *Just Noticing*

Set this book aside for 5–10 minutes to just sit quietly.

Notice what you are experiencing.

What do you feel in the body? What mental states and emotions flavor your experience now? What thoughts circulate in the mind?

With mindful awareness, explore each experience of body and mind, free of the elaborate stories they trigger.

Notice the thinking as just thinking—an energetic impulse in the mind.

Notice the feelings as just feelings, without explaining or justifying them.

Bring awareness to each precise momentary experience.

Turn your interest to the phenomenal process of the interaction of mind and body. Don't get stuck viewing experience in terms of personal stories about my day, my life, my friends, my family, my desires.

Let the mind rest, spacious and at ease, as mind and body processes are effortlessly known, arising and passing, disturbing no one, affecting no one, belonging to no one.

You may wish to let this exercise transition into one of mental relaxation.

Relax the mind.

Just relax.

Repeatedly relax.

Just relax and allow a naturally alert awareness to experience the nature of things.

PART III

How to Establish Meditative Absorption

CHAPTER 9

Happiness and the Five Factors of Absorption

One should remove all acquisitive craving, above, below,
and across in the middle. Whatever they cling to in
the world, by this itself Māra pursues a person.
—Sutta Nipāta, verse 1103

THE FORCES THAT CONFOUND our concentration are personified in the Buddhist teachings by a character named Māra. He represents the inner forces of temptation that hinder progress. This mythical symbolic figure arrives on the scene in various forms and represents a wide range of obstructive mental states that prevent concentration.[67] As we have noted, the mind must be free of such hindrances for stable absorption to occur. If we are able to counteract the forces of Māra and apply antidotes to the various obstacles to a stable mind, we can begin the entry into jhāna. This chapter and the next present instructions for dealing effectively with obstacles and creating the conditions necessary for entering jhāna. In preparation for absorption, these chapters take up in a more pointed, instructional way topics introduced in earlier chapters.

Classically, Māra manifested as fear, desire, or doubt just before a recluse approached jhāna or liberating insight. For lay people today,

Māra appears at critical junctures in our lives, when we stand at the brink of a choice. He might aggressively confront the unwary meditator with a stream of vengeful thoughts. He might be disguised as something pleasant, thereby seducing us with comfort, honor, and privilege. Māra may arise in a multitude of disguises: as friends cajoling us toward trivial activities; as temptations toward drink or distraction; as the rationalizations within our own mind that whisper, "You have too much to do today to waste time just meditating; accomplish something useful!"; as the inertia that reaches for the TV remote control rather than the meditation cushion; as the self-critical voice that condemns us before we try; or as the overconfident disposition that exaggerates our abilities and cannot accept defeat. When encountering any of these inner forces, you are metaphorically confronting Māra. To face Māra is to face your own shadow. Will we make the great stride toward liberating understanding or fall back again into the grip of habit? Vanquishing Māra you overcome the "inner demons" that threaten to limit your spiritual potential. Māra represents the challenges that test our mettle and spiritual maturity.

The depictions of Māra in the Buddhist scriptures offer an array of heroic stories that tell of the courage of meditators coming face to face with their darkest fears, including monks who surmounted lust when Māra appeared disguised as the alluring seductress and nuns who staved off their deepest fears when Māra accosted them in the forest.[68] Even the Buddha received a number of visits from this character. In each encounter there is a single antidote to all of Māra's antics: mindfulness. Mindfulness is the secret weapon for which Māra's army has no defense. Exposed to mindful scrutiny, obstructive forces always and inevitably weaken.

Māra provides a metaphorical image that can help depersonalize our relationship to hindrances. You might laugh when doubt arises, viewing the doubt as Māra playing a trick on you. You might poke fun at a tendency to find fault with your friends, seeing Māra appearing as the judge. You may cajole the greedy mind that buys needlessly, storing up possessions like a chipmunk stuffing its cheeks with peanuts, for this is Māra's mischief. And the time will come when, with faith clarified and confidence verified, you will return the challenge to Māra as Venerable Samiddhi did: "My mindfulness and wisdom are mature, and my mind well concentrated. Conjure up whatever forms you wish, but you will never make me tremble."[69] When we can stand firm in the face of Māra, we rest unruffled by whatever life may bring us.

WHERE MĀRA IS BLINDFOLDED

Jhāna is an attainment that is said to "blindfolded Māra" because it creates a field of unification in which hindrances of desire, aversion, and obsessive thoughts cannot arise. For the duration of the absorption, your energies are liberated from the struggle with hindrances and available to cultivate entirely wholesome qualities. Jhāna is an approach to training the mind in the absence of Māra, rather than in confrontation with Māra. In jhāna the strength comes not through rubbing up against obstacles, but through familiarity with a way of being that is unhindered by them. By turning away from the corruptions, the mind thrives in a range of purity temporarily unimpeded by malicious forces.

Prior to entering jhāna we learn about difficult mental states and work with them mindfully. Eventually we can set them aside without struggle or identification. Within jhāna, internal energies coalesce and strengthen. When you emerge, this well-concentrated mind is again ready to meet all variety of sensory contacts. Should you discover that you emerge only to be immediately ambushed by Māra (perhaps an attack of impatience or wanton greed) you need not bother to berate yourself for the occurrence of painful states—it is just Māra visiting again! We continue to work through the hindrances by facing them squarely whenever they arise. They may erupt with volcanic force or sneak up so gradually you hardly detect them. Although the refined mind might be humiliated by these unwholesome tendencies, little by little the integration of samādhi and vipassanā will wear away the forces of obstruction.

Confidence will flood the heart when you look into your own mind and can honestly declare, "No hindrance is present."

THE FIVE JHĀNA FACTORS

Access to jhāna occurs when hindering unwholesome factors are in abeyance and when five corresponding wholesome mental factors grow strong.

These five jhāna factors and the hindrances they overcome are (1) *the ability to direct the attention to a chosen object*, which overcomes dullness; (2) *the capacity to sustain the attention on the object*, which overcomes doubt; (3) *the delight and rapture that refreshes attention*, which overcomes aversion; (4) *pervasive feelings of happiness, peace, contentment, and joy*, which overcome restlessness; and (5) *the stability of single-pointed focus*, which overcomes lust and greed.

ᔕ *The Five Jhāna Factors*

Jhāna Factor	Hindrance Overcome
1. directed attention (*vitakka*)	sloth and torpor
2. sustained attention (*vicāra*)	doubt
3. rapture and joy (*pīti*)	aversion
4. happiness and pleasure (*sukha*)	restlessness
5. one-pointed attention (*ekaggatā*)	sensual desire

Each jhāna factor is an antidote to a particular hindrance. They are paired as opposites; the development of one automatically weakens the other, offering an alternative model for eroding obstructive

Working with Obstructive Energies

1. During your meditation, notice when hindrances or temptations arise. Recognize those forces and name them. Feel how each manifests in body and in mind. Precisely acknowledge each of these states by saying to them: "I see you Māra," or "I see you anger," or "I see you doubt."

   Observe their arising, how they change, and how they disappear.

   Notice the stream of associated thoughts or emotions that are triggered by hindrances.

   Notice how their arrival affects your degree of concentration and can distract your attention from the focus on breath.

   Consider Māra a mischievous neighbor who visits for tea. There is no cause for argument, yet his antics become tiresome, so you keep a keen watch over him when he is near, and you escort him to the door when the opportunity arises.

2. You are not plagued by hindrances every moment of every day. Notice any moments that seem empty of hindrances. When judgment, anger, lust, fear, laziness, restlessness, confusion, and doubt are not arising, what is the quality of mind? Allow the absence of hindrances to gladden the mind.

3. After recognizing the presence and absence of the
obstructive forces during silent meditation, bring the
exploration into your daily life.

During activities and interactions, notice when
the mind is affected or obsessed by unwholesome
forces and when it is free from obstructions.

forces. Much of a meditator's early samādhi training will be devoted
to developing these jhāna factors. Once they are established, the
progression through the jhānas follows systematically. When these
jhāna factors are fully developed, the mind cannot be overwhelmed
by hindrances.

The Buddha recommended that practitioners periodically review
their minds to assess if anything needs to be abandoned or developed. If when you look into your mind you discover a mind free
of hindrances, the instruction is to "abide happy and glad, training day and night in wholesome states."[70] Even after the hindrances
have been set aside, the jhāna factors must be fortified or absorption
will remain elusive. Don't hurry to get into jhāna; take your time
and cultivate the basic factors. They are a powerful resource with or
without the specific states of absorption.

The first meditation instruction given in chapter 1 was to be
aware of the breath at the nostrils. As you develop this basic exercise, be patient but diligent; each time the mind wanders, simply
bring it back to the breath. Being aware of the breath and returning
the attention when it wanders off constitute an exercise that cultivates the abilities to direct (vitakka) and sustain (vicāra) attention,
the first two factors essential for samādhi. With some practice the
mind will more frequently connect with and sustain attention on
the breath. As the momentum of sustained focus grows, attention
gradually becomes infused with joy (pīti) and pleasure (sukha), and

the mind settles down. When the mind stays with one object without straying, a feedback loop is created that further enhances stability and happiness. When delight, joy, or equanimity are available, the mind is less inclined to wander into thoughts of past or future. Consequently, when the first four factors gain strength, the experience of one-pointed focus grows, further unifying the mind with its object.

VITAKKA: DIRECTED ATTENTION

The first jhāna factor, *vitakka*, refers to the capacity to direct attention at a particular perception; it is the aiming or connecting function of attention. Think of this process as shining a light on an object in a dark room, striking a baseball with a bat, aiming a pistol at a target, or poking a needle through a buttonhole when sewing. It is the clear directing of attention to a chosen object. The *Visuddhimagga*, an ancient commentary written by Buddhaghosa in the fifth century, uses the analogy of a gatekeeper who inspects people as they enter and exit the gate.[71] The gatekeeper is not concerned with the business the merchants transact in the marketplace or which village they travel to when they depart. The gatekeeper simply checks each person as they pass through the gate. Just so, we direct our attention to the area between the nostrils and upper lip and examine what passes by. We don't need to follow the breath inside the body or contemplate external phenomena. We keep our focus precise.

The directed application of energy associated with vitakka has an invigorating quality that refreshes and revitalizes the mind. As the attention collects by consistently perceiving the breath, distractions diminish. It is not sufficient to want to feel the breath; nor will one connection be enough. You must repeatedly apply attention to the meditation object. You might aim and connect several times on the inhale and several times on the exhale. My first teacher likened this to training a puppy to sit. You have to repeat the lesson many times.

∽ More with Counting Breaths

Work again with the counting exercise introduced in chapter 2. Count the breaths from one to ten. Then from ten to one. Then from one to ten. As you count, emphasize the direct experience of the breath rather than the conceptual numbers. Give 95 percent of your attention to the actual feeling of the contact with breath, and the remaining 5 percent to maintaining the numerical sequence.

Then try another counting exercise. With each breath, silently repeat the count of "one" many times through the duration of the inhalation and exhalation, then silently repeat the count of "two" many times through the duration of the next breath, and then silently count "three" and so on. With every count, actively lift attention up to the breath during each inhalation and each exhalation. Repeatedly applying attention allows no opportunity for distracting thoughts to arise.

This traditional counting technique was inspired by the method ancient caterers used for measuring rice. A cook would repeat aloud the number of measures as he simultaneously pulled out bits of grass, straw, dirt, or pebbles from the rice batch. He would measure out one cup, saying "1, 1, 1, 1" as he sorted the debris from the grain. He would add a second cup, counting "2, 2, 2, 2, 2, 2," continuing to pull out bits of dirt. By repeating the numbers throughout the task of cleaning, the cook would keep track of the correct measurement and not become distracted by the related activity of cleaning the rice.

⤳ *Directing Attention*

Here are three ways outside of formal meditation you can playfully explore the remarkable capacity of attention to focus on and discern specific aspects of experience.

1. Listen to a recording of a symphony. Focus on individual instruments. Apply the attention to just the clarinet, then shift to the bass, then notice only the melody of the flutes.

2. Sit on a park bench for fifteen minutes or so. Choose four or five things to notice—perhaps the pressure where your thighs touch the bench, traffic sounds, the smell of cut grass, the warmth of the sun, and your posture. Systematically shift the attention through those items, spending about twenty seconds or so focused on the first sensory experience, then twenty seconds or so focused on the second sensory experience, and so on through your selected sequence. Rotate through the sequence of sense contacts several times at a comfortable pace while noticing the capacity you have to aim attention.

3. Sit in your home near an open window. Notice sounds that are close such as a heater, people in the building, plumbing, a gurgling stomach, the sound of saliva being swallowed. Then shift your attention to hearing far-off sounds: airplanes, distant traffic, unrecognizable street sounds. Notice the capacity to maintain a continuity of hearing while directing the range of that function.

Bring the pup back to its place and tell it again to "sit!" When it wanders, bring it back and again say, with patience and kindness, "sit!" After a while, puppies learn. So will your mind.

The function of vitakka is likened to ringing a bell with a striker. To produce a sound the striker must actually meet the bell: there must be a connection. Waving the striker around in the air would be unproductive. Only when there is clear aim, a directed swing, and contact between the striker and bell is sound produced. Similarly, it is not enough to have an idea about breathing; your attention must distinctly reach the breath. Many methods can strengthen this aiming capacity. Counting breaths is one popular tool. Counting maintains a clear focus. If the mind wanders off into thoughts of past or future, you come right back with the next number and continue your task. Repeatedly directing your attention to the presence of breath at the nostrils develops vitakka.

Vitakka is a subtle activity of thought that counteracts drowsiness and dullness. Māra shows up as the hindering force traditionally called "sloth and torpor." It is marked by a dull withdrawal, inertia, heaviness, lassitude, boredom, slumping, nodding, and, in its extreme form, sleepiness. Vitakka vividly connects to its object, allowing no opportunity for the torpor that dullness and boredom feed upon.

VICĀRA: SUSTAINED ATTENTION

The second jhāna factor, *vicāra*, the mate to vitakka, is the capacity of mind to sustain the attention on the object to which it has been directed. Vicāra is the quality of attention that stays with and penetrates the object of perception. When vicāra is strong, you can remain aware of the full length of the breath from the beginning, through the middle, and on to the end of each one. Vicāra sinks into its object and gets to know it with penetrative clarity. Because vicāra is an explorative aspect of thought, the term has been translated

⌒ *Moving Hands with Sustained Attention*

Choose a place to meditate that is relatively quiet.

Place your hand and forearm comfortably in front of you in a way that permits you to easily bend your elbow, raising your lower arm slightly in front of the body. The elbow can rest naturally near or against your waist. This movement will cause the hand to gently pass through the air.

Slowly move your lower arm and hand up and down while focusing your attention on the sensations in the palm of the hand. Keep the attention focused in the hand, sustaining awareness on these changing sensations.

Bring a penetrative quality to the attention so that your focus remains steady on the hand, even as the sensations change.

Encourage the attention to sink into the sensations and remain interested in the experience.

Gradually make the movements slower and smaller until the hand comes to rest on your lap.

Maintain the steady focus of attention with the sensations of the hand as the movement and sensations grow increasingly subtle.

Then shift the attention to the sensations at the point of contact where the breath enters the nostrils. Employ sustained attention to stay aware of the breath; allow attention to lock on to its object.

variously into English as "examination," "sustained thought," "pondering," "contemplation," and "investigation." In the context of jhāna practice, the specific function of vicāra is to sustain the attention on the chosen object. Sustained connection stabilizes consciousness.

Vicāra has been likened to the resounding of a bell. Vitakka directs the attention to the object (or strikes the bell), then vicāra sustains the attention (like the lingering resounding of a bell). Repeatedly directing attention to the breath brings a sustained knowledge of the breath. Vicāra holds the attention on a mental object, permitting concentration to deepen.

Both vitakka and vicāra are aspects of conceptual thought. They represent a skillful use of thought during meditation that focuses otherwise dispersed inclinations of the thinking mind.

Vicāra's function is to dispel the hindrance of doubt. By sustaining awareness long enough for deep contemplation, vicāra eliminates the opportunity for confusion and uncertainty to overtake awareness. The mind does not "back away" from presence, or wander off its subject, or separate from the investigation of things before the perception is thoroughly known. Sustained attention makes it possible to develop genuine confidence and a deeply penetrative knowledge of your meditation subject.

Pīti: Rapturous Interest

When vitakka and vicāra are steady, a feeling of lightness and pleasure naturally occur. The mind becomes bright and alert. The body will feel invigorated. The posture may be uplifted. This quality of pleasure, *pīti*, is infused with vibrant interest. *Pīti* is usually translated with terms such as "joy," "rapture," "delight," "pleasure," "zest," "happiness," or "bliss." Sometimes this pleasure will be intense, at other times soft and quiet. It is not necessary to effortfully rev up the bliss. Continuity of attention to the breath nourished by subtle pleasure is sufficient to support concentration.

Pīti manifests in many forms and not necessarily as the tantalizing electrified spectacle implied in such dramatic words as "rapturous bliss." Often pīti is experienced as simply an uplifting inner smile—a subtle joy that pervades the mind as attention settles with the breath.

⌇ *Discerning the Pleasantness of the Pleasant*

Find an experience that is pleasant: looking at a sunrise, feeling the smooth fur of a cat, holding a warm cup of tea, or any other such simple thing.

Practice moving your attention between the object and the pleasant feeling it elicits. Shift your attention between the object of pleasure (the visual image, feeling of warmth or softness) and the pleasurable feeling it evokes. Practice allowing the attention to settle within the experience of pleasantness without adding attachment.

If the desire for more arises, notice the attachment. Ask yourself—does attachment increase the pleasure or decrease it? Many people will recognize attachment by a characteristic feeling of contraction or separation. How do you discern attachment to pleasure as distinct from a simple awareness of pleasure?

Refocus attention and continue to move attention between the object of perception that is pleasant and the perception of pleasantness. Allow the pleasure to fill your awareness. Don't hold yourself back from the pleasant feeling. Allow the lightness of pleasant feeling to suffuse and nourish the mind and body.

Initially, some meditators experience goose bumps, shivers, tingles, vibrations, or surging and uplifting feelings. But as pīti matures, it becomes more subtle, not more intense. It should be recognized as a refreshing mental quality of buoyancy—a delight in the object; it should not produce distracting physical sensations. You will learn to identify the characteristics of pīti in its coarse, pervasive, and subtle manifestations.

You may need to ride some energetic waves of this bliss in the process of learning how pīti functions. Explore rapture without becoming agitated by the intensity of energy or impressed by personal meditative pleasures. When pīti develops into a quality that is full and steady—traditionally described as "all-pervading rapture"—it has matured into a force stable enough to be considered a jhāna factor.

This joy infused with interest lubricates the sustaining function of attention. Influenced by pīti, the mind grows increasingly cohesive. Rapturous interest produces energy that helps glide attention smoothly toward its chosen object of perception. As the rapt quality of interest draws mental and physical energy together, pīti becomes the catalyst and ally for the stabilizing of attention. While consciousness is saturated in delight and a feeling of fullness permeates the mind, the meditator is infused with joyful energy that inspires one's quest. Pīti is fulfilling its function of refreshing attention.

Pīti serves as an antidote that prevents Māra from appearing as the hindrance of aversion. Most people enjoy pīti at first. It is dramatically pleasant: a sharp contrast to the painful state of aversion. The struggle to direct and sustain the attention eases. Something finally seems to be happening in the meditation when this delightfully inspiring energy appears. The alluring pleasure of pīti attracts the mind, facilitating greater stability of attention and deeper unification with the meditation subject.

SUKHA: DEEP EASE OR PERVASIVE CONTENTMENT

Sukha is a quality of happiness that is much quieter and smoother than pīti. *Sukha* is usually translated as "joy," "contentment," "pleasure," "ease," or "happiness." Sukha has a sweet and smooth quality in contrast to the activated quality of pīti. Sukha is neither the jazz and thrill of delight nor the still calm of equanimity. When sukha

⤴ *Exploring Pleasant Daily Events*

For one week write a list of pleasant events that occur each day.

Make a note of the quality of the feeling: how the body feels, how the mind feels. Notice happiness wherever it arises. Be in touch with a felt sense of joy and contentment regarding the normal pleasant things that happen in a day—a hot shower, sunlight sparkling on a pond, the soft touch of fleece, a compliment from a friend, a good night's sleep.

Strengthen your capacity to sustain attention by mindfully observing simple pleasant daily experiences. Give your full attention to a conversation, play with your dog or cat without seeking alternative distractions, eat lunch with the intention to taste the flavors and feel the textures of each morsel.

If a pleasant experience sparks excitement, let the thrill settle. Then, focus on the quieter sense of happiness. Sukha is not revved up with interest and excitement; it is revealed by deeply settling into contentment. Rest into pleasant daily experiences and notice for yourself what aspects of pleasure agitate attention with the desire for more, or relax the mind with deep contentment that enhances the stability of attention.

is strong, the mind is exceptionally bright and undisturbed. It is the mental equivalent of submerging in a comforting warm bath: all-embracing contentment. Through intimate experience of sukha, you will discover a deeply settled state of ease that is not agitated by interest.

With the peace and contentment of sukha washing through the mind, the heart rests with confidence. When sukha is predominant, the meditator is undisturbed and feels no desire to get up at the end of the meditation: meditation sessions can last very long without distraction. The vastness of ease, a characteristic of sukha, overcomes the hindrance of restlessness. When sukha is strong, everything feels OK as it is. There is no restless lurching toward habitual planning or repetitive thinking. Deeply settled, content, pervaded by pleasure, the mind rests happily in present-moment experience.

EKAGGATĀ: ONE-POINTEDNESS OF ATTENTION

The fifth jhāna factor, *ekaggatā*, describes the capacity of mind to remain focused and one-pointed with a chosen object. Ekaggatā's characteristic quality is to lock onto the chosen object with an intimacy that rivets the attention, stills the mind, and settles into unwavering focus. The connection is so steady there is no impetus to wander. This singularity of attention does not diverge; it is not lured from its meditation subject by the seductive force of desire, lust, or craving. It is not thrown off its focus by the rattling energies of restlessness. Although it is described in terms similar to the sustaining factor of vicāra, ekaggatā has a steadier texture; it does not possess the explorative quality inherent in vicāra. Whereas vicāra is compared to a bee entering a single flower and buzzing around in the pollen, ekaggatā is compared to a nail or post that is anchored to one spot. Ekaggatā brings certainty, deep stability, and clarity: its one-pointed focus completely unifies attention with the object until consciousness feels virtually undifferentiated from its object.

The characteristic stability of ekaggatā transforms the hindrance of desire. Desirous energy tends to want more: it lurches to reach for the next good thing or clutch at present experience hoping it will last longer. Based in craving, desire is never satisfied, and the mind affected by desire cannot rest. No matter how much a person possesses, as long as greed arises the mind is discontent. The Buddha remarked that even if the Himalayas were turned into gold, it would not satisfy one man's greed.[72] After one pleasure is attained, the next is sought, perpetuating the fantasy of future fulfillment. In contrast, the focused intensity of one-pointedness needs nothing more. With ekaggatā there is no sense of deficiency, nothing lacking. The mind is completely unified and "one with the experience."

SETTING THE STAGE FOR ABSORPTION

These five elements of concentration—connecting, sustaining, rapture, pleasure, one-pointedness—take center stage during experiences of jhāna. Each level of absorption has its characteristic blend of these factors. Skill in entering and maneuvering through the levels of absorption depends upon cultivating these five factors.

These are not the only mental functions present in jhāna. In a detailed description, the Venerable Sāriputta lists each factor that can be observed during jhāna.[73] The primary jhāna factors—connecting, sustaining, rapture, pleasure, one-pointedness—are perceived. Contact, feeling, perception, volition, mind, zeal, decision, energy, mindfulness, equanimity, and attention are also present in jhāna. Notice that even within the state of absorption, mindfulness and attention remain present. These mental functions make it possible to clarify what is and is not being known.

In jhāna, consciousness is alert. Jhāna states are intensely clear. Absorption states do not resemble sleepy relaxation or dull spacey tranquility. Nor is absorption defined by the mere presence of rapture and happiness. It's important to note that the occurrence of jhāna factors is not synonymous with a jhāna state. Practitioners with a strong desire to succeed might mistake the simple arising of jhāna factors for absorption states. Sublime pleasures may seduce eager meditators; the development of the jhāna factors can turn them into distracting obstructions if they spark excitement, pride, or attachment.

At the same time, subtle meditative pleasures may go unrecognized; this lightness of pīti is easily dismissed by experienced meditators as just how meditation usually feels. It may take some time to discern the subtle significance of this familiar quality of joy in the shift from the more distracted mental states of worldly perceptions toward the protected seclusion of an inner abiding.

Developing jhāna factors can provide great benefits, even without the additional experience of absorption. In fact, busy lay practitioners who do not have the luxury of secluded conditions may opt to simply nourish the five jhāna factors in their daily meditation practice.

As you observe the maturing of the jhāna factors or the stabilization of the absorption states, you will come to know through direct experience what is present and what is absent in consciousness. You will recognize the changing clusters of mental factors that occur as concentration develops, and witness how different configurations of mental factors produce different effects on consciousness. You will learn how the jhāna factors intensify perception and are able to produce states of non-ordinary consciousness.

CHAPTER 10

Access to Absorption: At the Threshold of Peace

One who, whether walking, standing, sitting, or lying down, has calmed his thoughts and delights in the stilling of thought: a bhikkhu such as this can reach the highest enlightenment.
—Aṅguttara Nikāya 4:11

THE FIRST FORMAL INSTRUCTION I received for jhāna practice surprised me. My teacher told me to meditate in any way that supported the development of three qualities: mental brightness, spaciousness, and relaxation. I had expected the early instructions to emphasize vigorous focus on a narrow object. It soon became clear, however, that demanding effort can create tension; in the wake of tension, aversion and hindrances thrive. Conversely, a relaxed, bright, and spacious mind contributes to mental and physical ease and encourages a natural awareness of present-moment experience.

For concentration to deepen, the mind needs to relax. It cannot stay on the defensive. A mind that is glad is easily concentrated. In spiritual life gladness is not the giddy excitement expressed by titillation or thrill. The deeper forms of gladness arise when you trust your virtue. Happiness arises when you can trust the purity of your own heart's intentions. In short, it is a happiness of non-remorse.

⌒ *Thoughts of Kindness*

When I practiced in a Thai forest monastery, the other
residents and I were asked to generate thoughts of friendship and kindness for several minutes before leaving the
mosquito nets we slept under at night. We would bring
a person to mind and mentally recite a simple phrase of
goodwill—"May you be well, happy, and at ease"—or an
equivalent wish. With repeated practice, this simple reflection on kind wishes has the potential to soothe an ill temper, calm an anxious mind, and bring joy to the heart. Try
this throughout your day.

It is through sincere reflection and our inner ethical commitments
that we purify our intentions and grow to trust ourselves. If our ethical foundation is uncertain, tranquility will remain shaky, and the
mind will be unable to confidently settle into this living process of
purification.

We can improve the texture of the mind by influencing the kind
of thoughts we tend to think. When you observe thoughts that
diminish the qualities you appreciate, abandon those thoughts and
give a thought or two to something virtuous, respectable, joyful—
perhaps a thought of kindness.

BASIC INSTRUCTIONS FOR STABILIZING THE MIND

This book focuses on the technique of using the breath as your initial object for meditation. The Buddhist tradition suggests a number of objects for jhāna meditation, including colors, light, the basic

elements (earth, fire, water, and wind), foul aspects of bodily experience, or beautiful inner qualities such as loving-kindness, compassion, joy, and equanimity. Each object has the potential to raise the mind to correspondingly distinct levels of absorption. Traditionally, an experienced teacher tailors the meditation subject according to the student's disposition, meditative ability, interest, and intention.

The breath serves as a powerful, and popular, meditation subject. It can bring the mind through the four jhāna states. It is the preferred meditation subject for many practitioners. Although certain individuals might find jhāna easier to attain with a different meditation subject, the skills developed working with the breath can be applied to any meditative endeavor.

In the Buddhist tradition, the designation of a state called *access concentration* arose as a convenient term to describe the conditions that immediately precede jhāna. Although there is no direct reference in the discourses of the Buddha to access concentration as a distinct state, the conditions that lead to jhāna are clearly described—and when these conditions arise, access to jhāna is possible.

The following instructions for attaining access to jhāna refine the basic meditation instructions given in chapter 1.

⁌

Once you are sitting in a comfortable and alert posture, incline your mind toward qualities of brightness, spaciousness, and relaxation. You will experience a joyful sense of balance when your effort is diligent and relaxed. Allow the quality of your mind to be spacious and unconstricted, even while you are focused on a precise perception. Encourage an uplifting sense of mental brightness to support alertness, clarity, joy, perkiness, and enthusiasm for developing concentration and insight. Then, apply focused attention to experience the initial sensations of the breath touching the nostrils or upper lip. Direct your attention to the breath at the nostrils or upper lip area. The actual location will vary from person to person, depending on the angle of the nose, structure of the jaw, shape of the lips, and facial features; there is no best or correct place. Feel where the breath naturally touches you. Whenever the attention drifts off that point of sensation, guide it back, simply and diligently. Each time the awareness wanders off with thoughts of the past or the future, simply drop this preoccupation with thoughts by reaffirming the directed focus of your activity. Ignore everything else: environmental sounds, pain, thoughts, or plans. If emotions, great insights, a review of yesterday's shopping list, a plan for redecorating your kitchen, a replay of a movie you recently watched, or any profound or mundane thought should arise, invest no interest in these events and guide the attention back to the breath.

Although this instruction is simple to understand, within just a few minutes of practice you will notice that the mind tends to wander away from that point of contact where the breath is felt. It may wander through past thoughts, future plans, or a commentary on the present experience of sitting and feeling the breath at your nose. Whatever thoughts arise, interesting or boring, supportive or destructive of your self-esteem, let them all go unequivocally. The discipline here is to discard all entanglement without judging yourself and return happily to the meditation subject, with a spacious, bright, and relaxed mind.

Let sounds, sensations, and thoughts go their own way; there is no need to follow them. You may initially notice a multitude of perceptions: sounds might impinge, pain might be felt, thoughts might meander through consciousness. These are all normal sensory experiences. You don't need to push them away, but you don't need to maintain interest in them either. Keep sequestering the mind close to the breath, abandoning the urge to move toward the various sensory experiences that will inevitably arise. This streamlined practice, sustained over time, creates a powerful momentum of concentration by connecting and sustaining the attention on a chosen object.

Initially, the breath may appear with distinct physical properties: vibration, temperature, tension, pressure, and roughness, for instance. To develop concentration, remain steadily aware of the breath by connecting and sustaining attention with the breath, but without emphasizing the physicality of changing sensations. As the attention remains connected for longer periods of time without distraction, there will be a corresponding withdrawal of awareness from bodily sensations. Awareness of distinct sensations related to the sitting posture will diminish. Awareness of room temperature will fade. Sounds might occur as remote innocuous notes without pulling the attention toward them. Aches, pain, tensions, or twinges in the body will hardly be noticed. Gradually, even the sensations associated with the breath will fade and disappear. Parallel to this growing separation from physical sensory experiences, pleasant mental qualities of bliss, lightness, delight, rapture, pleasure, and happiness will grow, supporting the sustained connection. You will gradually experience clear awareness—samādhi is not a dull or drifting state—yet the objects you perceive will not be bound to the gross field of sensory perception.

As we've noted, meditation requires diligent effort and clear intention. You cannot demand that distractions vanish, but you can cultivate a deep willingness to repeatedly and happily let go. If you try to adhere to the breath and wrestle violently with anything that threatens that hold, you will quickly become tense and probably decide to quit before you have barely begun. But if you allow yourself to enjoy letting go of distractions, to feel happy to reconnect, and to meditate unburdened by pressure to accomplish a certain number of consecutive breaths, happiness will arise through the simple joy of relinquishment.

When attention is continuously applied, intrusive thoughts subside. If a thought should arise, there will be no fuel for proliferation.

It is just a tiny transparent thought that wisps through the mind without causing disturbance, like a momentary bubble on a stream or an ephemeral cloud in the sky. The few thoughts that do arise are entirely wholesome and often concern the meditation practice. Alertness thrives; the mind brightens. When access to jhāna is available, there are no hindrances in the mind: no craving, no judging, no doubt, no agitation, no greed. The pulsing activities of vitakka and vicāra continue. Relaxed, bright, and spacious, with a momentum of concentration supporting the process, the mind coheres around its object.

THE COUNTERPART SIGN

At some point, you will stop feeling tangible qualities of the breath. The mind will become collected through the repeated directing and sustaining of attention on a subtle knowing of breath, rather than on perceptions of tangible qualities such as temperature, movement, or pressure. Continue to focus the attention in the area of the nostrils or upper lip. You many perceive a subtle feeling of contact with breath or settle the attention in the space just off the body near the location where breath occurs. Stay focused on the whole breath—from the very start of the inhalation through to the end of the exhalation—without attention wavering. Be attentive to a continuous perception of breath as the object, rather than particular sensations associated with the breath.

The deepening of samādhi involves this distinctive shift from the physicality of breath sensations as the object of concentration to what is called the *counterpart sign* or *nimitta*. The nimitta may initially appear as a vibrating pearly bright light that occurs in conjunction with the in- and out-breath, or a soft luminous perception likened to cotton wool. Please don't jump to the conclusion that the first appearance of light in the mind is your counterpart sign. The mind progressively brightens long before the breath nimitta appears. Many meditators stall their progress by following after "false nimittas"—changing colors, changing images, flashes, motley fields of light, or visual impressions of light that remove the focus of attention from the breath-point to another location (most commonly above the eyes or in the head).

The breath nimitta usually appears as a stable, smooth, white radiance associated with the focus on the breath. It is a mental reflection of the breath and does not include physical sensations. The impression of inner light and the orientation to the breath may appear to have merged into a single mental experience. The breath nimitta arises as a result of the concentration and serves as the first landmark of a state conducive to absorption. By learning to notice when this sign arises, you will be able to retrace your steps in the future and attain jhāna when desired.

A skilled meditator should have the capacity to direct the attention at any time, either back to the physicality of the sensation of breath or to the mental experience of the counterpart sign. To confirm that you do have the option, it is helpful to sometimes choose the physicality and sometimes shift to the counterpart sign. If you decide to remain attentive to physical sensations, rapture will still arise, but it will be known as physical delight. If you accept the subtler luminous mental sign as the object for concentration, this shift to the subtler mental perception can lead to absorption. To attain access to jhāna, you would choose the perception of pleasant, radiant light as the new nimitta and allow the attention to remain steadily focused on this luminous perception.

Discerning the nimitta is the first step in stabilizing this refined mental object for concentration. To deepen samādhi, you will give no further attention to physical sensations of breath. Your meditation object has become the nimitta, the counterpart sign. It is known as a stable, luminous mental focus without sensation.

The momentum of samādhi naturally inclines toward the subtler experience of mental brightness, but skillfulness always includes options. Concentration can be very strong. The mind should never

> ⤺ *What Is Your Meditation Object?*
>
> Recognize how you perceive the meditation object of breath. Are you observing a tactile sensation, a visual experience, a sound, or a mental concept as you are observing breath? Ask yourself at the beginning, middle, and end of your meditation session, "How am I perceiving the breath?"
>
> Notice if the way you comprehend your meditation object changes as your concentration and mindfulness develop. Recognize how the meditation object of breath might manifest in a variety of modes and still be a perception of breath.

be propelled through this system nor sucked into a vortex of concentrated energies. Wise practitioners will moderate the pace and fully develop their meditative skills before moving to the next stage. By valuing both the release into a profound depth of experience and the insight that arises with dynamic proximity to the senses, you can explore the intertwined trainings of concentration and insight—simultaneously exploring how attention connects with both physical and mental objects of perception.

ACCESS TO JHĀNA

How strong does concentration need to be to be sure access is attained? Access to jhāna has been achieved when there is a sustained experience of a unified mind free of all hindrances and imbued with strong factors of vitakka, vicāra, pīti, sukha, and ekaggatā. Attention, undistracted by thoughts or sensory perceptions, remains intensely focused on the nimitta. The mind is utterly bright, the heart relaxed.

Fundamentally, *access concentration* describes an absence of hindrances conjoined with the presence of strongly developed jhāna factors. These conditions are recognized prerequisites to jhāna, as the Buddha describes:

> And when he knows that these five hindrances have left him, gladness arises in him, from gladness comes delight, from delight in his mind his body is tranquilized, with a tranquil body he feels joy, and with joy his mind is concentrated. Being thus detached from sense-desires, detached from unwholesome states he enters and remains in the first jhāna.[74]

With the absence of hindrances, in the presence of joy, happiness, tranquility, and concentration, there is a feeling of great relief. The feeling of relief characterizing access to jhāna increases to a sense of safety with the arising of jhāna: safe from distraction, safe from hindrances, or, as the ancient scriptures describe, removed from the forces of Māra.

The jhāna factors of connecting, sustaining, joy, pleasure, and one-pointedness will continue to strengthen. If your energy drops, you may find sounds or sensations intruding on the meditation. Gentle, joyful persistence is essential. If the mind becomes distracted, simply let the distracting perception be, and reconnect with the nimitta. Nurture equanimity; be happy to connect with the whole breath or the light nimitta; direct your attention to whichever object is apparent there. Reconnect repeatedly, clearly aware of gladness infusing the connection. Keep lifting the mind up to its object. Use this power of vitakka to refresh the connection whenever the energy sinks or the attention scatters.

When the prerequisites to jhāna are stable and sustained, focus the attention for just a moment on the distinctive absence of hindrances. Consider whether true happiness can ever be found

☞ Refresh the Attention with Skillful Breaks

If your mind feels tired of observing the breath, then periodically try other practices that might refresh your attention or perceive different aspects of breath.

For example, try focusing primarily on the in-breath, or focus only on the out-breath, or attend to the transition between the inhalation and the exhalation. You might notice how the whole body responds to breathing—feel the expansion and contraction of the rib cage; sense the belly rising and falling with each breath.

If you want a break from observing the breath, try cultivating the attitude of loving kindness, relaxing while hearing sounds, reflecting on the qualities of the Buddha or your virtues, or observing the flow of changing sensations from head to toe.

Although the classic and most direct instruction for attaining jhāna is to focus exclusively on the mental sign of breath, your mind may not always cooperate and agree to observe only this one object. Feel empowered to develop a variety of practices that support your mindfulness. After your attention is refreshed by a different perception, you might continue with the practice of developing concentration with the breath. Periodic brief, skillful breaks will help you to enhance mindfulness, maintain interest in the practice, and gradually cultivate conditions that are conducive to concentration.

through sensory experiences. Once you achieve the certainty that happiness will not be found by getting more sensory pleasures or thinking more interesting thoughts, your commitment to inner exploration will deepen. Recognize that this variety of seclusion is a source of joy and relief. After reflecting in this way, continue to develop the basic practice of connecting and sustaining attention on the light that infuses the breath perception.

Let go with relief and allow the withdrawal from thoughts, personal concerns, and sensations to continue, unforced and unbroken. Mental brightness will continue to increase. A sense of cohesion and mental unification will grow. Since at this stage concentration is still fragile, this deep release is often interrupted by distraction. Quickly but gently enhance your energetic interest and strengthen the connecting and sustaining activity.

With this practice, the mind is preparing itself for the altered state of jhāna—a deeply absorbed state of mind that can retain its unity without effortful striving. When vitakka and vicāra are strong and infused with delight, you won't need to continually refresh the connection or fuss with the energy. It is natural for the mind to stay attentive to that which is delightful. So harness this power of happiness and let it totally permeate the nimitta, allowing the mind to become increasingly stable, cohesive, and bright.

These references to delight, gladness, happiness, and rapture could cause you to expect dramatic ecstatic pleasures. The process is more subtle than that. A unified mind experiences such refined pleasures that, although the quiet presence of sublime happiness permeates consciousness and accompanies each stage of jhāna, the jhāna factors will barely be noticed while in jhāna. They are discerned primarily in the moments prior to absorption and upon emerging from jhāna.

Are there thoughts and hindrances that you can set aside, or is there an absence of hindrances in the mind? When you perceive the genuine absence of hindrances, you will feel happy: the happiness I've described as a great relief. Become sensitive to the subtle pleasant quality of rapture when connecting with the nimitta. When attention is quiet and steady, pīti does not have to be gloriously exciting. You will need only just enough joy to keep your interest in the breath or breath nimitta fresh. Enjoy the ease of a mind that is growing in purity and stability.

CHAPTER 11
Fearless Abidings—The First Jhāna

*Secluded from sensual pleasures, secluded from unwholesome states, I
entered and dwelt in the first jhāna, which is accompanied by thought
and examination, with rapture and happiness born of seclusion.*
—Saṃyutta Nikāya 28:1

IN NORMAL WORLDLY ACTIVITIES, we naturally orient our
perceptions toward sensory impressions. Jhāna, by contrast,
represents a radical reorientation: perception recedes from its
conventional relationship to sensory objects and gains support
from the particular mental factors characteristic of each stage of
jhāna.

As you approach the first jhāna, thoughts are few and far between.
Those that do arise are light and quickly dissolve. Without effort,
the mind automatically resettles after each thought passes.

Perception still functions, brightly and with alert mindfulness,
but during absorption you are unaware of sounds and other sensory impressions. Your attention is unified with the breath and supported by the buoyant energy of pīti, the gentle contentment of
sukha, and the various mental factors of alertness still active in the
field of jhāna. Hindrances of desire, craving, and aversion cannot
arise. Energy is balanced, and effort feels effortless. There is no need

to vigorously refresh the connection with the nimitta, because the attention is already stable.

Readers who have not personally experienced deep absorption may consider the details that I share in chapters 11–14 irrelevant to their practice. Please read these chapters even if you are struggling with hindrances or find concentration elusive. It can be useful to gain a conceptual introduction to these states prior to experiencing them. Even simply reflecting on the potential of deep samādhi may nourish conditions that support your concentration. And the chapters pertaining to insight that follow this section on jhāna are relevant to all practitioners. Don't worry if some of what I describe is beyond your actual experience today; read on, and allow your practice to gradually mature.

The First Jhāna

Aloofness from the hindrances gives rise to the characteristic happiness of the first jhāna: *happiness born of seclusion*. Detached from the hindering forces, consciousness is elated. By consciously experiencing the absence of the hindrances during access concentration, you have at your disposal a wholesome cause for generating greater happiness. Traditional descriptions of jhāna include observations such as these:

> Having reached the first jhāna, ... whatever sensations of lust that he previously had disappear. At that time there is present a true but subtle perception of delight and happiness, born of detachment, and he becomes one who is conscious of this delight and happiness. In this way some perceptions arise through training, and some pass away through training.[75]

Recognizing the perceptions that arise and cease in your process of cultivating concentration will help you recognize and nurture the conditions that support concentration. For example, you might have noticed that during the access stage the habitually restless wandering mind settles down. There was a presence of calm and an absence of restlessness. Noticing what is present and absent is a simple function of discernment that supports the integration of concentration (*samatha*) and insight (*vipassanā*).

The first jhāna, like the state of access concentration, contains the subtle activity of initial and sustained attention (*vitakka* and *vicāra*) and is infused with rapture and happiness (*pīti* and *sukha*). The purification of mind becomes palpable. Brightness increases. The connecting and sustaining of attention function with a gentle ease. Far from the threat of hindering disruptions, the one-pointed focus (*ekaggatā*) intensifies, and consciousness smoothly relaxes into absorption.

Comingling of the happiness factors of pīti and sukha also marks the first jhāna. Often *pīti-sukha* is first experienced as a simple lightness in the mind; it need not be ecstatic bliss. If pīti-sukha arises, even slightly, let it suffuse your perception of breath. Allow your entire experience to be suffused with this rapture and pleasure born of seclusion. Let this happiness cleanse, protect, and purify the mind.

Notice how you discern pīti and sukha. Is the pleasure located in the body or mind? Is coolness or warmth associated with this pleasure? Do you experience the pleasure as a vibration or wave-like phenomenon? Does it seem to be rippling, tingling, or showering through your body? Does it seem to subtly pervade your mind? Interest in pīti may strengthen the pleasantness of the experience, but excessive interest in pīti can become a distraction. As pīti matures, it becomes less thrilling and more subtle. Gentle interest and trusting attention are enough to nurture the wholesome factors of pīti and sukha and allow them to become pervasive and refined enough to support absorption.

Before entering the first jhāna and upon emerging from absorption, you may recognize pleasant physical manifestations of pīti and sukha, but these will not be perceived while fully immersed in jhana.

> ⌐ *Similes of Bath Powder*
>
> Reflecting on the simile of the bath attendant who kneads the soap powder so that the soap particles cohere, you can remind yourself to collect your attention to prevent distraction and mental agitation from dispersing your focus. What helps your mind collect itself during meditation? What helps prevent scatteredness, agitation, and distraction in your daily activities?
>
> Remember the simile of the soap powder and draw your attention back into a composed and settled experience of the present moment. Do not let thoughts loiter with distractions or cravings ooze out toward sensual entanglements. Whenever your attention wanders, repeatedly and gently bring your attention back to the task at hand.

In jhana, attention will be absorbed with the counterpart sign of the breath rather than bodily sensations or changing feelings.

A sense of cohesion, confidence, focus, and unification harmonizes the energies. The traditional simile used to describe this unification is the skilled bath man or his assistant who kneads a mass of soap powder into a bar or small ball. He blends, kneads, and sprinkles it with water, until it is unified, congealed, and bound with oil, such that nothing oozes or escapes.[76] Allow the gentle activity of connecting and sustaining the attention to continue amassing mental energies, drawing in the energy of thought that might otherwise leak out. Like the bath man kneading the mass of soap powder, trust the capacity of directed and sustained attention to collect the mind so that no thoughts ooze out. Concentration condenses the diffused tendencies of feeling, thought, and perception into a cohesive, unified, and cooperative force.

The first jhāna is deeply restorative to the mind and body. It is a wholesome and healing state of consciousness. Dwell within its domain for some time, saturating your being with this healing state.

HARNESS THE POWER OF RESOLVE

The critical skill for encouraging the development of the jhāna factors and negotiating the shifts between jhānas is invoking the power of intention, determination, and resolution. The effect of intention is dramatically amplified in the sublime refinement of an undistracted mind. Resolution is directed through wholehearted dedication; it is an orientation of collected mental energies more than an attempt to accomplish a task. To gain access "at will without trouble or difficulty" to levels of jhāna concentration, you shift your reliance on the gross activity of energetically connecting and sustaining (vitakka and vicāra) to a subtler power of mind that inclines toward the direction of your resolve. This subtle shift of effort releases consciousness into an absorption with the nimitta and resolutely lets go of any competing distraction. Once you form the resolve in mind (about which I say more below), you don't need to do anything more. In the limber mind near jhāna, what we resolve upon appears to happen without additional striving. Yet setting a resolve does not itself create the new experience; rather, when you trust the wholesome power of your intention, all possible diversions are abandoned, and the energy of mind orients toward the resolve.

Although specific resolutions may appear to be verbal requests or instructions, you may not need to use words to express your resolve; you may find your own way to focus your determination and crystallize your intention with images, feelings, or mental gestures. Determination is not a verbal instruction that we give ourselves and then set out to accomplish, and the essential feature of resolution is not contained in specific verbal expressions but in the focused power of energetic intention. A verbal expression, image, or feeling may help to coalesce the energetic resolve, opening your heart to your aim and supporting a disposition that eliminates all competing distractions.

The resolve may be inserted after access to jhāna is firmly established—that is, when the jhāna factors are strong and clearly discernible, the hindrances are at bay, thinking is minimal and not distracting, and the attention rests steadily and happily on the nimitta. At that point, you strengthen the earnestness of your commitment by making a strong determination to enter the first jhāna. You might silently aspire with thoughts such as "May I experience full absorption," "May I attain the first jhāna," "May the first jhāna arise," or "May my mind be absorbed in the happiness born of seclusion." You could also reflect with energetic resolve on the traditional description of the first jhāna: "Being thus secluded from sense pleasures, secluded from unwholesome states, may I enter and abide in the first jhāna, which is with applied and sustained thought, and has happiness and pleasure born of seclusion."[77]

Although jhāna can certainly arise without the impetus of a resolution, a little skillful nudging can escort the mind into the first jhāna. A clear resolution can also crystallize the delineation between access and the first jhāna. When you can move the mind through the light touch of intention, coarse applications of effort fall away. An intention gracefully planted when conditions are conducive is like a well-sown seed in a fertile field; it will grow on its own. Nurture the unfolding of jhāna and enjoy its sprouting.

Be observant as this altered state of consciousness called the first jhāna arises—and at the same time, do not consider it a problem if it does not arise immediately. Happily continue to connect and sustain the attention on the breath infused with rapture and happiness. This is the fundamental practice that brings clarity and calm. Give your attention to the breath with or without absorption. You might periodically resolve for the strengthening of each of the jhāna factors nonverbally or with the wish: "May each jhāna factor grow strong."

A useful precaution is to set the resolve for a balance of factors: "May pīti and sukha be balanced and firm." Pīti can easily get revved up, whirling you right out of a calm balance and into intensely agitated bliss. Even if you don't consciously know which factors need to increase or decrease, setting the intention encourages intuitive wisdom to operate. Trust your nervous system to restore its equilibrium, allowing the jhāna factors to thrive in the background as your attention is consistently established upon the breath nimitta.

Consciously directing the mind through resolve is not cheating, forcing, or contriving the experience. One of the mysterious powers of intention is that it can accomplish things you don't consciously know how to do.

DISTINGUISHING ABSORPTION FROM ACCESS

The transition between access to, and absorption in, the first jhāna is one of the most difficult to discern. Most meditators will experience the absorption several times, moving back and forth between access and first jhāna, before clearly distinguishing the two stages of concentration. The difficulty resides in the fact that the mental factors present in access and first jhāna are identical. Both are marked by applied and sustained attention, rapture and happiness, and a coherent and unified focus. And yet a distinctive shift in consciousness occurs in the first jhāna: the focus is settled deep inside the mind, utterly unconcerned with outer phenomena. Some people recognize the first jhāna only after emerging from it by noticing its effect on consciousness. A distinctive swell of energy accompanies jhāna. Calm and largely unnoticed during the period of absorption, the mind-body system is recharged in a way that is quite different from what sleep, caffeine, entertainment, good news, or any worldly spike of energy can accomplish. Please appreciate this inspiring restoration; it stands in stark contrast to the exhausting pursuits of a distracted mind.

Although it may be difficult for beginners to identify the transition between access to jhāna and the first jhāna itself with certainty, discerning the qualities of genuine absorption will clarify the path of concentration enabling you to attain jhāna in the future. The effort to discern these states and factors also facilitates the direct perception of impermanence, which I will address in more detail in chapters 17 and 18. Although shifting back and forth between first jhāna and access to jhāna might initially appear to stall the progression, the clarity that arises through a patient engagement with the essential features of absorption is a valuable support for transformative insight.

When Does the Mind Become One-Pointed?

The boundary between access to jhāna and full absorption in the first jhāna is a subject of historical debate among Buddhist scholars and practitioners. The controversy centers around a discrepancy between the standard description of the first jhāna found in early discourses, which does not specifically list the presence of ekaggatā (one-pointed attention), and later discourses[78] and commentaries[79] that define the first jhāna as possessing all five jhāna factors, including ekaggatā. This discrepancy has led to a range of opinions regarding the question of whether one-pointed attention must be present for absorption. And if so, to what degree?

As scholars debate where the line between access, first jhāna, and second jhāna is drawn, distinct schools of practice have evolved. Some teachers define the first jhāna as a relatively light stage of concentration; they will confirm attainment of the first jhāna when hindrances subside and the first four jhāna factors are developed, even if thoughts, sensations, and sounds still impinge on consciousness. Other teachers require a deeper absorption and do not declare the first jhāna attained until one-pointedness has strengthened to such a degree that engagement with thoughts, sounds, and sensations is suspended. Do these approaches describe two valid but different jhāna systems within the Buddhist tradition? Different teachers have drawn the line in significantly different ways, leading to controversies regarding a range of experiences that have been attributed to the first jhāna. Some teachers move students through the stage of first jhāna quickly, giving greater emphasis to the more intense factor of pīti in the second jhāna. Other teachers require prolonged absorption in deep states of the first jhāna, milking that attainment to develop mastery over the entrance and exit from absorption, to clarify subtle mental factors, to wear away potential enchantment with pleasure associated with seclusion or personal success, and to permit the first jhāna—as the basis of each further attainment—to mature.

Although my personal practice explored a number of approaches, I have come to value the sustained experience of the first jhāna and now teach students to remain with the first jhāna until it is very well established, it is attainable with ease, and the transition between access to jhāna and absorption in jhāna has been experienced many dozens of times. However, I do not want to assert a definitive interpretation of exactly where the line must be drawn. Instead, I suggest that noticing what constitutes *an absorption* enables the student to enter the systematic jhāna progression whenever they wish, given suitable conditions. Exploring the distinction between, on the one hand, a mind that is free from hindrances and possesses strong jhāna factors but is stimulated by perceptions from the sensory field and, on the other hand, a mind that is equally without hindrances and possesses strong jhāna factors but is removed from sensory perceptions clarifies the unique experience of absorption.

We cannot know for certain what the Buddha actually taught; however, it seems clear that he did not specifically define the unfathomable depths of absorption. There are various depths of concentration, each having its own use and meaning. But for the cultivation of jhāna, I believe that we can set this academic debate aside.

⤳ *Focusing on Daily Tasks*

To help identify the intensifying jhāna factors, notice how they operate during ordinary activities. Choose a project, such as cleaning a drawer, cooking a quiche, or writing a report at work. Notice that you are applying and sustaining your attention. Allow ease and pleasure as you focus on a simple task. Remain one-pointed and prevent the mind from becoming distracted with other activities until you have completed your project.

The jhāna factors may not be very strong in ordinary activities, but they can be valuable assets, even in mild forms, to support your daily activities. See how focusing helps calm and soothe the mind and remove distractions to clear the path to our goal.

The different definitions do not need to interrupt our practical attainment of jhāna. In my practice, I often experience qualities associated with concentration rather quickly on retreats. Some teachers consider these qualities a mark of the first jhāna and recommend shifting to the second jhāna to swiftly continue through the sequence of attainments. However, I have consistently found that when I simply continue to focus attention on the breath nimitta, all five jhāna factors develop and lead to deep clear irrefutable absorptions. Sometimes it takes several days of sustained attention for this shift to what I call *full absorption* to occur; however, when the shift happens, there is a sense of inner clarity and complete confidence regarding the absorption.

Ekaggatā is subtle and difficult to discern in the early stages of practice. The coarser activities of vitakka and vicāra tend to obscure it, but this does not imply that it isn't present. Ekaggatā's function becomes more apparent after these first two active jhāna factors subside through the progressive development of concentration. This suggests that one-pointed attention is present in all the jhānas and is a defining feature of absorption. Therefore, I shall continue to describe the first jhāna as possessing all five jhāna factors: vitakka, vicāra, pīti, sukha, and ekaggatā.

SAFE AT LAST

Access to jhāna can be likened to a radio whose volume is turned very low: the impact of sensory stimulation is minimal and obstructive states have dramatically diminished. With the arising of jhāna, the volume is turned down even more—below the threshold of hearing. The delineation of absorptions can be imagined as a fence around the mind that prevents the hindrances from entering awareness. When access is established, the hindrances don't arise, but they are not far away. The mind is brightened by their absence, but you would not dare let down your guard. The seclusion of jhāna separates the mind much further from obstructive states. In that depth of aloofness, you rest: safe at last. The heart is glad and happy. This is the happiness born of seclusion: a fearless abiding.

Traditional teachings consider absorption achieved when the jhāna factors of vitakka, vicāra, pīti, sukha, and ekaggatā are so powerfully present that one can stay secluded from sensory experience and undistracted by thoughts for a long time without the need to refresh the attention by diligently returning to the breath. The *Visuddhimagga* describes this period as being the length of a night and a day. Whether one chooses to take that time frame literally or not, jhāna is stable, undistracted, and undisturbed.

Contemporary teachers suggest resolving to remain in absorption for increasing durations of time. Start with twenty minutes of absorption uninterrupted by thought. Once that is easy to establish and repeat, make a determination for thirty minutes, then forty-five minutes, then one hour, two hours, and three hours. For a beginner to jhāna practice, the nimitta may remain stable for only five or ten minutes before a thought or perception interrupts the absorption; often it is a thought about the meditation itself. But as practice deepens, consciousness will remain absorbed for a long time without difficulty. One Burmese master I studied with requested sustained absorption, without the intrusion of a single thought, for more than one hour of each sitting, during all meditation sessions in the day, for at least three consecutive days before he would give the instruction for the next jhāna. Although I have not found any particular amount of time to be critical, jhānas are stable states of deep absorption, not brief encounters with bliss. In jhāna, there is no restlessness; nothing is present that would disturb the tranquility. A meditator should be able to sit without internal disturbance for very, very long periods of time.

THE FIRST JHĀNA AS A BASIS FOR INSIGHT

Insight, for our purposes, does not refer to an intellectual understanding. In the context of meditation practice, insight refers to an undistorted clear perception that has the potential to liberate the mind from ignorance. Chapters 17 and 18 are devoted to the exploration of insight after emerging from jhāna. This section briefly presents the practical shift between the concentration practices and insight practices so that each jhāna can be used sequentially as a basis for insight as you progress through these levels.

Strengthened by absorption, concentration becomes the basis for insight. Immediately upon emerging from absorption, observe the impermanent, changing nature of the jhāna factors as they change or fade. Then bring mindfulness to whatever mental and physical phenomena enter your awareness. If a sound arises, it is known as a moment of hearing: impermanent, undependable, and impersonal.

As physical sensations occur, they are known according to their specific qualities: hardness, heat, coolness, or movement. They are also known by their general characteristics: inconstant, unsatisfactory, and empty. Whatever occurs—thoughts, emotions, hindrances, or harmless thoughts—is met with mindfulness and the wisdom that apprehends them without attachment.

Commonly the meditator establishes jhāna during the earlier portion of a sitting meditation session and then shifts to a vipassanā mode for the later portion. You may find it useful to divide your meditation session in half. Or you may weave back and forth between samādhi and vipassanā practices as you feel inclined. Sometimes you might let the concentration grow by anchoring the attention with the breath for a few moments but not necessarily reentering absorption. At other times you might enter and exit jhāna several times, tasting the deliciousness of a still mind and emerging again to experience the changing nature of the dynamic world. In this exploration of perception, you learn to sensitively escort the mind between the seclusion of jhāna and the clarity of engaged contact.

The shift from unified absorption to the diverse explorations of insight will be discussed in greater depth later in this book, but you may periodically incorporate insight or wisdom practice throughout the development of the jhāna states. You don't need to wait until you experience all four absorptions before you see clearly. Use whatever degree of samādhi you have accumulated and direct that stability of mind toward investigating how suffering comes about and how it can end. Insight that arises out of the steadiness of first-jhāna concentration can be enough to end all suffering.[80] Play in the terrain that is secluded from Māra. Frolic with a joyful heart, courageously exploring this undependable fleeting world.

If, after moving in and out of absorption many times, learning to enter and exit without trouble or difficulty, and using the first jhāna as the basis for insight, the mind is not totally liberated, you have another option. You may grow disenchanted with the relative coarseness of applied and sustained thought. Interest may arise to further deepen samādhi. Rather than shifting out of jhāna to practice vipassanā, aspire to attain a more sublime degree of samādhi. With dispassion toward the first jhāna, relinquish that quality of happiness and aspire to attain the second jhāna.

⟡ *For Reflection*

Consider your relationship to the sensory field, now informed by a period of time secluded from sensory pleasures.

What is this body? What are feelings? What is your relationship to pleasure? Can happiness be found through the body?

After the meditation session, reflect upon the experience. What are the most significant qualities of the jhāna state? How does jhāna affect the condition of your mind?

CHAPTER 12
Drenched in Delight—The Second Jhāna

He enters upon and abides in the second jhāna, which has self-confidence and singleness of mind without applied and sustained thought, with rapture and pleasure born of concentration.
—Majjhima Nikāya 141:31

WITH THE FIRST JHĀNA well established, you may progress to develop more refined and sublime states of concentration. In the second jhāna, the agitation of directed and sustained attention ends, and the pleasure of pīti stabilizes into a powerful experience of inner tranquility.

From the second jhāna onward, connection with the meditation object is sustained by trusting one-pointed unification with the object. Now, vitakka and vicāra have fallen away, and pīti and sukha have taken center stage. The mind locks onto its object and settles with rapt interest. This absorption into the second jhāna is characterized by a refined quality of pleasure as the mind is submerged in this field of happiness. The traditional description of entering the second jhāna says:

With the subsiding of thinking and pondering, by gaining inner tranquility and oneness (unity) of mind, he

enters and remains in the second jhāna, which is without
thinking and pondering, born of concentration, filled
with delight and joy. And with this delight and joy born
of concentration he so suffuses his body that no spot
remains untouched.[81]

Pīti is an effervescent quality of pleasure that refreshes attention.
The discourses of the Buddha describe it like this:

Just as a lake fed by a spring, with no inflow from east, west,
north or south, where the rain-god sends moderate show-
ers from time to time, the water welling up from below,
mingling with cool water, would suffuse, fill and irradiate
that cool water, so that no part of the pool was untouched
by it—so, with this delight and joy born of concentration
he so suffuses his body that no spot remains untouched.[82]

When pīti first becomes apparent, it might thrill novice meditators. You might feel energized by the intensity of what is happening.
Your posture might spontaneously align upward, buoyant against
gravity. You might feel like a bright smile dominates your expression,
even though your facial muscles do not visibly move. Pīti can become
a distraction if it draws attention toward its dramatic or physical
expressions such as ripples, waves, excitement, and bubbling energies.
Whether pīti manifests with intensity or mildness, you must understand the function of pīti—to refresh attention. Do not allow it to
draw your attention away from the breath or breath nimitta.

Throughout the practice of jhāna, the object of perception
remains the same; the mind is concentrated on breath or breath
nimitta—not pīti or sensations. Keep your attention focused on
breath or breath nimitta while allowing subtle joy to accompany
that focus. Do not abandon your meditation object by allowing
attention to chase after the sensory effects of pīti.

Resolving for the Second Jhāna

When you wish to shift to the second jhāna, reflect on two disadvantages to the first jhāna and one advantage to the second jhāna. The first jhāna has the disadvantages of being dangerously close to the hindrances, especially restlessness and distraction, and of relying on the relatively coarse factors of vitakka and vicāra.

The second jhāna has the advantage of being quieter than the first; rapture, happiness, and one-pointedness are more peaceful. Make the clear and firm resolve, "May the second jhāna arise," "May I attain the second jhāna," or "May my mind be absorbed in the happiness born of concentration." Or use the phrasing of the sutta descriptions: "With the subsiding of thought and examination, I enter and dwell in the second jhāna, which has internal confidence and unification of mind, is without thought and examination, and has rapture and happiness born of concentration."[83] This resolve may be the boost the mind needs to allow its reliance on vitakka and vicāra to fade. Make the resolve, then let go. Let resolve do the work without interfering further.

Clear resolve can strengthen each state and its associated jhāna factors. If absorption is *almost* happening—the factors are present and stable—but the attention is pulled to the fringes of absorption, employ the simple resolve "May the second jhāna strengthen and deepen" or "May the factors of the second jhāna grow in clarity and balance." Supported by rapt interest in the meditation object, attention can settle upon the breath nimitta and become absorbed.

The second jhāna is characterized by this particular blend of pīti and sukha called the *happiness born of concentration*. Practice moving back and forth between the first and second jhāna to sharpen your ability to distinguish happiness born of seclusion in the first jhāna from happiness born of concentration in the second jhāna. You don't need to analyze every minute distinction; in fact, such detailed analysis could unravel into a discursive thinking process.

⤳ *For Reflection*

Observe how you experience these characteristic blends of happiness: happiness born of seclusion and happiness born of concentration. How do they differ? What aspects are clearer or more intense in each? Is your experience physical or mental? What is the quality of the pleasure—rippling, tingly, wavelike, pulsing, pervasive, smooth? What is the texture of mind in the second jhāna as distinct from the first jhāna? Is there any change in body posture? What is present and what is absent in each stage of consciousness?

A joyful mindful interest in what is and is not present is enough to highlight the processes that unify the mind. By developing these first two jhānas, you will acquire the skills needed to progressively refine the mind.

MOVING TOWARD THE SUBTLE

The thrill of pīti—drenched by delight, suffused with happiness—might at first be tantalizing, enthralling, even fun, but its intensity can give rise to annoyance. In comparison to the distractions of worldly life, any jhāna appears smooth. From the perspective of higher absorptions, however, the first and second jhānas are relatively agitated states. This does not diminish their importance; they are incredibly useful states for rejuvenation, for inspiration, and as foundations for insight. After exploring the second jhāna and shifting repeatedly between the first and the second jhānas, intentionally use the experience of the second jhāna as a basis for a new perception of reality. Emerge from the jhāna and allow the jhāna factors to change. Observe how the experiences of mind, perception, and

⟿ *A Fresh Encounter with the World*

When you emerge from the jhāna, experience the impact of bodily sensations and sensory perceptions. How do these contacts affect your consciousness?

Feel the touch of your clothes; notice the sound of the refrigerator; experience the effect of light; sense the movement of air and the different temperatures at different points on your body.

Let life flow in.

There is nothing you need to do with sensations and sounds. Let these phenomena be as they are: fleeting, impersonal, continuously flowing by.

During the hours that follow the meditation session, notice how you experience daily encounters with sight, sound, social interactions, sensations, and activities.

Did the previous experience of jhāna have an impact on your everyday perceptions?

In my own experience, I found each jhāna left a residue that inclined my experience in distinct ways. How do you experience the moments that followed absorption in the second jhāna as distinct from the moments after the first jhāna?

environment change. Dedicate time in your meditative process to discern the qualities of that concentrated state. The second jhāna is a powerful foundation for direct insight for the very same reason it is considered less stable: because of its proximity to thought. Vitakka and vicāra are close by, readily available for your wise use. Engage them with the strength of a buoyant, energized, undistracted mind to perceive the true nature of all things.

If, however, you are not completely liberated from all forms of clinging when using the second jhāna as a basis for insight, incline toward a more sublime state, even if you don't know what comes next. When pīti fades, the mind prepares for a greater depth of samādhi. Because the concentrated mind is inclined to release whatever it perceives as coarse, development of higher consciousness progresses through successive stages of letting go.

CHAPTER 13

Absorbed in Joy—The Third Jhāna

[W]ith the fading away of delight [the meditator] remains imper-
turbable, mindful and clearly aware, and experiences in himself
that joy of which the Noble Ones say: "Happy is he who dwells with
equanimity and mindfulness," and he enters and remains in the third
jhāna. And with this joy devoid of delight he so suffuses his body that
no spot remains untouched.

—Dīgha Nikāya 2:79

S UKHA WAS ALREADY PRESENT during access concentration and the first and second jhānas, but only after the grosser
factor of pīti is stilled can the subtler factor of sukha take the
spotlight. Since pīti no longer thrills, intrigues, or impresses, dispassion toward the coarseness of rapture grows. Perception simpli-
fies, attention remains single-pointedly focused on the nimitta, and
sukha comes to the fore. At this point, consciousness is devoid of
delight, infused with pleasure, and unified.

The traditional description of the third jhāna points to a specific
subtle pleasure that comes from a mind at rest in equanimity: the happiness of unreactive mindful awareness. As you prepare to enter the
third jhāna, sukha shines brightly, filling consciousness with a smooth
sense of contentment. Sukha has a deeply balanced quality of peace

that is thoroughly but subtly happy. Distinctly different from the dazzling grandeur of pīti, sukha feels creamy, like the texture of a perfectly prepared dessert pudding or sweet butter. Translators seeking English words to describe this ambiguous blend of happiness and equanimity, pleasure and equality, turn to such terms as "contentment," "happiness," "pleasure," or "joy." When dissatisfied with these renderings, some teachers prefer to use the Pāli term "sukha." I have found that as we repeatedly experience this absorption, practitioners sense for ourselves the unique quality of third-jhāna happiness. You will come to know sukha through your experience of it.

A gentle lingering delicacy to sukha melts consciousness into its object, affecting the quality of attention even beyond the duration of the absorptions. When sukha is strong, conceptual divisions seem inconsequential and indistinct. Sukha tends to temporarily dissolve them, eliminating even subtle feelings of fragmentation or alienation. Experience feels seamless and without the usual arbitrary divisions between consciousness and perceptions. There is virtually no content in the mind: no personal thoughts, no personal stories, no distracting or fragmenting perceptions. Social conventions, such as the use of calendars and clock time, will hold little relevance to the practitioner whose mind is saturated with sukha.

When consciousness is affected by the pervasive presence of sukha, nothing disturbs you. There is no sleepiness, no dullness, no energetic imbalances to shake the stability of this state; environmental sounds do not disturb the attention, nor does cold or heat. If physical discomforts such as chronic back pain should arise, the mind remains undisturbed. Although the meditator may recognize sensations of pain, pain may not be perceived as unpleasant, due to the saturation of consciousness in contentment. Muscle spasms can be recognized and wisely responded to, but the mind will be free of any unpleasant associations.

After deep experience of the third jhāna, sukha will begin to permeate perception between meditation sessions—in any posture and activity. During this phase of my jhāna retreat, happiness saturated every aspect of the day. Deep contentment pervaded the experience of folding laundry, walking in the snow, standing in line, touching a doorknob, and exercising. When a meditator is saturated with the feeling of happiness, there is no opportunity for an unpleasant experience to occur.

One can sustain jhāna for very long periods when consciousness is supported by sukha. You will not want to end the meditation session. This pleasant abiding is soothing, healing, and completely wholesome. It brings consciousness into a full absorption. Such a pervasive experience of sublime pleasure can deeply transform the tendencies of mind, restructuring the tendencies of perception toward happy states. After a deep experience of concentration, students may find that habitual patterns of grumpiness and depression are replaced by the lingering residue of joy and equanimity. Prolonged contact with sukha, periodically intensified by the potent field of jhāna, can diminish conditioned tendencies toward depression, irritation, and crankiness. You can let sukha suffuse your entire being.

As the Buddha says:

> Just as if, in a pond of blue, red or white lotuses in which the flowers, born in the water, grown in the water, not growing out of the water, are fed from the water's depths, those blue, red or white lotuses would be suffused, filled, and irradiated with that cool water—so with this joy devoid of delight the monk so suffuses his body that no spot remains untouched.[84]

Allow the coolness of sukha to saturate every aspect of your being, like lotuses completely suffused day and night, inside and out, by cool pond water. Melt into it, welcome it, and let it purify your heart and mind. Drink deeply of this pleasure. Grow familiar

---

Noticing Feelings of Pleasure

Several times in your daily meditation, ask yourself what feeling tone accompanies whatever you are observing. In particular, highlight the subtle pleasure that often accompanies the calm ease of mindful awareness. So, when you are mindful, notice the feeling associated with mindfulness. Let the pleasure of mindfulness saturate your awareness.

At the end of the meditation session, you might make notes in a meditation journal describing how you experienced feeling tone. Identify the subtle cues that helped you to recognize meditative pleasure.

Also, spotlight pleasant events in daily activities. Focus your attention on the experience of pleasure. Did this pleasure arise from a pleasant sensual stimulus, or did it arise from virtue, concentration, letting go, kindness, or meditative development?

Notice how pleasure affects the mind. Does sensual pleasure have a different effect than meditative pleasure?

---

with this unperturbed mind. Notice the extraordinary stability of the mind in the third jhāna. Absolutely nothing about the third jhāna is unpleasant.

RESOLVING FOR THE THIRD JHĀNA

The third jhāna may arise naturally with the fading of pīti in the second jhāna. You can easily accelerate the process, however, by intentionally relinquishing the coarser jhāna factor. In the transition from second to third jhāna, that would require letting go of pīti. Make a definite resolve to allow the factor of pīti to fade. Withdraw attention from it. Reflect on the coarseness of pīti and the proximity that the second jhāna has to the coarser qualities of the first jhāna. Consider the greater refinement that sukha and ekaggatā offer.

Then reconnect with the nimitta to enter the third jhāna. Direct attention toward the nimitta with disinterest toward pīti and interest in sukha, resolving, "May I attain the third jhāna," "May the third jhāna arise," or "May my mind be absorbed in sukha." Or use the traditional language: "Mindful, clearly aware, and equanimous, may I enter and abide in the third jhāna, experiencing happiness devoid of delight."

USING THE THIRD JHĀNA AS A BASIS FOR INSIGHT

There is no need to hurry through the third jhāna. Few people will want to rush once they taste this expansive and spacious happiness. Although the third-jhāna happiness is deeply calm, there is still a relatively coarse quality. The feelings are entirely pleasant, so one does not experience the common coarseness of unpleasant feeling. In fact, third-jhāna happiness is so wondrously calming and joyful to the heart and mind that there is nothing distinctly unpleasant arising in this state—no aversive feelings of boredom, no agitation like the slight irritation of the incessant delightfulness of pīti, no involvement with thought fragmenting the attention, no striving effort draining the energy, no craving to be anywhere else.

Nevertheless, sukha does begin to feel relatively coarse after some time. The fragile, conditioned nature of the jhāna becomes obvious, and with that recognition, dissatisfaction with the conditioned state arises, even though it is a thoroughly pleasant conditioned state. Satiated, the mind will naturally turn away from pleasure and incline toward something much stiller.

Many students find it difficult to fathom the possibility of growing tired of deep and pervasive contentment. Thus some may linger in this stage, unaware of their subtle attachment to pleasure.

At some point in this distilling process, you must honestly reflect, "Am I willing to relinquish pleasant feeling?" Until you confidently embrace relinquishment, the happiness of the third jhāna will remain seductive.

Jhāna is a pleasant abiding. The purpose of developing samādhi, however, is to create the conditions most conducive for liberating wisdom. Be wary of the seductive danger of third-jhāna happiness. Many meditators discover it as the most sublime happiness ever known, and you may too—but please do not stop there. As wonderful as contentment feels, it is not a reliable foundation for abiding happiness.

Since it is conditioned and volitionally produced, this sublime joy is ultimately undependable. Realization of this frees the mind from the seductive enchantment of pleasant states and prepares it to look elsewhere for freedom. The mind wants to be free, not simply experience temporary pleasures. Develop conviction in the potential of release, and you will be able to allow this sublime pleasure to fade. Although there is no aversion to the third jhāna and no craving for a different state, the mind naturally inclines toward a quieter stillness.

When you feel ready, allow the jhāna to end and observe the changes that occur. Watch closely as the factors of the jhāna (in this case, primarily contentment and unified singularity of mind) shift in the transition from altered to normal consciousness, from seclusion to sensory contact, from samādhi to vipassanā practice. This is your opportunity to carefully observe the impermanence of subtle mental factors. Notice how you can distinguish a jhāna state from regular consciousness. Observe whatever is happening. And then, with a mind energized, clear, and refreshed by concentration, dedicate the remainder of the meditation session to recognize the true nature of mental and physical phenomena.

If your mind becomes excessively distracted while you are observing changing objects, or if you feel it would enhance clarity to return to jhāna, permit yourself to enter and exit jhāna states at will. You can move among the first three jhānas, clarifying and strengthening each attainment. You can interweave the samādhi and vipassanā practices in various ways, or structure the meditation sessions to methodically begin with samādhi and end with vipassanā. Individual meditators will become sensitive to their energetic rhythms and can determine for themselves when to enter or exit the secluded states of jhāna.

After developing the third jhāna and using it as a basis for insight, you might grow curious about more refined levels of concentration. What state is beyond the happiness of a mind imbued with mindfulness and equanimity?

☜ *For Reflection*

After exploring the third jhāna during meditation, notice whether there are any effects on your disposition during daily activities.

For example, has your patience during political discussions increased? Has appreciation of spouse, partner, or intimate friends grown? Has your tolerance of an infirm relative changed? Notice the implications of being saturated with sukha and how this experience informs your life.

Reflect on the following questions:

Is your happiness dependent on particular conditions, relationships, events, possessions, or attainments?

What do you really need to be happy?

CHAPTER 14

Radiant Calm—The Fourth Jhāna

*With the abandoning of pleasure and pain, and with the
previous passing away of joy and displeasure, I entered and
dwelt in the fourth jhāna, which is neither painful nor
pleasant and includes the purification of mindfulness
by equanimity.*
—Saṃyutta Nikāya 28:4

B Y THE TIME you have reached the threshold of the fourth
jhāna, the quality of your mind will be smooth, quiet, and
exceedingly refined. After the third jhāna, pleasure is relinquished, and the heart is washed with the coolness of equanimity,
upekkha. A very gentle inclination of interest is sufficient to realize
the fourth jhāna. You need to do nothing except look beyond the
happiness of pleasurable states.

The mind that is near the fourth jhāna is extremely responsive
to intention. Consciousness instantly molds to the suggestion,
whether your intention is to enter, focus, release, deepen, or relax.
You are not creating equanimity. There is no need for striving. The
energetic penetrating function of directed thought that supported
the attainment of the first jhāna is far too coarse to apply now.
Such vigorous endeavoring would feel rough at this refined level of

consciousness. The fourth jhāna is an opportunity to surrender to your deepest spiritual aspirations.

Quietly reflect on the two disadvantages of the third jhāna: it is perilously close to the agitation of the second jhāna, and sukha is relatively coarse. Consider the advantages of the fourth jhāna, namely that equanimity and one-pointedness are more peaceful. Gently give rise to a resolution: "May I attain the fourth jhāna," "May the fourth jhāna arise," "May my mind be absorbed in equanimity," or "Beyond pleasure and pain, beyond happiness and sadness, may I enter and abide in the fourth jhāna with mindfulness purified by equanimity."

These resolutions support the withdrawal of interest in sukha and incline the mind toward the feeling of equanimity. As sukha diminishes, it is replaced by a neutral feeling of equanimity. Give single-pointed attention to the breath nimitta infused with this quality of equanimity. Allow the mind to become absorbed in this stable yet vibrant state of equipoise.

Recognizing the Fourth Jhāna

The fourth jhāna is characterized by a single-pointed focus with a neutral and equanimous feeling, a deep unification in this state, and the strange sense of not much else going on. Consciousness is pervaded by a feeling that is neither pleasant nor unpleasant. The mind remains composed within itself in quiet still awareness, very remote from sensory contact. There is no excitement.

It is not a particularly pleasant state, but there is nothing to find here that is unpleasant or harmful. The bliss of the third jhāna pales in comparison to the deep rest, sublime peacefulness, and profound sense of OK-ness at this stage. In the sublime stability of the fourth jhāna, sounds, sensations, and other occurrences will pass unrecognized. If intrusive external phenomena are perceived, breaching jhāna and pulling consciousness briefly into contact with sensory stimuli, the experiences will be known from the perspective of equanimity.

For instance, if a loud sound is perceived, it will not trigger conditioned responses of desire or aversion. On structured group retreats, the lunch bell might be the most exciting moment of the day. Although it might ring nearby and briefly break the absorption state, it won't trigger the conditioned impulse to get up to go to the meal. The sound may be loud enough to intrude into consciousness, and with that contact there is awareness of hearing and the intelligent comprehension that it is the bell signaling the day's meal, but no habitual reaction is attached to the awareness. No urge is present to move from the meditation.

Unaffected by conditioned reactions of desire or aversion, the meditator's attention emerges only momentarily from absorption and easily resettles back into jhāna. In retreat conditions, few environmental objects are intrusive enough to penetrate the detachment of the fourth jhāna; those that do will arise and pass without disrupting this deeply balanced equipoise.

In the fourth jhāna, you will feel as though you could sit indefinitely, like the yogis of old who sat unmoving for days at a stretch. There is no cause for disturbance while absorbed in this neutral feeling and steadiness of mind. Conventional body sensations are not registered. The breath becomes very, very shallow. Mindfulness continues with precision, and there is no reduction in attentiveness, but the physical field is beyond the boundaries of interest to the mind absorbed in the fourth jhāna.

Experience this complete physical relaxation; however, out of compassion for the health of your spine, you might explore entering the fourth jhāna with the resolve to relax with an uplifted spine. Let this profound equipoise saturate your consciousness, permeating every cell of your being with the unified experience of equanimity. As the Buddha's illustration states, "Just as if a man were to sit wrapped from head to foot in a white garment, so that no part of

ᕲ Noticing When Your Mind is Spacious or Contracted

In ordinary activities as well as in meditation, you might find that in some moments you sense a quality of spaciousness, while in other moments there is a sense of contraction. Sometimes the mind is fascinated by diverse sensory objects, sometimes it's lost in an internal narrative, and sometimes it seems to rest in a spacious, empty experience. In your meditation session and throughout the day, notice moments of mental contraction and moments of mental balance, quiet, or spaciousness. Periodically ask yourself what you are aware of so that you clearly recognize the object that your attention is focused on. Notice how the nature of the object affects the quality of the concentrated state.

Investigate the following:

- What are you aware of? Is your attention focused on feeling? On matter? On consciousness? On a concept?
- What are the conditions that support spaciousness and stillness of mind?
- What triggers contraction?
- How does the mind recover from contraction to find ease again?
- What is present and what is absent in the mind?
- What enables the qualities of spaciousness and focused attention to occur simultaneously and support each other?

- Are you experiencing joy? Ease? Fear? Anticipation? Equanimity? Pride? Contentment? Agitation? Curiosity? How do these qualities affect the flexibility, calmness, and effectiveness of your mind?
- Do you expect something specific to happen next?
- Are you trying to make something happen?
- Is your practice affected by an open-minded attitude or a narrow motivation?

him was untouched by that garment—so his body is suffused, filled and irradiated . . . so that no part remains untouched by it."[85]

The mind can become so far removed from bodily experience that sensations may seem distant even after you emerge from the jhāna. Equanimity can become so pervasive through deep absorptions that feelings normally associated with pain or pleasure simply carry a neutral quality. After emerging from absorption, the meditator may experience strong sensations as primarily neutral.

Take the time to mindfully reconnect with the body and the world; gently stretch your limbs and feel the touch of clothes and the contact with water as you wash your hands. After emerging from jhāna, *do not sustain a state of disconnection* with the world: bring active energy to mindfulness on contact and invigorate your connection with the senses. Systematic withdrawal from worldly expressions is an important feature of jhāna, but it would be a disadvantage for insight if sensory seclusion were sustained beyond the range of absorption. Insight frequently arises when mindfulness infuses sensory contact.

After emerging, give attention to embodied awareness, sensitively guarding the senses with the clarity of mindful presence.

Experiencing Equanimity

If your experience of the fourth jhāna is deep and sustained, a strong sense of equanimity will continue between meditation sessions in relation to all contacts. Explore how equanimity feels in relation to weather, temperature, food tastes, other people's peculiar habits, broken equipment, and daily choices of what to drink or wear. Equanimity supports a deep comprehension that things in the world are just following the way of the world. Things are the way that they are. As the Buddha said, "Such it is."[86]

Equanimity is not the static feeling most people imagine it to be. At this stage, you can explore equanimity through its contrast to pleasure by shifting between the third and fourth jhānas and jumping between all the previous levels. By comparing the qualities associated with each state, you can discern each factor and the feelings as they change. Recognize exactly what changes in each transition. Specifically notice what happens when the feeling-tone of sukha is exchanged for the feeling of equanimity. The feeling-tone of equanimity is not bland or mediocre, but it does not have the upbeat quality of sukha and certainly not the intensity of pīti. With the first four jhānas as a basis, you have four distinctively different states to explore. By moving through the jhānas in reverse order, you may learn about equanimity, contentment, and delight from a new perspective.

Equanimity is an extraordinary quality of the heart, necessary in life and vital in practice. It cools the heart and lets the mind rest completely—steady and undisturbed. Following a deep absorption in the fourth jhāna, the mind can feel so imperturbable that it is difficult to imagine ever reacting with desire or aversion. Many ardent meditators, saturated with this profound encounter with equanimity, briefly wonder if they have attained enlightenment. But enlightenment occurs with the realization of the unconditioned. The fourth jhāna, like all the previous states experienced in the development of concentration, is conditioned. Like all mental states, it will change.

One of the profound teachings of the Buddha is that all conditioned things are unreliable and unsatisfactory. This truth becomes vividly clear with the support of the stability of fourth-jhāna samādhi. The mind is not busy fabricating stories, making excuses, weaving commentaries, developing strategies, or manipulating its relationship to all things in the futile quest to minimize the unpleasant. There simply is an absence of those ingrained reactions that fruitlessly attempt to adjust worldly conditions to support personal preferences and views. When the mind is profoundly balanced with equanimity, there is no averse reaction to the basic fact that nothing in the material world can bring satisfaction. The mind does not require further elaboration. The struggle ceases.

For example, in jhāna you might sit unmoved for many hours at a stretch. In the course of time, your mouth might dry; when the absorption ends you will feel thirsty. The sensations of thirst may or may not carry an unpleasant feeling tone. Influenced by equanimity, these sensations would not be coupled with craving, desperation, fear, or aversion. There may be no desire to quench them. The sensations will simply be known as they are, and a wise course of action will arise in response. You will simply drink some water, without the extra drama that an unsettled mind might interject into the moment.

A spasm or cramp is merely tension or pulsating heat. It is not terrible. It may not even be unpleasant. It can be known simply as a series of changing sensations. You might clearly feel sharp stinging sensations but not consider them painful. For the untrained mind, an added experience of aversion strengthens the motivation to change, seek help, or protect the body. However, with equanimity as your resource you won't need pain or aversion to protect yourself. Rather, intelligence determines a skillful course of action—to move, massage, or stretch a straining muscle. Wisdom is a sufficient guide.

When still saturated by equanimity after the fourth jhāna, you might hear a spring bird song with magnificent detail—discerning fluctuations of melody and interactions with the wind. When mindfulness has been purified by equanimity, you will know whatever is perceived in its bare simplicity, without the extra involvement of liking or not liking, without the distortions of personal preferences, comparisons, and judgments. Equanimity is a deeply sublime and preferred experience. It is not the happiness of a pleasant feeling, but it could be described as a kind of happiness that is realized through the absence of unpredictable swings of pleasure and pain and the agitating reactions of desire and aversion.

Experience the positive and lingering effect of equanimity on consciousness. Go about your daily routine without the desire to control experiences, without demanding that things be your way. Confidence is based on the direct experiential knowledge that you don't need the biases of aversion, judgmental criticism, and personal greed to function peacefully in this world.

PURIFICATION OF MIND BY EQUANIMITY

In the quietude of the fourth jhāna, the primary event is the progressive purification of awareness by equanimity. As the jhāna is sustained, the power of mindfulness is clarified through the non-reactive qualities of this state. A mind influenced by equanimity is not buffeted and dulled by desire and aversion; it achieves a stillness that sharpens attention and clarifies awareness.

As the mind quiets, observe how equanimity affects your experience of things. How does equanimity affect the precision of mindfulness? How does the absence of desire and aversion affect your energy, focus, and concentration?

A consciousness influenced by a recent abiding in the fourth jhāna feels extraordinarily spacious. Look into the mind and recognize what is there and what is not. Confidence develops when there is no craving, no aversion, no judging, no agitation, no preoccupations with self-interest, and no unwholesome forces of any kind. Complete confidence is essential for the further development of samādhi. This confidence will be found by looking into the mind and clearly discerning that there is actually nothing to fear. Notice what is present. Notice what is absent.

There is a path to peace, and the mind will naturally incline toward whatever is deeper and purer. This inclination has been guiding you away from the gross aspects of worldly pleasures through the initial four jhānas. You won't need to coerce your mind down the path, cajole it, or bargain with it. By this point in the process, there is a momentum in the practice. It may feel as though the mind is finding its way home, and you are just coming along for the ride. Watch the natural settling of the mind as it follows its innate inclination toward peace.

A mind purified by jhāna is beautiful!

USING THE PLIABLE, MALLEABLE, WIELDY MIND

From the stability of the fourth jhāna, several options are available for further development. The ancient discourses present the possibility of using the fourth jhāna as the springboard for wielding "the various kinds of psychic potency,"[87] such as mind-reading, seeing into the future, recollecting past lives, duplicating the body, or flying through the air. Although these possibilities are interesting, this book limits itself to discussing the two other traditional options. By continuing in the scheme of absorptions, you can experience a further sequence of *four formless attainments* that are explained in chapter 19. More importantly, you can use the fourth jhāna as the basis for insight to purify the mind of all forms of attachment, defilement, and delusion.

The mind in the fourth jhāna is extraordinarily agile, malleable, unified, clear, and stable—very fit for the work of insight meditation. It has become an effective tool to direct toward the resolution of suffering. After sufficiently permeating the mind and heart with the calm clarity of the fourth jhāna, turn your now limber attention to the dissolving of the jhāna. Observe the jhāna factors as they change. Observe all phenomena. Again you may enter or exit the jhāna, or return to lower jhānas as you feel so inclined. Sense for yourself what supports the clarity of insight into the nature of things.

Samādhi sharpens the mind. Use it to develop an undistorted comprehension of life.

⌐ *Equanimity and Engagement*

When you emerge from the fourth jhāna, direct mindfulness to the basic components of experience: pleasantness, unpleasantness, and neutrality of feeling.

Observe the feelings carefully.

Notice what reactions they trigger.

Practice fully experiencing the clarity of feeling without the extra formations of desire, aversion, and delusion.

Allow a feeling to simply be a feeling, without adding attachment.

Continue your discernment of experience and development of insight as you go about your daily activities.

What does the experience of deep equanimity reveal about your engagement with life?

CHAPTER 15
How Deep Is Deep Enough?

*Those who have grasped perceptions and views
wander in the world creating friction.*
—Sutta Nipāta, verse 847

CONTROVERSY HAS HISTORICALLY surrounded the practice of jhāna. The primary point of contention is the depth required to designate a state as jhāna: How deep is deep? How stable is stable? How secluded does the mind need to be before the experience can reasonably be considered a jhāna?

Some teachers in Asia and the West recognize fairly light levels of samādhi (unified concentration) where bright joy steadily infuses perception. They liberally apply the term jhāna to any arising of the designated configuration of jhāna factors. Other teachers reserve the term jhāna for a depth of seclusion that permits no sensory impressions whatsoever. Most teachers fall somewhere between the two extremes.

Although the jhāna states are succinctly described in the discourses of the Buddha, the question remains: "What exactly entails an experience of jhāna?" One teacher[88] illustrates this controversial issue with a simile of eight pools of water. A meditator may skim the surface of the water, wade in, swim on the surface, or dive in deep.

However one enters, to whatever depth, the pools of water are still the same pools. The eight attainments remain the same even though the depth of experience differs depending upon how one engages with them.

The controversy over what constitutes a distinctive jhāna experience raises several questions. Should *no* thoughts arise—or only wispy thoughts that don't move the mind off its chosen point of focus? Must practitioners hear *no sounds* in jhāna, or do they simply find that the mind is unmoved by the sounds that are perceived? Is there any perception of body and posture in jhāna? Is physical perception suspended in the higher jhānas but not the lower, or is bodily perception abandoned as a basic precondition of the first jhāna?

Teachers offer various views based on their experiences. I am not sure that strict objective criteria can be applied to all absorption experiences. I prefer to let individual practitioners explore varying depths of stillness for themselves. With practice, you can gauge for yourself how liberally or conservatively you wish to apply the term "jhāna" to your experience.

It is my hope that the question of "How deep is deep enough?" will become inconsequential when one comes to understand jhāna practice as a progression of relinquishment. By stabilizing the mind and growing familiar with the jhāna factors, you'll soon come to a functional determination yourself. A personal sensitivity coupled with experientially developed criteria for absorption will be more useful for deepening concentration than taking sides in traditional debates. You must learn to steer your own process. You must learn when to rest the attention deeper in absorption, when to intensify the factors of concentration, and when to shift between jhānas or dissolve the seclusion entirely and see things as they are.

If we get trapped into arguing over the definition of a jhāna's depth, we miss the opportunity to abandon at least some unwholesome forces and cultivate a degree of wholesome states. It is simply

How Concentrated Is Your Mind?

In Meditation: Notice the quality of your attention at the beginning and end of your daily sitting meditation. What signs indicate that you are concentrated or distracted? Notice to what extent your mind feels stable, workable, efficient, flexible, uplifted, confident, interested, attentive, balanced, quiet, and calm.

In Daily Activities: Periodically examine your mind during daily activities to monitor when your mind is concentrated and when your mind is entangled, agitated, hurried, dull, or distracted.

There are many kinds and degrees of concentration that may be more or less suitable for particular situations. Become familiar with the state of your mind while you are engaged with ordinary activities as well as when your attention is focused during meditation, and consider how much concentration is sufficient for the task at hand.

wiser to dwell with a mind suffused by joy or equanimity at any depth and to any degree than to indulge the comparing tendencies of mind or cower under the weight of historic controversies.

The depth that is possible for a concentrated mind is unfathomable. The Buddha listed depth of concentration as one of the four conditions that were incomprehensible and unfathomable: if obsessively considered it can never result in an answer, only in insanity.[89] However, should you choose to apply the term jhāna liberally to states lightly saturated by jhāna factors, please don't presume that such states represent the full potential of jhāna. The early discourses of the Buddha describe deeply secluded states.

For example, a student of Alara Kalama was once bragging that his teacher had sat unmoved by the roadside while five hundred carts passed by. Upon questioning, Alara Kalama stated that he was fully conscious and awake and yet did not hear or see the five hundred carts passing nearby, even though his robe was splattered with mud. The Buddha then shared his experience of sitting through a violent rainstorm with thunder and lightning that killed two men and four oxen. He also described being fully conscious and awake, yet did not hear or see the storm.[90] Deep absorption describes a state removed from conventional sensory perceptions; however, it is not a dull or mindless state. Attention is keenly aware of the subtle mental phenomena that characterize each jhāna. During jhāna, the Buddha was steady, unmoved, and apparently unaware of external commotion—with mindful attention focused internally, he remained happily absorbed in jhāna.

The early discourses contain a description of the chief disciple, Venerable Sāriputta, sitting absorbed in meditation when a passing mischievous spirit clobbered him on the head. He remained entirely undisturbed by it—only later commenting that he had a slight headache.[91] Physical assault is certainly an extreme test. You do not need to be attacked to have confidence in sustained states of consciousness that are flooded with exquisite purity, delight, happiness, and equanimity. For prolonged periods there can be exceedingly refined states of alertness during which bodily and postural sensations are completely excluded from awareness. There are no feelings of pain, no sense of touch, no perception of temperature, no sounds, and no awareness of birds, doors opening and closing, bells ringing, people walking in and out, or heaters turning on and off. There is no consciousness of day shifting into night or night into day, although the events occur.

Such depth of seclusion is certainly possible. When absorption is terminated and consciousness emerges from this controlled withdrawal, a dramatic moment of heightened awareness occurs—everything is sensitively and vividly known. One recognizes light, sounds, sensations, and the flow of dynamic life as they actually are. Consciousness, purified by the temporary seclusion of absorption, opens to meet this precious and fleeting existence in supreme clarity.

While developing this methodology, you may often observe periods in which the jhāna factors are strongly established but you don't feel an altered state of absorption. The jhāna factors are vibrant and dominant, and yet the mind seems slightly removed. It may feel like you are watching them from a slight distance or through a glass window. Sometimes the only mental factors in your field of view will correspond to standard descriptions of jhāna. If asked to describe what was present and absent in your mind, you might offer a textbook description of jhāna, but you don't feel genuinely confident.

In a phase such as this, hindrances won't arise, due to the vibrancy of the jhāna factors. Everything looks right on the surface. However, the meditator's relationship with jhāna is still tenuous—thought, effort, and sensations periodically intrude. The mind has not completely released into the cradle of jhāna; it is not full absorption. To understand the quality of this phase, imagine yourself standing on the threshold of your house. You are looking inside through the open front door but have not yet stepped inside. You are looking inward, but you can still feel the outside temperature. This phase marks a natural transition; I would not call it jhāna until a deeper immersion has occurred. When conditions for absorption do occur, the experience is like entering the house and closing the door behind: you feel more relaxed, safe, confident, and at ease in the welcome seclusion.

Even after absorption is established, you may experience your detachment periodically weakening as a result of an influx of minor thoughts or environmental intrusions. Then that detachment may effortlessly reestablish itself. Like an ebb and flow the mind momentarily surfaces from the depths, or returns to the thinner fringes of a concentrated field, then effortlessly sinks back, deep and centered. It is as though there is a minor breach that quickly closes by itself, or a tiny leak in concentration that is immediately plugged. Although imprecise, these images convey a general sense of the way altered states can fluctuate without disturbing the evolution of concentration.

Each level of attainment presents a new opportunity to consolidate the energies of mind. Working each jhāna, you strengthen the absorptions while simultaneously developing a mind that is malleable and wieldy. There is no need to abbreviate this process for the sake of efficiency. Each attainment should be thoroughly developed and examined before resolving for the next jhāna.

During a daily practice at home, meditators may find that although they can attain stable states of unification supported by strong jhāna factors, these states lack the sensory withdrawal characteristic of deep jhāna. Seclusion can be supported by choosing a quiet and solitary location for meditation, closing and locking the door, meditating in the early morning before family members wake up, unplugging the telephone, and turning off computers, cell phones, faxes, and any other equipment that produces sound. For many practitioners, retreat conditions are necessary for deeper detachment. And even in retreat conditions, some practitioners will find that their minds simply do not enter absorption, even though they practice diligently. Nevertheless, the mental composure cultivated through concentration practice and energized by jhāna factors will add an exponential degree of clarity to vipassanā practices regardless of whether or not deep absorption is attained.

Spend whatever time you need to fully explore each state; don't rush through this system. The Buddha compared a meditator who hurries on to higher jhānas to a foolish mountain cow who wanders seeking greener pastures.[92] This mountain cow does not know the terrain and is not skilled in moving about the mountain. She leaves one pasture but gets lost and is unable to find that greener pasture or return to her home.

It is essential to lay a strong foundation of skill through practice in these first four jhānas before advancing to the more subtle formless states. Learn precisely how the nimitta develops; balance your effort; refine your mindfulness skills. Examine the concentrated mind after each jhāna and assess your observations to determine whether they highlight consistent aspects of that concentrated state. Confirm your understanding through repeated reflections. Diligent practice will enable you to "obtain at will, without trouble or difficulty, the four jhānas that constitute the higher mind and provide a pleasant abiding here and now"[93]—the classic description of an adept.

After attaining stability in the jhāna and clarity regarding its components, scrutinize the jhāna even more closely until you genuinely recognize the conditioned aspect of concentrated states. Reflect that the state has been volitionally produced, is impermanent, and is subject to change. Once you recognize the undependable quality of all conditioned states, you cease to adhere to things that are changing and conditioned—which you have probably figured out by now includes just about everything! Even if conditioned states are exquisitely delightful and pleasant, a mind intent on peace and freedom will look beyond their fleeting pleasures.

Undertake this investigation with an infusion of a gentle but potent interest. When you are interested in something, you naturally look very closely to understand the true nature of what is perceived. Observe the experience of jhāna with the innocent interest of a child fascinated with the movement of a beetle walking over pebbles. Or take your inspiration from the astronomer who repeatedly gazes through a telescope and patiently considers the movements of stars. Adjust the quality of investigation so that your observation does not impede the functioning of the subtle states. Overly vigorous investigation can agitate the mind.

Look Closely

When the mind is concentrated, conditions are superb for clear seeing. If, however, you remain too long in deeply still absorptions, the factor of investigation can grow sluggish, inert, or dulled through disuse. Perception might feel rusty rather than agile if it remains sunk for too long in deep seclusion. The mind sometimes can feel stretched thin by excessively sustained absorptions, perhaps too thin to want to encounter chaotic confrontations with sensory phenomena.

Attentive to the dynamic balance of calm unification and mindful interest, a wise meditator moderates the duration and depth of absorption and adjusts the practice to obtain a useful blend of energy, tranquility, and clarity. This may require moving between the jhānas more frequently, entering and exiting the jhānas in shorter intervals, intertwining the practices of samādhi and vipassanā.

Develop the ability to move flexibly, like an accordion, flexing and extending awareness. Once this system is learned, meditators will find it remarkably easy to slide into deep states. There is no value, however, to falling into jhāna like soiled linen tossed down a laundry chute. No skill is involved in going straight down. At all times each state should remain responsive to the meditator's intention and afford a flexible basis for insight. Jhāna produces a profound peacefulness. This peaceful mind is flexible, balanced, and responsive. If attention emerges from seclusion disoriented, or with the critical faculty of mindfulness dulled or impaired, it is not the right concentration taught by the Buddha.

ꙮ *Cultivating Mastery*

The following exercises drawn from the traditional teachings can strengthen the absorptions and cultivate mastery in jhāna. I recommend that meditators engage with these exercises from the time that the first jhāna is well established, exploring and enhancing their concentration regarding each jhāna before advancing to the next level.

Exercise One: Develop the skills to sustain absorption for a long time and to emerge at a predetermined time. These skills develop with diligent practice. First, learn to stay immersed in the jhāna for long periods without the intrusion of distractions, thoughts, sounds, or sensations. Next, practice remaining absorbed for specific durations. To refine this ability, prior to entering an absorption you will establish the intention to remain for a specific period of time, and then check the time when you emerge. If you overstayed your intended duration, you may be indulging in the pleasures of the jhāna state. If you fall out too soon, your concentration is not yet strong. Practice with short and long durations until you can remain absorbed for as long as you wish.

Exercise Two: Know clearly what is present and what is absent in each jhāna. After emerging from absorption, consciously notice the presence and function of the jhāna factors. Notice the texture of mind: is it malleable, flexible, limber? In addition to the primary five jhāna factors, take note of any mental factor that accompanies jhāna. Become aware of how these mental factors function in the altered state of jhāna. How does energetic effort affect the quality of the absorption?

Recognize mindfulness functioning when no sensory object is present. Let interest discern which faculties are active or dormant. Through these explorations you will know from your own experience, without the slightest hesitation, without referring to ideas or texts, what characterizes each jhāna and how to distinguish each state.

Exercise Three: Work with a very soft whisper of intention to move between the jhānas. The mind near jhāna is so malleable that even a subtle intention will have a dramatic impact; the bare arousal of a simple resolution will be quite enough. Learn what is enough and what effort is too coarse for the refinement of each state. Incline toward doing less; trust the gentler options. Let these shifts happen without force and without difficulty. Notice how your attention responds to your intention.

After establishing at least the first three jhānas, incorporate the next two exercises.

Exercise Four: Clarify the entrance into and defining features of each jhāna by moving back and forth through the sequence of jhānas. Develop skill and greater awareness by moving in forward order, reverse order, by systematically skipping first through the odd numbers (jumping from the first to the third jhāna and then back to the first jhāna), then through the even numbers (jumping from the second jhāna to the fourth jhāna and back to the second jhāna), and then jumping between jhānas in a random order.

Exercise Five: Attain each jhāna directly from access: access to first jhāna, exit and return to access; access to second jhāna, exit and then return to access; repeat this process through all levels of jhāna. You can achieve this most easily by connecting with the whole breath before and after each absorption.

CHAPTER 16
Summary of Meditation Instructions

There are these roots of trees, these empty huts.
Meditate, do not delay, or else you will regret it later.
—Majjhima Nikāya 106:15

B EFORE MOVING into the final stages of our exploration of the jhānas as a means to liberation, it would be valuable to review the meditation instructions we have covered in this book. This chapter provides a checklist for jhāna practice that you can refer to as you establish the sequence of the four meditative absorptions.

INITIAL ATTITUDES AND CONDITIONS

1. Guard the mind with mindfulness.
2. Establish a stability of mindful attention in the present moment.
3. Have a clear intention to focus on your meditation object: the breath.
4. Incline the attitude of the meditation toward stability and composure.

5. Understand the practice as a refinement of relinquishment rather than an accumulation of attainments.

6. Enjoy any opportunity to abandon an unwholesome state or repetitive thought.

7. Cultivate mental attitudes that are bright, spacious, and relaxed.

8. Temporarily set aside other meditation systems while you are establishing this singularity of focus. Permit your meditation practice to be utterly simple.

9. Cultivate confidence that this practice works—jhāna is attainable. For over 2,600 years meditators have used these techniques to discover profound peace. Trust that the practice will work for you too—your mind is no exception.

Beginning the Focused Meditation Technique

1. Connect and sustain the attention at the point of occurrence of the breath with diligent penetrating interest.

2. Count 1–10–1, 1–10–1 for a few minutes to strengthen the focus on the breath.

3. If distracting thoughts persist, count 1, 1, 1, 1, 1, 2, 2, 2, 2, 2, 2, 3, 3, 3, 3, 3, 3, . . . reconnecting repeatedly as you attend to the whole breath.

4. Learn to abandon all unwholesome states.

5. Notice mind as it brightens and coheres. Notice the arising of the jhāna factors.

6. Infuse the awareness of breath with delight and happiness while steadfastly focusing on the breath.

7. Examine the experience of the absence of hindrances to become familiar with the quality of an undefiled joyful awareness.

ESTABLISHING ACCESS TO ABSORPTION

1. Gladden the mind with the perception of the absence of hindrances; learn to trust your mind by abiding without hindrances.
2. Continue to direct attention to breath or breath nimitta. Stay attentive to breath without necessarily perceiving sensation. Let go of the habit of interpreting breath through physical sensation.
3. Notice when the physicality of the sensations diminishes and a dominant luminosity arises in the mind: the appearance of the counterpart sign (nimitta).
4. Resolve for the growth and increase of the jhāna factors.

SEQUENTIAL PROGRESSION

1. When the mind is very bright, cohesive, undisturbed by thoughts, and unhindered by desire, aversion, or doubt, insert the resolve "May I enter and abide in the first jhāna."
2. Let the mind rest in the purity of this state.
3. Observe the inward quality of mental cohesion in the first jhāna.
4. Allow vitakka and vicāra to settle, then focus with rapt interest on the nimitta to attain the second jhāna.
5. Become dispassionate toward pīti as it fades in order to shift to the third jhāna. Let the mind unify with the subtle happiness of sukha.
6. Relinquish any attachment to sukha to attain the fourth jhāna.
7. Follow the single-pointed stillness into a stable absorption characterized by a neutral expression of equanimity.

Strengthening Absorption

1. Sustain the jhānas gently, with joy, interest, and ease.
2. If the seclusion begins to weaken with the influx of a few thoughts, infuse attention with interest to maintain the unification.
3. When protecting seclusion, avoid trying to adjust the jhāna. If distractions interrupt the absorption, a gentle equanimous recognition of the breach may restore your dedication to the wholesome state of concentration and usher the mind back into absorption.
4. Upon emerging from each jhāna, notice the qualities of stability and clarity, and the presence or absence of the jhāna factors.
5. Develop the agility to enter and exit each state without difficulty.
6. Jump between the levels of jhāna.
7. Rest deeply in each of these pleasant abidings.
8. Relax. Trust the concentration to deepen without forceful striving.

Using Jhāna as a Basis for Insight

1. Relinquish the seclusion after each absorption. Let the jhāna dissolve and observe the dissipation of the jhāna factors and the secluded state.
2. Upon emerging from absorption, examine the qualities and mental factors that are present and absent in the mind.
3. Become mindfully aware of perceptions, sensory experiences, and mental activities as they naturally occur.
4. Use each stage as a basis for insight before aspiring to the next level of jhāna.

5. Take a moment to consciously bring each meditation session to a close with a dedication toward an altruistic purpose, reflection on the quality of mind during the meditation session, recommitment to your aim, or contemplation of the relevance of the meditative experience for your life.

6. Allow the experience of jhāna to consciously inform the decisions that you make and the actions that you perform in your daily activities.

PART IV

DOING THE WORK OF INSIGHT

CHAPTER 17

Three Doorways to Insight

*Whatever is conditioned and volitionally produced
is impermanent, subject to cessation.*
—Majjhima Nikāya 52

I T IS UNLIKELY THAT insight will occur as a spectacular event marked by celestial music and fireworks. It will be much simpler: seeing things without attachment, as they are, rather than as we wish they were.

There is a story about a wisely foolish Sufi saint, Mullah Nasrudin:

Mullah was walking down the village street when some street kids began to throw stones at him.

"Don't do that, and I will tell you something that will interest you," Nasrudin said.

"All right, what is it? But no philosophy," the street kids replied.

"The Emir is giving a free banquet to all comers."

The children ran off toward the Emir's house as Nasrudin warmed to his theme, ". . . the delicacies and the delights of the entertainment . . ."

He looked up and saw them disappearing in the distance. Suddenly he tucked up his robes and started to
sprint after them. "I'd better go and see. It might be true
after all."[94]

Too often we ascribe reality to our desires and lose touch with
what is true in the present moment. Is your experience of seeing,
smelling, hearing, thinking, and sensing clear, or is it distorted by
misperception?

Imagine you are walking along a forest path at dusk and see something partially coiled and partially stretched across the path just a
step or two ahead. Startled as the thought of a snake occupies the
mind, you stand frozen with fear. As you are caught in the grip of
this perception, your heart races, fear overtakes your mind, and
then—afflicted with a flurry of emotional responses—your mind
jumps back and forth between strategies of escape and scenarios of
danger. As you stand motionless, wondering which way to step to
avoid the snake, you notice that the snake has not moved. Looking
more carefully you discover that it is not a snake; it is only a rope.

The story of the snake and the rope is a familiar rendering of the
problem of seeing clearly. This ancient teaching story has been retold
for thousands of years reminding us that problems are solved by clear
seeing. We don't turn a snake into a rope. We don't need to make
things different than they are. We simply bring our attention to the
reality of things. When encountering conditioned phenomena, we
observe their fundamental characteristics as *impermanent, unreliable*, and *not self*. Armed with the striking clarity of this knowledge,
the mind can find nothing to cling to, crave for, or identify with.

IMPERMANENCE, UNSATISFACTORINESS, AND NOT-SELF

The Pāli term *vipassanā*, generally translated as "insight," literally means "clear seeing." Vipassanā is not simply a meditation

technique. Vipassanā is fundamentally about clear perception. Liberating insight may manifest when a meditator clearly recognizes three specific characteristics—*anicca* (impermanence), *dukkha* (unsatisfactoriness), and *anattā* (not-self)—because this recognition diminishes the tendency to cling.

Everyone has experienced phenomena changing. Weather changes. Bodies alter with age. All material and mental conditions are impermanent and inconstant. Things increase and decrease, expand and contract, begin and end. Awareness of change is not shocking to most people. Few, however, penetrate this fundamental perception sufficiently to arrive at a state of liberation through not-clinging.

Undoubtedly you have experienced the unsatisfactory, undependable, and stressful quality of things as they decay, break, or are lost. Pain is an obvious expression of suffering. Dukkha, more subtle than mere physical or mental pain, reveals the underlying undependable aspect of things. A deeper understanding of dukkha arises when we recognize that impermanent experiences cannot be a reliable basis for happiness. You might experience this quality of dukkha not only through explicit suffering, but also in the subtler discontent of, perhaps, wanting just a little more.

Whether you realize it or not, you have probably experienced the absence of an inherently existing essence we call *self*. You are not who you were yesterday. Your cells change. Experience changes. Ideas, opinions, and feelings change. Which one, if any, of these provides a stable definition of you? Examine your perceptions to discover if you can find someone behind your experience. Is there a fixed essence called *self* to whom your life happens? We all taste, but who or what knows the taste? We see, but who or what sees? Look deeply into your experience of perception. Does this sense of self that we conventionally call "I" have color, shape, location, or attributes? Is there an intrinsic being lurking behind the face, inside the rib cage, or in the elbow who would claim experiences as *I*, *me*, or *mine?* Usually the sense of a continuous self arises when we identify with thoughts, affiliations, or possessions. Yet when we examine our experience closely, nothing can be found that allows us to say, "This is really self."

Confusion arises when the term *anattā* is misunderstood as *no-self*, rather than *not-self*. The language of *no-self* sometimes creates a false impression that Buddhist teachings negate existence, whereas the teachings of *not-self* invite a precise investigation into what exactly the concept of self relies upon. What does the term *self* refer to?

Insight into anattā does not require a blanket negation of self-constructs. Through investigation we discover that every experience of body, mind, perception, or feeling is in fact not self. Self does not exist as a thing; self does not exist in anything. When we have clearly perceived this, identification with experience fades and the mind rests in profound detachment and ease. The insight into anattā manifests in the moment you are not taking life personally.

Mindfulness of breathing, bodily sensations, emotions, perceptions, and mental states can heighten awareness of the three primary characteristics. When directly perceiving anicca, you do not cling. When deeply perceiving dukkha, you do not cling. When clearly perceiving anattā, you do not cling. Shine the spotlight of attention onto these three characteristics until your attentiveness results in liberating insight.

Recognizing these three characteristics is called *seeing with wisdom.* When you see with wisdom, your former infatuation with sensory experience is replaced with an attention that is markedly disenchanted. This is an important distinction for the meditation practitioner to perceive. You do not *practice* disenchantment. You practice clear seeing; disenchantment naturally ensues. When you see with wisdom, the deluded view that seeks gratification through the senses ends. The connection with the senses continues, but it is

---

ᗏ *The Perception of Impermanence*

This perception of impermanence is the basis of liberating wisdom and the cornerstone of vipassanā practices. To draw attention toward this insight, notice what you are aware of right now: perhaps it is a cold sensation in your hands, or the sound of rain landing on the roof, or a throbbing sensation in your shoulder, or a planning fantasy. Recognize that the experience is changing; look closely to observe the changing elements and factors that constitute it:

- The material qualities might change as heat increases or decreases, as pressure causes contraction or expansion.
- The degree of pleasantness or unpleasantness might fluctuate.
- Your attention may be riveted to it now but might lose track of it when a competing perception arises.
- You might be conscious of it one moment and completely unaware of it the next moment.

Notice both these material and mental aspects to recognize vividly that the experience is changing.

---

altered by this perspective of disenchantment. Observing the fragile qualities of existence, you become disenchanted with conditioned things as a foundation for happiness. When you recognize that fleeting phenomena are not under your control, your enchantment with self-grasping ceases. When you perceive clearly, you discover a liberating disenchantment.

This transformation constitutes insight.

Fettered by Desire

To experience liberating wisdom, you do not need to abandon particular objects. Objects and experiences are not the problem. The trouble lies in the indulgence, attachment, infatuation, and confusion that presumes "things" can be the basis of lasting happiness. Don't let go of objects; release the grip of clinging and attachment instead.

A simile the Buddha repeatedly used describes a black ox and a white ox yoked together.[95] One would not say that the black ox is the fetter of the white ox, or that the white ox is the fetter of the black ox. The yoke is the fetter. This simile can be applied to our experience. Thoughts and experience are the black and the white oxen; desire, titillation, and clinging constitute the yoke that fetters. We abandon the yoke; thoughts and experiences remain.

Sometimes people don't recognize the fetter of desire because they are entranced by the hope that *this* sensation, *this* idea, *this* sight, *this* taste, *this* meditative experience will be the one that will "do it once and for all," that will bring ceaseless happiness. As you review your previous sensory experiences, consider how many sensory contacts you have already had in your lifetime. Were any capable of providing secure pleasure? If these didn't make you happy and peaceful, why would another one do it? Have you learned from your experience that conditioned phenomena are not a cause of lasting joy?

The selective attention that jhāna depends upon must eventually be relinquished as the mind opens in a full response of living insight. Ultimately the path leads beyond the force of grasping, beyond the duality of this and that, things and nothings, confinement and spaciousness, form and formless, and beyond any subset of concentrated states. The freedom of release reveals something beyond the equipoise of equanimity and concentration.

Insight can arise at any time—in the midst of mundane daily interactions or during profound spiritual quests. A flash of insight

᎗ *Highlighting Disenchantment*

Observe the quality of disenchantment as it occurs in simple ways: perhaps as you turn away from attractive perceptions or change tasks throughout the day.

What does the mind feel like when it is enthralled with a sensory experience?

What occurs when that seduction ends?

As you walk around the block and see a beautiful sunset, or as you savor a delicious meal, notice the moment when you are seduced into the experience.

Then observe the moment when the mind releases that enchantment and moves on to the next thing. No one exists transfixed the entire day by a single sensory pleasure.

Observe disenchantment occurring as you move from one activity to the next; as you are attracted to and then fail to notice various sensory stimuli; as you make this food choice, then that; and as you alter your recreational preferences.

Highlight and study mundane experiences of disenchantment in your daily routine.

Then, during formal meditation, observe this same dynamic. Disenchantment plays an essential role in the practices of both jhāna and insight. Notice how disenchantment makes the seclusion of the first jhāna possible. Notice the function of disenchantment in the transitions between jhānas, as each factor is released. Observe closely as it arises in a moment of clearly perceiving the impermanent, undependable, and empty nature of things.

may bring new perspectives to personal psychological patterns or inspire creative ideas for a project at work. A surprising vision might arise and inspire a painting. Or, you may find yourself mysteriously oriented toward something utterly sublime. As your awareness expands beyond self-interest, you might awaken to a realization of what the Buddhist tradition refers to as the unconditioned, the ultimate, the inexpressible, the immeasurable, the deathless—the end of all distress.

IN THIS FATHOM-LONG BODY

The Buddha taught that everything you need for liberating insight can be found by looking into your own experience. "It is, friend, in this fathom-high carcass endowed with perception and mind that I make known the world, the origin of the world, the cessation of the world, and the way leading to the cessation of the world."[96] Don't look for fancy insights or expect huge openings of heart. Rather, just see what happens when you allow your basic relationship to sensory experience to be relaxed and free of grasping.

If we expect freedom to be a far-out and spectacular experience, we may miss the intimacy of the timeless expression of an unbound mind. Repeatedly the Buddha referred to liberation not as an isolated, reified state, but as something more accessible: a wise and peaceful encounter with everyday sensory contact. He taught that "the supreme state of sublime peace" manifests as wisdom regarding all sensory contacts, and he summarized it as "liberation through not clinging."[97] Whatever understanding we have must be brought to bear on our sensory experience. Since it is in our sensory contact where grasping may erupt, there is where we will come to know a profound absence of clinging.

⌒ *Sensing Present Awareness*

Right now, as you are reading these words, sense present awareness, that natural open knowing of things as they are.

Feel the contact with your chair, feel the temperature of the body, feel the sensations of the breath moving, notice the sounds in the environment, sense the texture of the pages on your fingertips.

As you experience the simplicity of present-moment contacts, without dwelling on or preferring any particular perception, feel the factual flow of experience.

Notice what you are experiencing in this moment.

Experience now, without past or future, and see if there is any problem with the present.

Let this experience of simple and clear presence register within.

Look into the present moment and see what it is.

What is your relationship to present-moment experience?

BENEFITS OF CONCENTRATING THE MIND

Many benefits come with practicing jhāna: making space in the otherwise hectic bustle of your days, learning to disentangle yourself from chronic distraction, and enjoying the pleasures of a unified mind. These are alluring and valuable aspects of concentration practice. From a Buddhist perspective, however, they are merely the fringe benefits, not the reason for concentrating the mind.

The only reason for developing samādhi genuinely worth your time is that it supports liberating insight, insight that will ultimately allow you to become free from all distress. Concentration is the ground out of which liberating wisdom arises. The Buddha advised us to develop concentration, because "one who is concentrated understands things as they really are."[98] Understanding the interdependence of wisdom and concentration is fundamental to creating an effective and balanced spiritual life.

Supported by the steadiness of samādhi, your awareness can penetrate subtler aspects of experience: the pervasiveness of change and the undependable quality of conditioned things. With a stable mind, you will see beyond your familiar patterns of distraction. In particular, you may discover the subtle forms of clinging, where the illusion of "I" arises and clings to perceptions. Samādhi supports this sustained inquiry so that deep truths can be realized.

The traditional instructions describe jhāna as the process that makes the mind "fit to be worked" or "fit for work."[99] The Buddha used the analogy of purifying gold to describe the purification of mind. Gold is worked until the metal becomes pliant, strong, malleable, pure, and ready to be shaped into any ornament or object the goldsmith desires to produce.

> There are these five corruptions of gold, corrupted by which gold is neither malleable nor wieldy nor radiant but brittle and not properly fit for work. What five? Iron is a corruption of gold, corrupted by which gold is neither malleable nor wieldy nor radiant, but brittle and not properly fit for work. Copper . . . Tin . . . Lead . . . Silver . . . These are the five corruptions of gold, corrupted by which gold is neither malleable nor wieldy nor radiant but brittle and not properly fit for work. . . .
>
> So too, there are these five corruptions of the mind, corrupted by which the mind is neither malleable nor wieldy nor radiant but brittle and not rightly concentrated for the destruction of the taints. What five? Sensual desire is a corruption of the mind . . . ill will . . . sloth and torpor . . . restlessness . . . doubt is a corruption of the mind. These

are the five corruptions of the mind, corrupted by which the mind is neither malleable nor wieldy nor radiant but brittle and not rightly concentrated for the destruction of the taints.[100]

The meditative process enables you to overcome these classic five hindrances, to purify the mind and make it pliant and responsive to your deepest intentions, until nothing remains to corrupt attention. The traditional texts describe the quality of mind that is ready to work as "concentrated, purified and cleansed, unblemished, free from impurities, malleable, workable, established, and having gained imperturbability."[101] The seclusion of jhāna preserves mental energies, and the mind grows remarkably bright, malleable, and fit for work. Thus, jhāna prepares the mind to solve the problem of suffering.

As a child I enjoyed sharpening my pencils—cranking the handle of the sharpener that was mounted on the classroom wall and watching the shavings fill the container below. I'd sharpen a bit and then inspect the point, sharpening more and more until I was satisfied with the point. Sometimes I would sharpen away the better part of the pencil seeking a refined point. Now I have a small battery-powered pencil sharpener on my desk that stops shaving when the point is sufficiently sharp. It reminds me of the purpose of concentration. Concentration sharpens the mind; it serves no purpose, however, to seek a perfectly refined state. Once the mind is sufficiently clear and sharp, use it. Just as it is childish to enjoy sharpening pencils so much that we shave until the pencil finally disappears, we should not fritter away our time just playing with jhāna. We can apply whatever degree of mental refinement we develop to a purpose: attaining liberating insight.

Time goes by, retreats end, health fades, and inevitably death comes. Life progresses quickly. How much concentration is needed for insight will depend upon the practice conditions, inclinations, interests, and disposition of each individual. There is no objective measurement for how sharp a pencil needs to be to write or how deep an absorption needs to be for insight. A pointy pencil that sits in a desk drawer is of little value. A concentrated mind that merely abides in pleasant states is frivolous. Whatever degree of concentration you are able to establish will be your resource for awakening. Use it to free the mind!

WHAT IS THE WORK THAT NEEDS TO BE DONE?

Even though astonishing, almost miraculous powers can be generated through jhāna concentration, the Buddha forbade his monastics from displaying such attainments. We don't develop the mind to feel concentrated or impress friends.

The Buddha's teachings guide our attention toward those particular insights that have the potential to liberate. A mindfulness practitioner is trained to observe both the specific and the general characteristics of phenomena. For example, anger is specifically characterized by heat, agitation, tension, pressure in the head, coarseness of thought, and rudeness of speech. Pain is specifically characterized by sharpness, burning, searing, pulsing, and stabbing. The characteristics associated with lustful fantasies are longing, infatuation, clinging, and greed. When we are truly mindful of these experiences, we know anger, pain, and lust; we understand how these emotions function.

And as I've said, vipassanā meditation also encourages the recognition of general characteristics: impermanence, unsatisfactoriness, and emptiness. For example, when your attention becomes entangled in a planning scenario, investigate your thinking by noticing the particular qualities that characterize that thought—it might be excited, joyful, resentful, pleasant, or peaceful. Then observe how thought is subject to change. Perceive the beginning and ending of thoughts. Recognize the universal fact that thought is an unreliable foundation for happiness: because it changes, thought cannot be a lasting source of security. Investigate the lack of intrinsic essence to thought; see that there is no permanent entity to whom this thought refers. A willingness to investigate makes it possible to discriminate specific and general characteristics in any perception and to open to the universal qualities that all things share.

And yet, it is important to resist the urge to grasp insight. Observe all perceptions with detachment. If you become fixated on a vipassanā technique, jhāna attainment, or perception of impermanence, you are just as trapped as if you were attached to a tuna-fish sandwich. Fascinated with observing change, otherwise diligent students sometimes falter. Stagnation can occur if repeated observations of impermanence are hailed as the markers of success. Any form of attachment, to the pleasures of jhāna or to the brightness of insight, can halt progress. The self will try to take a stand upon these attainments, creating an illusion that it exists through association with meditative accomplishment. Then the entrapping concept of "being a meditator" is born. Recognize this construction; it presents the dangerous first step toward attachment to the concept of "a realized self."

Sometimes you may have great insights—and indeed insight can feel so pleasing, vast, and luminous that one confuses it with the satisfaction of completeness. Vigilance is necessary to see whether the liberation is truly lasting, or whether it rigidifies around a view of enlightenment. Observe whether the ease truly ends clinging or is merely the recollection of a peaceful moment that passed. Continued alertness in the midst of profound "aha" experiences keeps the examination alive until you are certain that there is no more work left to do and that your deepest intention is fulfilled.

Let go of every fixation. Ultimately this is a path of release. The mind may attempt to construct itself on any foundation: through attachment to blissful jhāna states, by becoming "the one who lets go," or by being "the meditator who understands change." Observe and laugh at the antics of the mind. Coax it to release its hold, even its attachment to good things. Uproot any place you find yourself stuck, whether it be with the pleasures of the tranquil mind of jhāna or in the clarity of insight. Resist the urge to keep score of your insights. Assessing your meditation practice only fuels grasping.

Willingness to let go is indispensable. Every stage of this path requires a complete relinquishment of both the struggles and the delights, pleasant experiences and painful ones. Even the states of samādhi that you diligently cultivate must, in the end, be relinquished.

The refined sublimity of the final formless state is considered "the best object of clinging,"[102] but the Buddha encourages disciples to not cling even to the base of neither-perception-nor-non-perception, because only one who "is without clinging attains Nibbāna."[103] Any form of clinging, even to concentration, is undesirable. As you see the limitations of each conditioned state, the state will dissipate. Every refinement you cultivate will dissolve. Regarding all the wholesome and wonderful developments of concentration, including all the levels of jhāna, the Buddha said, "That, I say, is not enough. Abandon it, I say; surmount it, I say."[104]

This discipline is not a practice of preferring one thing over another, of taking the subtle and leaving the gross, or of trading petty sensual desires for the bliss of jhāna. In mastering the jhānas, you will have sequenced through an extremely refined system of relinquishment to develop the capacity to let go. One of the greatest insights regarding things is also obvious: "Whatever is subject to origination is subject to cessation."[105] Whatever perceptions arise cannot be clung to. The Buddha's instruction was "to abandon desire for whatever is impermanent, suffering, and not-self."[106]

You don't really need to let go of much—only the delusion of misperception. In doing so, you will quickly discover the ultimate peacefulness of the Buddha's instruction, "Abandon what is not yours; this will lead to your happiness for a long time."[107]

Insight is immediate recognition that moves consciousness beyond the fragmentation of the conceptual mind. It is an order of knowing neither bound by the intellect nor limited to ideas and concepts; very often it cannot be reduced to language. Yet insight has the power to release the tension of attachment and end the strain of clinging.

Seeing things as they are will open you to the truth of being. You will rest at peace in the fluidity of sensory contacts while in the midst of active living. Insight does not depend on retreat conditions, silence, or secluded absorption states.

Insight transforms our lives!

CHAPTER 18

A New Way of Seeing

As he dwells contemplating impermanence . . . fading away . . .
cessation . . . relinquishment in those feelings, he does not cling
to anything in the world. Not clinging, he is not agitated.
—Aṅguttara Nikāya 7:61

THE MIND THAT EMERGES from absorption is remarkably stable, agile, and energetic as it meets the dynamic flow of sensory experience. The concentration you accumulate through samādhi can be your vantage point for insight.

This chapter explores the transition from the stillness of concentrated states to clearly understanding sensory contact, from samādhi to vipassanā.

Sustained absorption in happy states affects the tendencies and patterns of the mind, inclining it toward joy and ease. Concentration alone, however, does not have the power to make us free. We must join concentration, mindfulness, investigation, and wisdom to generate an unshakable deliverance from suffering. Concentration temporarily suspends preoccupation with desires and aversions and provides relief through a state of desirelessness. However, this peace is born of seclusion, not wisdom. It depends on specific conditions and hence is vulnerable to change.

The effort it takes to sustain jhāna reveals the defect of jhāna states. Notice what you must do to sustain absorption in jhāna. That subtle intentional effort reveals the limitations of the conditioned state: jhāna is produced through volition and effort and hence vulnerable to change.

The moment jhāna dissolves—the shift from the seclusion of absorption to sense perception—provides a strategic opportunity for insight. Thoughts, sensations, and images arise. How this flood of impressions is perceived will have a deep impact on the mind. This is due to the purity that accrued during jhāna. When a mind is concentrated, it feels less "sticky," less prone to grasp at things it likes or react against things it does not like. This dispassion provides a bridge between the peaceful secluded state and direct, wise contact with worldly life. Insight backed by the potency of jhāna has tremendous strength to free the mind from suffering.

EXAMINING THE DISSOLUTION OF JHĀNA

When the mind is absorbed, there are no distractions. In other words, there is not much going on! Mindfulness is still functioning within jhāna, although one is not mindful of ordinary sensory contacts. The mind is vividly alert, but sensory stimulation is not perceived. Hindrances may arise before or after jhāna; however, whenever the jhāna factors are dominant, the mind remains at ease.

The Pāli Canon likens the investigation a meditator performs when emerging from jhāna to the training with a straw target that an archer undertakes before going into battle.[108] A meditator who observes the characteristics of impermanence, unsatisfactoriness, and not-self revealed within the less complex conditions of a concentrated mind later applies that understanding to the potentially confusing encounters of worldly life. The limited range of factors present in a concentrated mind makes for safe and easy practice. In particular, subtle insights that arise in the wake of jhāna attainments are often related to this narrow range of pleasant states. We can see, for example, the impermanence of rapture, the undependability of sustained attention, and the impersonal quality of consciousness. In the safe practice ground of a mind freshly emerged from absorption, the meditator can explore the unreliability of pleasure as a basis for real happiness and then boldly look beyond the conditions of this refined state to realize that pleasure is *always* unreliable.

Notice how you perceive the sensory world as jhāna dissolves. Many changes occur as the factors of concentration diminish. Notice how qualities of happiness, pleasure, cohesion, concentration, one-pointedness, and equanimity change during the transition from deep jhāna to sensory experience. These qualities may increase or decrease. They may disappear altogether. The energies of pīti, sukha, and upekkha may take on a more physical quality, with energy pulsing through the body. Observe the impermanence and conditionality of the dominant jhāna factors during this transition.

As a meditator, you have invested a great deal of time and energy to cultivate these jhāna attainments and refine your mind. You can now watch the factors that you have so lovingly nurtured dissipate. This is the pivotal moment for investigation: *Is there any clinging or attachment?*

Attachment to the pleasant experience of absorption is an inherent risk in jhāna practice. Look carefully for any attachment to happiness, rapture, and concentration. The very investment made in achieving absorption creates the opportunity for attachment to slip in.

Practicing jhāna as the basis for insight is a little like the practice of the Tibetan sand mandala. These extraordinary ornate paintings are made of colored sand. Their construction demands years of training and diligent attention. No matter how perfectly formed, the painting is ritually destroyed and literally brushed away shortly after completion. We carefully construct samādhi, but lurking beneath our efforts may be an unseen desire for permanent satisfaction. As you move out of jhāna, experience the conditioned impermanent nature of every experience.

We cultivate wholesome states of jhāna within the broader context of practicing non-attachment. To a clear mind, even slight
attachments will be viewed as suffering. We develop strong jhāna
states in order to watch them dissolve, and thus we train the mind
in non-attachment. We strive for the best possible experience meditative effort can bring and then, by design, must witness its demise.
Jhāna, as the basis for insight, fuses development of wholesome conditions with relinquishment of every perception that consciousness
might fixate on.

The residue of absorption can bring a spacious clarity to vipassanā
practice. It is worthwhile to explore how the mind unified through
samādhi meets sensory contact. In the transition period immediately following absorption, observe the five jhāna factors change.
After they have diminished, gently allow mindfulness to meet
whatever else may be occurring in the body and mind. The breath
may become apparent. Attention may be drawn toward sounds. The
flood of sensory data sometimes feels intrusive, overwhelming, and
confusing; don't worry—quietly watch it all unfold. Simply recognize sensations and thoughts as they arise and change. With a calm
and stable mind, examine the nature of sense impressions and do
not be swept away by conceptual proliferation or reactivity.

Be curious as you meet the sensory world. What happens when
you hear a sound? During absorption you perceive no sounds, but
when jhāna dissolves, you hear all sorts of things: a person moving,
a bird outside, the drips of a water faucet, your own breath. How
does consciousness know it is hearing or what it is hearing? Inquire:
*Is this a simple experience of hearing, or does my mind move toward
the sound, constructing a relationship that postulates self, preference,
desire, or aversion?*

In jhāna there was no awareness of bodily experiences. In a post-
jhāna state, there may well be pain, pleasure, or sensations of warmth
and coldness. You will become aware of your posture. How are these
physical experiences known? Are they felt with a balanced mind,

or is there a critical commentary attached? In absorption, there are no hindrances of desire or aversion. But without the protection of seclusion, these mental states may arise again. Notice whether judgment, comparison, or confusion arises. Do perceptions stimulate desire, craving, fear, aversion, or agitation? Work with whatever hindrances you find. Having practiced letting go of attachment to tranquility, happiness, and rapture as an archer practices on a straw target, now you can use these skills to abandon coarser hindrances. Understand them as nothing more than changing mental states.

Explore how perception occurs. Notice whether the mind wraps itself around objects by conceiving of things as *I*, *me*, or *mine*. Observe very carefully what happens when you shift from a secluded state of absorption to the non-secluded state of sensory perception; the first moment is critical. Experience a fresh perception, before attention gets entangled in concepts. Examine whatever occurs as if this were your first encounter with life.

The higher jhānas do not necessarily yield better insights than the lower ones. For liberating insight, the first jhāna has all the conditions you will need. The first four jhānas plus three formless perceptions are traditionally used as a direct basis for insight, and insight from the perspective of the last formless attainment is gained through reflection. Whatever concentration is established as you move through the jhānas can be applied progressively to seeing the nature of things. It is always possible to create another vantage point for insight by deepening the concentration to the next level of absorption. On the other hand, you may be liberated in the early stages—after all, why not? It is a simple matter of not-clinging!

Exiting Jhāna

Within the field of absorption, perception is restrained. Absorption states are like a fenced-in ring, an arena where only certain factors are allowed inside. In order to establish jhāna, you guarded and restrained the mind. After absorption ends, sensations and thoughts arise uninvited. When no longer emphasizing tranquil and happy feelings, you can experience the present moment with an awareness that is vast and holds all things. Be aware of the flow of experiences with a mind that is balanced in the midst of it all.

The powerful energy accumulated through jhāna can meet any experience without losing equipoise. Be careful not to squander this concentrated energy. The momentum of attention as you emerge from absorption can be very strong. Channel this energy toward insight. Don't let it scatter. These initial post-jhāna moments may be disconcerting or invigorating. It matters little whether the perceptions are calming or agitating. As you encounter the world of sensory experience, examine that contact. The mind influenced by jhāna might be bold, curious, and fresh, or cautious, contented, and delicate. Respect the depth of absorption; take the transition slowly and gently. Feel your way into a mindful encounter with the dynamic world without force.

If you have been practicing with determining the time of absorption before entering each jhāna, you may well find that the jhāna automatically crumbles when the time period is reached. To exit jhāna, there is no need to actively abolish the jhāna state. Ceasing to hold the factors in one-pointed awareness is usually sufficient. If you need a stronger demarcation upon exiting, establish a resolve such as "May I abide in full awareness," "May jhāna dissolve and I see all things clearly," or "May I rest in open clear awareness of what actually occurs." Or, make a mental gesture of opening the mind as you would open your fist.

Let go of expectations that something marvelous will happen when jhāna dissolves. Don't be too disappointed if the world is just as wacky, painful, and imperfect as when you entered absorption. Of course it is! An explosive destruction of all defilements the moment you exit jhāna is unlikely to happen. More typically the quiet mind simply knows ordinary experience as it is. Nothing fancy. Awareness meets whatever is arising without craving for more or less. Experiences remain ordinary. It is the absence of agitation and discontent that is extraordinary.

Examine how the mind emerges and meets the phenomenal world. Notice how the mind naturally apprehends perceptions. Do experiences of seeing, hearing, smelling, thinking, and feeling construct a sense of becoming someone through sensory encounters? Are experiences possessed as *mine*?

Whatever you notice is OK; you needn't manipulate your experiences to gain preferred perceptions or feelings. Just bring enough interest to notice what this mind is doing and how it functions. Relax in full wakefulness; observe without trying to control phenomena. Trust the strength of samādhi and have faith in your aspiration to awaken. There are no preconceptions to impose upon the experience of the present moment.

Everything is known as it really is: empty ephemeral phenomena arising out of nothing and passing away into nothing, leaving no litter, no trail, no trace. What an amazing world! And it is continuously revealed to anyone ready to behold it. If mind attends to the various changing objects in the sensory field such as sounds and sights—fine. If mind attends to perceptual functions such as how things are known—fine. If it attends to jhāna factors such as the diminishing or intensification of sukha or upekkha—fine. If it recognizes habitual dynamics, such as self-grasping or what the Buddha calls "mine-making" and "I-making"—fine. If it rests in a deeply profound release of all suffering—fine.

More on the Insight Phase of Practice

During the insight phase of practice, you may employ a variety of vipassanā methods:

You may observe the rise and fall of sensations, feelings, and thoughts whenever they occur.

You may systematically move attention through the body, from the top of the head to the tip of the toes.

You may shift the attention between various touch points in the body.

You may rest with an open awareness of any present perception.

You may incline toward reflection.

You may contemplate death, observe the fluctuations of pleasant and unpleasant experiences, or contemplate how the mind is affected by moods, states, and dispositions.

You may focus on the apparent construction of self.

You may develop any of the many vipassanā techniques and satipaṭṭhāna practice preserved by Buddhist tradition.

You may systematically discern and analyze the conditions of matter and mind.

Or you may abide, simply noticing when there is clinging and when there is no clinging.

There is no single right way to experience the truth of the present. Some practitioners will be inspired to employ traditional systematic exercises; others may be inclined toward less structured or intuitive explorations. Trust the process to unfold according to the wholesome force of your intention. When the mind is not running away with thoughts and sense impressions, it is open to insight. Allow this potential for insight to manifest, supported by curiosity and direct observation of reality, with or without the superstructure of formal vipassanā techniques.

Simply observe the moment. Reflect: *Did you "organize" the present moment like this; did you somehow cause it to be this way?* When coming out of jhāna, you may be inundated with sudden bursts of sensations. Pīti and sukha may flood the body with pulsing sensations. In sharp contrast to the seclusion of jhāna, there may be a multitude of haphazard phenomena occurring at every sense door—birds twittering, dogs barking, heat, the tingling contact of hands, thoughts arising. Bare contact with sensory life can spark the simple but profound knowledge that all this is happening without your control. It is not constructed according to your personal design. Reflect: *Since you did not organize this, maybe you don't need to resurrect habits of worry, manipulation, and judgmental comparisons that dominate most human perceptions.*

The basic perception is simply that "I" did not organize it. "I" can't control it. It is not "my" personal story, not the defining feature of "my" life. You may then wonder, What is this "I" and "mine" anyway?

Observe: *Is experience simply being known?* Or is there a secondary process of "I-making" and "mine-making" intertwined with perception? "Not-self" is not merely a Buddhist concept to understand intellectually. It must be experienced. With the stability of a concentrated mind, you will know for yourself when, how, and whether self-grasping arises in a moment of contact. You will also know when perception is free from the distortions of what we can playfully call "*selfing.*"

Wisdom and equanimity encourage acceptance through a mindful relationship with whatever is happening. Can you be present with dullness as well as with clarity? Are you interested in irritation as well as appreciation? Are both the experience of the unconcentrated mind and the concentrated mind worthy of being recognized? Mindfulness is without bias, prejudice, and preference. It readily recognizes whatever occurs. Through that total acceptance, insight into all things unfolds. Insight can quench a craving heart, as a tall glass of lemonade on a sultry summer's day quenches thirst. It is distinctly refreshing, tantalizing, exciting—tart and sweet at the same time.

Tremendous happiness can follow insight. Experiencing change without the entanglement of attachment provides a joy greater than anything tasted in jhāna. Contemplate the fading away of attachment with a relaxed smile. Allow direct insights to resonate deep within the heart.

In the quest for liberation, the transitory delights of jhāna have a practical function, but these secluded states should not be confused with enlightenment. Enlightenment is defined as the eradication of lust, hate, and delusion. When you are in the midst of sensory contact, let insight dissolve any residue of lust, anger, and confusion and radically transform your relationship to life. This is the greatest seclusion; this is the end of all suffering.

Sit in the midst of things, occupying the vantage point tradition-ally likened to a great throne that overlooks the city from a palace high up on the hill. Here, perched above the kingdom, a monarch observes all the daily functions that keep the city prosperous and safe. Assume your royal seat; observe all that occurs from this perfect vantage point. Empty experience, unpossessed and uncontrolled, appears and disappears, forms and dissolves.

Throughout this book I have referred to two practices: samādhi and vipassanā. As facets of experience, they can be distinguished but not divided.

The descriptions and instructions for meditation may produce the impression that the calm abidings of jhāna are completely separate from a mindful investigation of perception; however, samādhi and vipassanā can develop simultaneously. Insight is a part of a wise and thorough approach to jhāna practice. You cannot contemplate the impermanence of body and mind while maintaining a full absorp-tion, but you will learn a great deal about your perception while you are cultivating the conditions for jhāna. When you emerge from each absorption, you can thoroughly examine that concen-trated mind. You will increasingly find it obvious that every per-ception and experience is impermanent, conditioned, volitionally produced, and not fit to be clung to. A wise undertaking of samādhi and vipassanā will refine mindfulness, develop wisdom, and incline the mind toward letting go.

Concentration and insight are inseparably intertwined in a lib-erating path. The stability of concentration supports direct insight into the impermanent and empty nature of things. When insight arises, you will meet experience without attachment. A stable clear mind is primed to make the liberatory leap of "having made release the object."[109]

Realization occurs as an undivided and limitless expression of not clinging—including not grasping views that separate samādhi and vipassanā.

ꙅ *The Experience of Non-Clinging*

There will be times when you experience a profound letting go, when constructions of I-making, me-making, and mine-making stop. Bring to mind a time when you experienced this release and feel the peace it brought to the mind.

In a moment when you let go of some attachment or desire, examine the quality of mind that is letting go, that is not-clinging. What does the experience of non-clinging feel like?

Whenever release comes to you, don't become fascinated by methods, hold on to meditation objects, or assess your personal progress. Instead, recognize the peace of non-clinging. Insight knowledge is also impermanent and empty of self. Insight knowledge is a powerful, beautiful, and wholesome expression of wisdom—worth becoming familiar with, but not worth clinging to.

PART V

EXPERIENCING THE FORMLESS DIMENSIONS

CHAPTER 19

Without Boundaries: Exploring the Infinite

My mind then launched out upon the base of the infinity of space and became placid, settled, and liberated in it, since I saw it as peaceful.
—Aṅguttara Nikāya 9:41

THE FIRST MILESTONE in the development of jhāna occurred when you achieved the transition between the stage of access to jhāna and genuine absorption in the first jhāna, radically reorienting your consciousness from the dispersal of sensory perceptions to an internal unification. The fourth jhāna brought feeling to its culmination in the neutrality of equanimity. To explore beyond the fourth jhāna, you will need to take another quantum leap.

The four formless absorptions share two factors with the fourth jhāna: equanimity and unity of mind. The perception that characterizes each successive immaterial state, however, is more peaceful than preceding perceptions. The higher attainments are aptly described by reference to their objects: the sphere of infinite space (the fifth attainment), the sphere of infinite consciousness (the sixth attainment), the sphere of no-thingness (the seventh attainment), and the sphere of neither-perception-nor-non-perception (the eighth attainment).

Before exploring these higher states in your meditation, ask yourself: *Am I willing to abide without any reference to material forms or the senses?* If you are not sure, then stay with the fourth jhāna. It is not prudent to force the formless spheres to occur. They are delicate states that some people find unnerving or dissociating. If you have a history of mental instability, drug use, depression, anxiety disorders, hallucinations, or if the four material jhānas are difficult for you to attain, it would be wiser to concentrate on developing a stable grounding in the four jhānas, which provide an excellent and entirely sufficient basis for insight.

The formless spheres are not needed for liberating insight. In fact, many practitioners find that the lower states provide a *more* effective basis for insight. The tranquility of sustained absorption in formless spheres can inhibit investigation, a factor vital to the dynamic examinations needed in insight practice. The teachings on jhāna in the early discourses frequently culminated with insight after the fourth jhāna. Only on selective occasions did the Buddha teach disciples to explore these subtle immaterial concentration states.

Since some practitioners enter into these formless states uninformed, I have chosen to include the immaterial attainments in this book. Some practitioners will find that after the saturation of happiness and peace of the four jhānas, the mind naturally inclines toward contemplating consciousness unsupported by form.

THE SPHERE OF INFINITE SPACE

> By passing entirely beyond bodily sensation, by the disappearance of all sense of resistance, and by non-attraction to the perception of diversity, seeing that space is infinite, he reaches and remains in the sphere of infinite space.[110]

This passage is the ancient instruction for attaining the base of infinite space. This occurs as an extension of the fourth jhāna.

Absorption in the fourth jhāna leads to release of interest in diverse perceptions and allows attention to incline toward the element of boundless space. If your concentration is ripe for this experience, the attainment will occur very easily.

The *Visuddhimagga* recommends resolutely directing attention to the space left by the removal of the previous nimitta, as though one is "striking at" the sign of space with the thought of "space, space" until absorption occurs.[111]

I recommend a less elaborate approach: bare relinquishment. This simple and relatively uncontrived approach will work when the mind is well prepared. From the fourth jhāna simply relinquish all engagement with the four aspects of perception listed in the Buddha's instruction: bodily sensations, resistance, attraction to diverse perceptions, and any defining boundaries. Give your attention to whatever aspect of space you may intuit as you sense space as infinite. Relax and observe the basic aspect of space. Like a waterfall filling a pond, mind rushes in to rest in the spacious expanse.

Space has no direction—it is neither up nor down, neither in nor out. In space, there is no relationship to body or breath, no physical vibrations intrude, and conventional references are inadequate to describe a spatial field. It is a perception of the absence of matter that is unconfined and without borders. Space is not big like a sky filled with stars; it is not small like a speck of dust. It is literally a perception without references, formations, structures, distinctions, or particulars. It is without bounds. Infinite space cannot be described by its proportions, measurements, or dimensions. It is neither infinitely large nor infinitely small. Referential distinctions don't apply. Since material forms are absent, nothing exists to create diversity.

This is a direct perception of the fundamental aspect of infinite space. It is not a concept, idea, or notion of what space looks like. It is, rather, the simple and direct awareness of infinitely extensive space.

⤳ *Exploring the Space Between*

As you go about your daily activities:
Notice the space between things.
Notice the pause between breaths.
Notice the gap between thoughts.
Notice the space around the furniture in a room, around the pieces of food on a plate, or around the branches of a tree.
Rest at ease with a spacious attention.
Notice the aspect of space whenever and wherever you can.

BOUNDARIES ARE MIND-MADE

Boundaries are arbitrary mind-made distinctions. In the perception of infinite space, the mind rests in the experience of non-locatability and non-confinability: the boundaryless nature of reality.

Contemplate space in contrast to material forms: What is the separation between your hand and this book? What is the distinction between your body and the chair you sit on? Where does one end and the other begin? The perception of space invites the recognition of the absence of matter. Space delimits matter.

Relative stability or instability of the formless spheres is determined by the texture of mind in the fourth jhāna. If your glimpse of infinite space is short-lived, if thoughts interrupt the seclusion, or the attention gets drawn out by sensations (even cooperative thoughts such as a thought about the meditation experience or mundane sensations related to the breath), then you have not completely turned away from the sensory sphere. You have not set aside fully your attraction to diverse worldly perceptions. Since there is nothing

---

⌒ *For Reflection*

In quiet moments after the concentrated meditation has ended, ask yourself:

What is the mind?

What are its boundaries, color, shape, location?

If you cannot find a location for mind, does this affect how you might conventionally refer to mind as a thing that you own?

---

to "do" in the formless realms, if you aspire to greater stability, the work must be done from the lower jhānas. Intensify the equanimity and single-pointed focus in the fourth jhāna, strengthen mindfulness and equanimity while engaged in everyday tasks, develop a dispassionate attitude toward material forms encountered during daily routines.

Attainment of these formless perceptions unleashes incredible energy. When the perception of form is released, tiredness vanishes; sleep might feel impossible. There is no agitation in either body or mind, yet one feels plugged into an unfathomable source of energy. Even though you may not feel the physical need to sleep, don't be fooled! The intensity of this energy demands that you care wisely for yourself. Everyone needs sleep to preserve sanity, maintain health, and sustain mental balance. You may need to moderate the amount of time spent in formless states so that sleepless periods are not repeated or prolonged.

Undertaking an exploration of the formless dimensions of consciousness is a delicate investigation, best done with wisdom, with a qualified teacher as guide, and in the protected conditions of retreat. If you are accessing formless perceptions, your consciousness is pretty far outside the ordinary framework of conventional mental functioning. Although this extreme saturation in peaceful and happy abidings may produce a sense of being invincible, you may not be as balanced as you think.

EXPLORATIONS OF EMERGENCE

What do you do when emerging from the stability of the base of infinite space? You might want to return to the fourth jhāna for a while, emerge from absorption, and then practice insight based on fourth jhāna concentration. Shift back and forth between the perception of space and the equanimity of the fourth jhāna highlighting the object of perception that changes between these two levels. You might sense the experience of equanimity in a new way. You might experience sensory contacts from a fresh perspective.

Notice how your experience of the base of infinite space affects perceptions subsequent to that attainment. Sometimes you will notice more by moving through the jhānas in reverse order rather than in ascending order. When you move in reverse order, the lower jhānas' sense of density enhances your dispassion. The pleasant qualities that previously seemed so divine can appear almost repulsive when viewed from the perspective of formless perceptions. This viewpoint can dislodge residual enchantment with pleasure and unbind the heart from attachment to conditioned forms. You will come to know that things are fundamentally unsatisfactory, even the ease of equanimity.

When even the exquisite states of jhāna feel coarse and unsatisfying, why would one cling to anything in this world? Again and again you will see there is no lasting happiness to be found through things, objects, ideas, and perceptions.

If you still haven't attained this insight, take the system to the next level. Perhaps the next perspective will convince you that nothing is worth clinging to. Although practice systems can become

---

⌐ *For Reflection*

From the perspective of infinite space what can be relinquished?

In what ways are you identified with form?

Is there attachment to your body, appearance, health, or particular thoughts?

Consider: Are you really those thoughts? Are you really this body? Can you be limited to those frameworks of conceiving?

---

exceedingly reified, the lesson to be learned is always the same: don't attach to anything!

THE SPHERE OF INFINITE CONSCIOUSNESS

The next stage does not add anything to experience; it would be absurd to even attempt to "add something" to space. What does occur is shedding the perception of infinite space. Then, what is left to perceive?—the consciousness that was aware of infinite space. You turn attention around to perceive that which knows space. Now infinite consciousness becomes the base through which the mind unifies. This consciousness is a brilliant expanse of unbroken knowing.

The transition from the perception of infinite space to the perception of infinite consciousness entails a miniscule shift. No strain is involved, no effort to push space away, no attempt to grasp hold of consciousness. You simply become aware of the basic lucid cognizant quality of mind. The traditional phrasing is: "By passing entirely beyond the sphere of infinite space, seeing that consciousness is infinite, [one] reaches and remains in the sphere of infinite consciousness."[112]

This shift reveals an awareness that is utterly radiant and without bounds. Unrestricted lucidity has no fixed dimensions. Luminous clarity abides undefined by space and time, unrestrained by particular objects. In this state, the mind is exceptionally buoyant, light, and bright. Energy continues to seem unlimited when the mind is not heedlessly consumed by binding consciousness to diverse objects of perception. There is enormous comfort in this undistracted state. Mind is quiet and content within itself. There is no agitation, nothing to resist, nothing to gain in this extraordinarily energized and potent state of complete relaxation. With nothing to disturb your ease of concentration, you can remain absorbed for many hours at a time.

Formless dimensions are too subtle to permit active investigation. Consequently, the intentional movement between these states provides conditions for contrast, for moments of reflection that can reveal the characteristics of each distinct state, and for potentially liberating insights into the nature of mind.

Rather than merely sustain long absorptions with the subtle perception of infinite consciousness, periodically move through the lower states in reverse order. Your mind may bounce up again into formless spheres, buoyant like a helium balloon, but coax it to return periodically to the first four jhānas. Let the experience mature by integrating your awareness of both form and the absence of form. Know consciousness in its infinite, unbounded, and unlimited aspect, and recognize how consciousness functions when engaging with mundane sensory perceptions and feelings.

Like the perception of infinite space, infinite consciousness is neither sweepingly large and expanded nor infinitesimally small and contained. It is not measurable or definable. Without boundaries, it cannot be condensed or disturbed. Affected by this bare perception of infinite consciousness, the texture of awareness grows very soft, open, allowing, and transparent.

After emerging from this absorption, you may find that sights, sounds, thoughts, and sensations come and go of their own accord with little or no interference from your mind. You might taste a prolonged experience of clarity without a fixed standpoint for perception; knowing is activated without grasping particular things that are known.

After some time, however, sensory impact may stimulate familiar attachments, personal views, and comparisons. This is an opportune time for contemplating perception. The perspective gained by experiencing the infinity of consciousness is a wonderful platform for calling into question the habitual association of consciousness with its objects.

When grasped by the mind, perceptions can become the basis for constructing a sense of being yourself. Not only is the external experience grasped, but an internal attachment to the one who experiences is formed. Habits of self-grasping construct a personal standpoint. This is the habit of the mind. Remembering the infinitude of consciousness, you will recognize that this formation of self-grasping is unnecessary, and then you will relax. Clinging is not inherent to perception. Self-grasping is merely a superfluous function, utterly trivial from the perspective of the infinite evenness of consciousness.

There is much to learn through these rare perceptions. Touching an infinite capacity of awareness casts age-old habits of identification in a new light. Let yourself laugh at the amazing absurdity of a mind that tries in vain to cling. From the perspective of infinite consciousness, grasping things is ludicrous. Why would a mind without bounds, vast beyond the concept of vastness, ever reduce itself to identification? Why would consciousness restrict itself to the knowledge of some particular thing?

Infinite consciousness is a profound perception. Although the experience is softer and more subtle than the knowing of space, it is not entirely peaceful. When you recognize the conditioned aspect of the base of infinite consciousness, you will realize how to move beyond its limitations. The way into the next state will be spontaneously apparent.

⤳ *For Reflection*

Is knowing defined by what is known?

Can you know only objects or is there a knowing beyond objects?

What is the nature of knowing?

When the subtle veil of infinite consciousness lifts, no-thingness is instantly exposed.

THE SPHERE OF NO-THINGNESS

To examine the next stage of concentration, drop the perception of infinite consciousness and notice what is left. Nothing remains! Directly perceive the absence of things. You will notice that perception is still functioning; however, it is not meeting any particular object. To describe the base of no-thingness, the *Visuddhimagga* uses the illustration of entering a hall where everyone has left. Upon entering the hall, you perceive that there is nothing there. You do not think about the people who have left. Rather, you experience a clear steady perception of the absence of things. The concept of absence will become the subtle object for attention.

As the Buddha said,

> By passing entirely beyond the sphere of infinite consciousness, seeing that there is no thing, [one] reaches and remains in the sphere of no-thingness, and [one] becomes one who is conscious of this true but subtle perception of the sphere of no-thingness.[113]

Mind does not need to be defined by things. In the seventh absorption state there is no thing to grasp, no thing to be, no place for consciousness to land. From this perspective of voidness, also called a perception of emptiness, the coarse desire for sensory pleasure is incomprehensible. The perception of emptiness can shatter a lifetime of preoccupation with protecting our roles, reputations, successes, and possessions. What really matters in life? Exploring the empty essence of mind puts one face to face with the barest of facts. In the face of no-thing, what matters?

Contemplate this question, letting it mature in your heart with unlimited love and compassion. Align your life with the knowledge of what is of deepest significance. Discover what can hold its value in the face of the extraordinary clarity of emptiness. When you are motivated by wisdom, compassion, profound love, or a commitment to awakening, steadfast courage will be unstoppable. Supported by the unshakable quality of emptiness, you will be undeterred by the transient hardships that compassionate service often requires. Graced with knowledge of the true nature of things and no-things, we find our relationship to everything is clarified. The fundamental misperception of things that creates the illusion of *I*, *me*, and *mine* is unraveled. Nothing exists with which to identify a self-concept. Nothing exists to claim as mine.

THE SPHERE OF NEITHER-PERCEPTION-NOR-NON-PERCEPTION

To explore samādhi further, turn the attention away from the absence of things and allow it to alight on that which took no-thingness as its object. From the knowing of no-thingness, turn mindfulness back on that which was aware of no-thing. This requires that you withdraw from the *movement of perceiving*.

Imagine this as the function of perception folding back into itself without turning itself into another object of perception. The *Visuddhimagga* suggests one use the thought "peaceful, peaceful" to strike at the "nonexistence of no-thingness." Unruffled awareness pervades the dimensionless knowledge of this attainment. The mind stills, imbued with trust, utterly relaxed and unmoved.

In this attainment, the absence of things is not perceived. Awareness is clear and steady, but you cannot say what the steadiness is fixed upon. It is a state of deep stillness, completely free of elaboration. It is even more removed from the ability to make intentional effort than previous levels of absorption. Here most mental functions rest in abeyance.

This sphere of neither-perception-nor-non-perception is referred to as *not non-perception*, because you *can* recognize it. It is referred to as *not-perception*, because you *can't* recognize anything about it. Hence a state that is a perfection of simplicity has gained a rather long and awkward name.

This state of neither-perception-nor-non-perception is, for obvious reasons, difficult to describe. Although there is little that can be "known" about it, it creates a profoundly smooth texture in the mind. The general experience is one of incredible softness of mind. The mind simply rests, soft and stable, simple and quiet. There is absolutely nothing to do in it. In fact any activation of intention, feeling, resolve, or mental activity abruptly ends the absorption. Nothing is there to relax into or let go of, so even the subtle intention of release has no merit. Only a residue of mental factors is present, and this is in a partially dormant condition. You will know the attainment and its effects upon consciousness by means of reflection after emerging from the sustained perception.

Two traditional images try to describe the subtlety of this state. The first image is of a bowl with a residue of oil in it:

An attendant wants to serve his master some rice gruel. He tells the Master, "I have brought rice gruel, but your bowl has oil in it."

The Master replies, "Go get that other bowl and pour the oil into it, so this bowl can be used to serve the gruel."

The attendant responds, "There is no oil to pour out."[114]

This is the analogy for the base of neither-perception-nor-non-perception. Just as there is neither oil nor non-oil, but a residue of oil remains, so it is with the base of neither-perception-nor-non-perception: perception is not engaged by taking up objects, and yet perception is not absent. There is a residue of the functions of feeling, perception, mental formations, and consciousness; however, all are temporarily dormant.

The *Visuddhimagga*'s second example uses water as the metaphor:

A novice and an elder monk who is nearly blind are traveling between villages. The novice sees water on the road ahead and says to the elder, "There is water ahead sir, get out your sandals."

The elder responds, "Good, let us take a bath. Where is the towel?"

The novice responds, "There is no water for bathing."[115]

The illustration of the presence of water that is not usable tries to describe the residue of formations that are suspended and inactive. Perception is arrested in a state in which it cannot perform its function.

If you cannot accomplish anything, you might wonder: Of what use is attaining the sphere of neither-perception-nor-non-perception? The base of nothingness is actually considered the supreme base for insight. The base of neither-perception-nor-non-perception is too subtle to use as a ground for direct insight. One must emerge from this absorption, then turn the attention back in a reflective process to comprehend that it, too, is conditioned and volitionally produced. So why bother to develop it?

By virtue of its greater degree of peacefulness, absorption in the base of neither-perception-nor-non-perception will provide a dispassionate view toward the perception of no-thingness. The exquisitely pervasive peacefulness of the sphere of neither-perception-nor-non-perception naturally ends any residual attachment to the previous attainment of the sphere of no-thingness. There is no direct defect in the base of neither-perception-nor-non-perception to contemplate, except that you can't stay there, because it is conditioned and volitionally produced.

Otherwise it might be utter perfection.

THE CESSATION OF PERCEPTION AND FEELING

Most references in the early discourses to deep concentration include only the four jhānas. In some, however, all eight attainments are elaborated: the four material jhānas and the four formless perceptions. In a few discourses, a ninth state is presented: the cessation of perception and feeling. It is the final attainment in the sequential distilling of mind and might be understood as the crowning achievement of the samādhi sequence. The discourses report that upon emerging from this cessation attainment and seeing it with wisdom, the mind is liberated from all the taints.

Venerable Sāriputta's experience illustrates this as follows:

> Again, bhikkhus, by completely surmounting the base of neither-perception-nor-non-perception, Sāriputta entered upon and abided in the cessation of perception and feeling. And his taints were destroyed by his seeing with wisdom.
>
> He emerged mindful from that attainment. Having done so, he recalled the past states, which had ceased and changed, thus: "So indeed, these states, not having been, come into being, having been, they vanish." Regarding those states, he abided unattracted, unrepelled, independent, detached, free, dissociated, with a mind rid of barriers. He understood: "There is no escape beyond." And with the cultivation of that attainment, he confirmed that there is not.[116]

This description treats the cessation of perception and feeling like the absorptions, as a temporary state that is attained through the relinquishment of previous states, and suggests that it can be used as a basis for insight through reflection.

For the adventurous, the *Visuddhimagga* suggests a simple method for entering this attainment. It is traditionally recommended that before meditators enter this secluded state they should take precautions to protect their bodies and property from fire, robbers, and weather; invoke protection from deities; and make a clear determination regarding the time of emergence from the attainment. Then, upon emerging from the base of no-thingness, and prior to entering the base of neither-perception-nor-non-perception, they should resolve to attain cessation. In response to the resolve, consciousness will momentarily pass through the sphere of neither-perception-nor-non-perception and then perception and feeling will cease. As a samādhi attainment, the greater degree of refinement of this state can dislodge any residual attachment to the base of neither-perception-nor-non-perception; it may serve as the final purification of perception in preparation for the realization of nibbāna.

An impressive degree of insight, as well as concentration, is a prerequisite for this attainment. The Theravada tradition suggests that only a person who has reached the third stage of enlightenment by eradicating the defilements of personality view, doubt, greed, and hate is capable of attaining the cessation of perception and feeling. Due to the extreme subtlety of this state, I do not recommend striving for the cessation of perception and feeling. Instead, I recommend cultivating concentration through the eight attainments and using that concentration to support insight practices.

The cessation of perception and feeling is so refined that nothing can be perceived while in it, or about it, and yet the texts tell us that Sāriputta reflected upon it. How can "seeing with wisdom" occur, as Sāriputta described, in a state that has no perception? Freed from entanglements with feeling and perception, nothing remains to cling to. Upon emerging from the samādhi state of the cessation of perception and feeling, the mind would swiftly incline to the truly liberating cessation: the complete and final ending of craving, attachment, and suffering.

NOT A MARK OF SKILL

Meditators engaged in long-term practice may abide in these boundless dimensions fairly easily, sometimes suddenly and deeply, like sliding down a laundry chute. The mere experience of rarified states is not the mark of skill. They occur as a natural result of a momentum of concentration. When they arise, it is essential to work skillfully with them so that they mature as an attainment, not as another passing altered perception to amuse the self and add status to the spiritual persona.

Some personalities latch on to the dramatic occurrence of formless perceptions with pride, attributing significance to their practice simply because these perceptions arise. Other personalities withdraw in fear, overwhelmed by the altered state of consciousness. Some people ride into this energy in the spirit of full abandon. Some are curious, comparing the experience with what this book says on the subject. Others resist the powerful vortex of this extraordinarily empty power. Some wander, bewildered and confused by the intensity of the occurrence, intermittently drawn in by its power and uncertain whether it is a good thing to do. These differences in temperament are insignificant because all these reactions are mere superficial personality traits. Some children love to ride roller coasters; others cry. So what?

Once the perception of form has been released in the transition from the fourth jhāna to the immaterial bases, the draw can feel like a powerful vacuum pulling you into its realm. There is no particular value to being sucked in. Gravity naturally pulls all children down the playground slide; the energy of formless spheres naturally pulls the concentrated mind into its field. Skill develops through the ability to enter and exit without trouble or difficulty. The skilled practitioner should be able to emerge from absorption at any time. These states are described as "controlled perceptions" in the Buddha's discourses. They are not seductive episodes to glorify the concentrated practitioner.

Do not limit your practice to *surrendering* to these states: *examine them!* Withdraw from the stability of the attainment and then establish it again, absorb and emerge, move in and move out many times, according to your resolve. Let your resolve guide your exploration of these transitions, at your choosing. Contemplate and reflect upon the attainments. This is the work to be done regarding the formless spheres.

You can do nothing to strengthen or deepen them, but your skill and insight can still grow in proximity to this dynamic empty expanse.

DIFFICULTIES AND DANGERS OF FORMLESS DIMENSIONS

What you experience in these attainments influences your ordinary perceptions. If absorption with the formless perceptions is sustained for excessively long durations, a meditator might feel vulnerable, disoriented, easily startled, or nauseated when emerging from concentration. Normal daily tasks might seem confusing. Decision-making might become difficult. It is important to be connected with the senses and the body after emerging from absorption.

Be gentle with the transition from deep meditation to the complexity of daily tasks. Immaterial jhānas are not something to dive into right before a staff meeting at the office or before piloting an airplane or scuba diving. They are certainly not to be undertaken for frivolous recreation. If you feel vulnerable or if there is any difficulty reestablishing embodied awareness, give careful attention to how you emerge.

Come out slowly, gradually shifting sequentially through the lower jhānas, restoring perception and each mental factor one by one, until your consciousness regains its orientation to physical life. Limit the time you spend in any of the higher attainments. Develop mastery by predetermining the duration and emerging according to

> ⌒ *For Reflection*
>
> With these higher states (and indeed with any meditative attainment) you gain another perspective on reality and access a potential platform for liberating insight. After emerging from each level of concentration, activate the mind by asking yourself:
>
> What does this teach me?
>
> What does this reveal about how I live?
>
> Is this experience conditioned and subject to change?
>
> What is the significance of this experience?
>
> What does it show me about the end of suffering or the nature of mind?
>
> What is there to cling to?

your timed intention. Enjoy conscious movement practices during the day, like walking, yoga, or *qi gong*, to maintain a parallel embodied practice.

If they are balanced with mindfulness and investigation, the formless attainments can provide a fascinating and powerful view into emptiness. But, if recklessly sustained for too long, they can backfire, temporarily diminishing the meditator's capacity for investigation. For the skillful meditator, formless perceptions can provide experiential knowledge of consciousness without boundaries: an intimate realization of emptiness. Despite their conditioned and fabricated nature, these states lead to an experience of an unwavering clarity, pure like space—timeless and dimensionless.

The transformation of perception in these formless states is quite marked. Altered perception usually lingers, informing later sensory contacts. You may feel quite light, as though you are gracefully floating through your routine rather than walking. The entire visual world may appear transparent and insubstantial. Trees, buildings, traffic, people—all might appear substance-less, coexisting like an exquisitely choreographed dance. They interact but lack the density that creates conventional demarcations.

This is not a state of confusion; one clearly knows the distinction between a tree and a fire hydrant. The mind functions, intelligence operates, but consciousness is filled with an infinitely extensive radiance that pervades all perceptions. It is not helpful to try to sustain these lingering effects of formless attainments, nor to replace conventional perceptions with these "spiritually advanced" perceptions. Their value is simpler. They provide an opportunity to stop clinging to conventional perceptions. They should not lead to attachment to an altered perspective.

Just Let Go, Again

By progressively releasing, consciousness inclines toward the subtlest states. To gain access to jhāna, your consciousness had to recede from obstructive states of mind, such as desire, aversion, and restless thinking. To establish the successive jhānas you abandoned the grosser factors. The agitated movements of vitakka and vicāra were released, the excitement of rapture fell away, and the gentle pleasure of sukha diminished until you rested in the utterly still unification of mind in the fourth jhāna.

The shift from fine material jhānas to formless states required the release of binding fascination with diverse perceptions. When the perception of infinite space was dismissed, infinite consciousness shone brightly. Once dispassion toward infinite consciousness developed, no-thingness came to the fore. With the release of the perception of absence, the function of perception itself tranquilized.

You can read and comprehend descriptions of each level. But you cannot know successive levels for yourself until the previous coarser faculties fade. Although it may seem that these are things that you do, enforce, or make manifest, you do not make these states occur. Like love, they are dimensions of unwavering trust that do not obey commands.

You can't do much in any of these formless spheres of perception. You might try to "let go" but even the attempt to release is effortless. There simply is nothing to push against, nothing to resist, nothing for the effort to rub up against. Finally, humbled, you allow every concept of effort to fall away. Awareness shines with spontaneous radiance.

Relax, let the practice mature; allow it to guide you through the experience of emptiness.

This is the inevitable inclination of awareness.

CHAPTER 20
Realizing Emptiness

That should be seen as it actually is with proper wisdom thus:
"This is not mine, this I am not, this is not myself."
—Majjhima Nikāya 28:6

W HEN MAGNIFIED TO metaphysical proportions, the concept of emptiness, sometimes called "voidness," can seem bewildering—yet the *realization* of emptiness is profound in its simplicity. The realization of emptiness is a perception of pristine purity; it is neither complex nor abstract. It is a profound encounter with the nature of things.

Nothing actually exists the way we conceive of it. As the Buddha said: "In whatever way we conceive, the fact is ever other than that."[117] The failure to understand emptiness keeps people enthralled by the stories the mind fabricates as it wanders in a trance of hallucinated narratives. Reality cannot be perceived with such distortion. A concentrated mind has the strength to penetrate the layers of conceptual proliferation and allow a direct experience of reality to occur.

> ⌒ *For Reflection*
> _____
>
> What do you assume the realization of emptiness describes?
>   Is it a place? A thing? An experience?
>   Is it a fascinating attainment that will elevate your self-esteem, fix your personality quirks, and resolve personal problems?
>   Is this an experience that you fear or desire?
>   How would you recognize the experience of emptiness?
>   Why is the realization of emptiness considered a spiritual attainment?

THE THOUGHT "I AM"

Thoughts determine our personal experience of the world. Our concepts affect the way we perceive our lives. When you are mindful and bring attention directly to meet a thought, what do you find?

Meditative investigation explores, among other things, these questions: What is a thought? Does a thought have color or shape? Is it housed in a location? Does it travel a certain distance?

The greatest illusion created by the thinking mind is the concept of itself. If I asked you, "Who is thinking?" you might reply, "I am thinking." What is this "I" to whom you attribute your activities? The thought "I am" is the fundamental concept obscuring the void nature of things.

Buddhist tradition considers the thought "I am" to be the great catastrophe of birth: a birth that leads inevitably to death. Every time "I" arises in a moment of sensory contact and claims experience for itself, this birth of self recurs, caught in the cycle of dualistic formations. Without the deluding dualistic concepts of self and other, what would conceal the exquisite purity of the empty space of all phenomena? Suffering arises as we try to sustain the illusory creation of self. When we finally stop trying to maintain the illusion, the mind awakens to a knowing beyond knower and known; it opens to a timeless lucid awareness.

One of the fundamental instructions my teacher H. W. L. Poonja gave was to "follow the *I-thought* back to its source and stay there." Catch the "I-thought" and trace it to its root. Where did it arise? Where does it cease? What is its basis and support? Follow the "I-thought" back and you will rest at ease—at home. Worldly attractions may arise and pass like a magic show. The mind, without the tether of identification, however, is not allured by diverse concepts.

Mindfully observe where, when, and how a thought arises and disappears. Ponder: *What is a thought?* This inquiry need not produce specific answers. By inquiring into thought, you will recognize the patterns of illusion that have been giving credence to the formation that is conventionally assumed to be *self*. You'll discover that each distinct thought of *I*, *me*, *mine*, and *myself* is impermanent— thoughts change and end.

The Buddha declared, "Bhikkhus, I do not see even one other thing that changes so quickly as the mind. It is not easy to give a simile for how quickly the mind changes."[118] Beliefs that are constructed on rapidly changing ideas are unreliable foundations for consciousness. Anxiety proliferates when consciousness tries to rely on the unstable support of ever-changing concepts. Thinking about ourselves, we are preoccupied until death. This cycle of unrest agitates the mind and prevents concentration.

MINDFUL OF NON-CLINGING

Wisdom replaces foolish responses with considered, skillful actions. But you can go further than reconditioning your mind to respond with wisdom. It is also possible to realize a quality of wisdom

⌒ Investigating I-Making and Mine-Making

Notice in your daily activities when the constructs of I-making and mine-making form. Watch for occasions when your mind assumes possessive relationships to experiences. As you learn how identification and possessiveness operate, you will find they occur when a sensory contact is met without wise attention.

For example, when you enter a room and take a seat, consider if there is a possessive relationship to that place. Do you think of it as "my seat"? Who do you choose to sit next to and why? If there is any attachment to being the one who has a place or exists in relation to another?

When you spot your favorite tea mug on the shelf, is it an experience of simply seeing? Or is the seeing infested with mine-making?

When you feel a stinging sensation on the arm, is it a simple sensation? Or are you outraged, complaining that "a mosquito is biting me!"

When a feeling of grief sweeps over the heart, notice if there is an unadulterated wave of grief, or if the mind constructs elaborate stories based on the memories of beautiful moments shared and lost.

Is your self-image threatened when illness affects the body?

Observe when I, me, and mine form in the midst of experience, and ask yourself, "Am I this thought? Am I this feeling? Is this emotion me? Is this sensation what I am? Is it mine? Does it belong to me?"

Whenever you notice that you have identified with something, are attached to something desirable, or are withdrawing from something painful, ask yourself: "Really? Am I really this thought? Is this sensation really me? Is this tension really mine? Really, am I that?"

Noticing the fabrication of I and mine can enhance the intimate experience of seeing, hearing, smelling, tasting, touching, or thinking. It strengthens mindfulness of the encounter, free from the distorting intrusion of self concepts.

more profound than skillful manipulation of old patterns: a direct encounter with life, beyond concepts, beyond thought, beyond the personal, and beyond mind. So, how do you cross over from skillful and wise reflections on the conditioned to a realization of what is unconditioned?

When you let go of a desire or reaction and feel the peace of release, at that moment examine the quality of mind. Are you still focused on the release of an object, on the letting go, on the wise action you took? Or can you simply rest within the release of the not-clinging? Informed by wisdom, you took the appropriate action: you considered cause and effect, repeatedly reflecting on the wholesome and unwholesome roots of your endeavors. But did you stop there to marvel at how well you handled the situation? Or, in that moment of deep peace, did you look deeper? What is the nature of the experience of non-clinging itself? Look into the direct experience of liberation through non-clinging without being fascinated by methods, meditation objects, progress, or feelings. Get to know those moments free of clinging as the release that is the manifestation of wisdom.

Often the mind comes in at critical junctures and either doubts your path or claims the experience for itself. Even after a profound insight, you may find a little thought arising that clings to the

⌐ *Observing the Self-formation*

It is normal and healthy to have a sense of self—to know our values, duties, and individual roles in this world. But notice what your identity is based upon and bound to. Are there moments in your day when you sense a subtle threat to your identity? Reflect on your response to situations that disagree with your story of self.

For example, you may become aware of your identification with physical strength and health only after you are injured and discover that your pride, as well as your body, is hurt. You may notice your identification with a political party when you unconsciously make a politically oriented statement or joke assuming that everyone in the room will agree with you. You might recognize your identification with race, class, generation, or gender when you walk into a crowded room, look around for a place to sit, and don't see anyone "like me."

Witness this process of self-formation in ordinary daily activities. See if you can drop the story of self, just being with the raw, conditioned experience of the present moment—without imagining that experience is happening to a reified self. How does this change of perception affect the quality of your awareness?

skillfulness of your action or attributes significance to your experiences, turning an otherwise profound encounter with reality into just another conceptual story with a spiritual subplot. Reveling in the spiritual experience, you might think about how that profound event arose, or how lucky "I" am to have had this awakening.

At this juncture, having discovered a meditative tool to use and apply, people often want to test their new tool by advising others about how to fix their problems. Sharing your wisdom may seem generous, but it can also stop the exploration before it is complete. Subtle identification with spiritual experience keeps us grasping at the methods and techniques. Meditators can become attached to the path and stop short of the triumphant goal.

The Buddha described the dangers of self-grasping infiltrating the profound experiences of peace. He warned, "And when this venerable one regards himself thus: 'I am at peace, I have attained Nibbāna, I am without clinging,' that too is declared to be clinging."[119] Experiences of profound peace will occur in the course of a meditation practice. But the Buddha pointed the way to a liberation beyond any definable state, beyond any formation where the concept of I might arise to distort experiences through self-grasping.

Beyond the Practice

When letting go is understood as a practice that is done over time, it is seen as conditioned. The decision to let go is informed by wisdom. This act of letting go, however, is not the ultimate expression of release. Go beyond letting go. Let go of this approach too. Don't turn release into another method to cling to.

The Buddha's famous simile of the raft is one of the great illustrations of wisdom and letting go. The Buddha described the building of a raft to use to cross the river of suffering. Arriving at the other shore, one does not carry the raft on one's shoulders but leaves it on the bank and travels unburdened, liberated from all attachments, even the attachment to what helped one arrive at the destination. You must untangle and release any clinging to method, technique, rights and rituals, views, concepts, knowledge, and experience—once they have done their job.

Spiritual experiences may occur, jhāna can be attained, insights may be won, but you needn't be proud of yourself on that account. In one discourse, Sāriputta is described in discussion with the Venerable Samiddhi, whose clarity and able manner while engaging in Dhamma discussion elicited great praise from the chief disciple. The sutta ends with a wonderful reminder: Sāriputta remarks to Samiddhi, "Good, good, Samiddhi! When you were asked such questions, you answered well, but don't become conceited because of that."[120]

Attainments can easily become a basis for self-grasping with the thought, "I attained" or "I did not attain," distorting the experience and entrapping the mind yet again in the age-old pattern of self-interest. Sāriputta describes his emergence from each jhāna without any sense of *I*, *me*, or *mine* in relation to those attainments. He describes each jhāna and remarks, "Yet friend, it did not occur to me, 'I am attaining the first [second, third, etc.] jhāna,' or 'I have attained the first jhāna,' or 'I have emerged from the first jhāna.'" And Ānanda speculates, "It must be because I-making, mine-making, and the underlying tendency to conceit have been thoroughly uprooted in the Venerable Sāriputta for a long time that such thoughts did not occur to him."[121] Sāriputta had abandoned these notions of *I*, *me*, and *mine*, in relation to all things—even refined spiritual abidings. Whether you are immersed in the chaotic encounters of everyday living or in the refined absorptions of jhāna, keep a watch out for any formations of *I*, *me*, and *mine*, where you may become ensnared. These formations of self-grasping are among Māra's many baited hooks.[122]

Although on many occasions we confront obstacles, we often abide free of clinging, identification, and misperception. Experience those moments of non-clinging; they point to something beyond the repetitious practice of alternately clinging and letting go. When the mind is naturally settled in a stable and open clarity, it is ripe for contemplation. What happens, then, when you ponder what is unconditioned, uncaused, beyond cause and effect, the end of the path?

Let your love of freedom carry you into an inquiry beyond the known. It will guide you safely from the conditioned to the unconditioned, from the relative aspects of wisdom and skillful living to realizing something beyond mind, effort, and actions. The desire to be free is not the kind of desire to abandon midstream. The desire for liberation inspires the practice—and leads to the end of desire.

As H. W. L. Poonja said, "Have only one desire in your life, the desire for freedom. Only this desire will not allow any other desire to trouble you."[123]

Abiding in Voidness

There are several dialogues recorded in the early Buddhist scriptures of an awed companion exclaiming that the Buddha or his chief disciple Sāriputta exhibited a radiant glow that permeated their complexions.[124] In reply, the Buddha or Sāriputta explains that they often "abide in voidness" and that it was this abiding that produced the radiant appearance. Perception beyond mundane fixation on objects will have an effect on consciousness, mind, and body. This may manifest as the radiance depicted by artists in paintings of saints with halos, surrounded by auras, rainbows, and lights beaming in luminous glory.

Ānanda, who served as the Buddha's attendant for the last twenty-five years of the Buddha's ministry, once asked the Buddha to elaborate on the remark, "I often abide in voidness."[125] The Buddha described three general avenues into the perception of emptiness: (1) knowing things as void of what is absent; (2) knowing as present only what is there; and (3) knowing just that amount of disturbance that is actually occurring in the current conditions. This means a meditator will recognize what factors are present, what factors are absent, and accurately identify the gross factors that agitate the current state.

In a progression that parallels the development of jhāna, the Buddha described increasingly subtle experiences of emptiness,

ᕲ Self Feeds on Comparisons

Try to notice when your mind conjures up thoughts or judgments that in some way laud yourself or disparage others for an activity, ability, or personal quality. People compete around both great and trivial things, so notice how any moments of competitiveness, comparing, or criticizing arise in your mind and promote a sense of self. Look for the little comparisons you might make as you go through the day.

For example:

- Do you compare how far you bicycle each day with the distance your friend cycles and judge yourself by comparison?
- Do you praise your own intelligence, productivity, or performance at work and perhaps subtly negate the contributions of others?
- Do you stew in jealousy when a friend wins an award?
- Do you assess the worth of your spiritual life by comparing your spiritual progress to traditional stages of progress you've read about?
- Do you ever feel angry when someone achieves something you have also been striving for?
- Do you feel relieved when you hear a Dhamma teacher describing their struggles or enjoy seeing someone you respect display their failures?
- Do you feel personally wounded or bitter when someone you feel is inferior to you is chosen for a position instead of you?

Whenever you notice a pattern of comparing, competing, or criticizing, examine the way that thought fuels the construction of self. In idle moments, notice if your mind is still conjuring stories that retell events and reinforce your self-image by comparing yourself as superior, inferior, or equal to others.

beginning with the simple departure from the complexities of urban life by retreating to the forest, progressing through the stilling of conceptual proliferation and stabilizing of concentration, experiencing the formless perceptions, and finally culminating in a profound experience of emptiness.

At each level the meditator is instructed to reflect upon perception: recognize what is present in each state; recognize what is absent in each state; know each state as conditioned, impermanent and subject to cessation. This is the same process used to reflect on the defects of each jhāna. We examine every experience until we have stabilized the recognition of craving's absence.

With the undistorted knowledge that craving is absent, one is capable of realizing liberation. With this understanding comes the distinct and specific knowledge, "It is liberated." This instruction points to an interesting distinction between the absence of craving and the "positive knowledge of liberation." Direct and clear knowledge is a crucial step. Without it, our conditioned perception may think, "There is nothing here," rather than recognize the potential for freedom. Like a fish that does not know it is in the water, a mind that is often lost in concepts may fail to realize emptiness when it applies the label of emptiness or becomes satisfied with a conceptual knowledge of emptiness. The freedom inherent in emptiness may go unrecognized if we are holding ideas about emptiness or looking for an experience to attain. The subtle searching for something to happen in our meditations may cause us to miss the liberating realization of emptiness.

In this teaching on the gradual descent into voidness, the Buddha's guidance continues with indefatigable detail. The meditator is asked to recognize not only what is absent in the liberated mind (i.e., craving for sense pleasures, self-construction, and ignorance), but also what is present (i.e., "It is liberated"). The only disturbance to be found is "connected with the six sense bases, dependent on body and conditioned by life." Life continues; our senses, bodies, and minds function; only the causes of suffering have ended. This sequential reflection on what is absent and what is present, and what degree of agitation (coarse factors) remains, constitutes the structure of examination that we apply to every level along the approach to emptiness. The Buddha summarizes this progressive reflection with a simple instruction on how to realize emptiness: "Regard it as void of what is not present and understand that which is present as 'this is present.'" These instructions are not mysterious, esoteric, or confusing. As you follow the approach to jhānas presented in this book, you will reflect in the same manner upon the presence and absence of formations at every stage of concentration. Knowing what is present and absent, the heart relaxes with the deep stillness of acceptance. Non-attachment, non-struggle, and non-contention pervade both the practice of jhāna and the realization of emptiness.

The Tibetan master Dilgo Khyentse Rinpoche described all the events of life, whether pleasant or unpleasant, kind or critical, as "just the echoes of emptiness."[126] Just as there is no reason to feel elated or depressed if you shout flattery or insults at a cliff and those words are echoed back, so it is with all of our experience. All the sounds, sights, and sensations of the entire universe "are without any real essence. They are just ungraspable empty echoes."[127]

Many classic illustrations of emptiness refer to the tricks of magicians. Things seem to appear and disappear, but the magician, knowing his tricks, is not fooled by his own performance. Like the magician, we live in the world but are not fooled by it or by our own contrivances. It is possible to experience the physical senses and think with the mind and not be deceived by the antics of grasping.

There is a traditional story of a parent standing with a child under a clear night sky and pointing to the moon. If the child fixes her attention on the pointing finger (that is, the concept or practice method), she will never perceive the moon for herself. She must turn her attention away from the pointer in order to recognize the moon. This shift from fixation on the finger to a direct perception of the moon requires an act imbued with faith and curiosity. It is a movement from the known to the unknown, from the familiar to the unfamiliar.

We have refined perception through our systematic exploration of the jhānas. Now we can turn the attention away from things that are defined by form or formless perceptions to discover what is beyond this dualistic spectrum. Freedom is not found in the secluded states of absorption. The Buddha described this movement from the known to the unknown in this way:

> He considers whatever phenomena exist there pertaining to form, feeling, perception, volitional formations, and consciousness as impermanent, suffering, an illness, a boil, a dart, misery, affliction, alien, disintegrating, empty, and non-self. He turns his mind away from those phenomena and directs it to the deathless element thus: "This is peaceful, this is sublime, that is, the stilling of all activities, the relinquishing of all acquisitions, the destruction of craving, dispassion, cessation, nibbāna."[128]

Here we meet the term *deathless element*. This is not a place or a thing, but rather an experience of the end of the solidifying formations of grasping. The term describes an insight in which life is vividly apparent, but not set in opposition to decay and death.

The mind lets go of the attachment that has kept it bound to the cycles of birth, decay, and death. Once you know beyond all doubt that jhāna, although sublime, is subject to conditioning, birth, decay, and death, the mind naturally will seek another route to freedom. The method is utterly simple: turn the attention from all that is conditioned; don't grasp a concept of the deathless. This is the meaning of the metaphorical instruction to turn one's attention from the finger to the moon. Following upon relinquishment, the entire mass of conditioned perceptions may fall away, revealing the potential for a liberating recognition of the deathless element—also called an experience of emptiness.

THE LAND-FINDING CROW

As I have emphasized repeatedly, the discourses of the Buddha tell us very simply what we must do to have the experience of emptiness: don't cling.

The *Visuddhimagga* offers additional instruction in the illustration of an ocean-faring ship that keeps a land-finding crow on board.[129] Periodically the crow is released to fly free while the sailors observe the direction of its flight. If the crow does not return, the sailors assume it found land and steer the ship in the path of that crow. This analogy suggests that a meditator, in releasing consciousness from the cage of identification with mind-body processes, allows the mind to fly unburdened by desires, fears, personality formations, or concepts. This opening of the mind beyond fixation invites the realization of what is unbound—"the other shore" of the ocean of suffering.

If the mind is released from fixation but does not discover the deathless property, it returns to a state of deep equanimity, just as the land-finding crow returns to its nest on the ship until the next opportunity to fly free occurs. When your mind is very still and equanimous, release all holds. Abandon all fixation—to the subtle as well as to the gross. Then observe the flight of the mind. Let go of the pleasant absorption of jhāna and fearlessly send the mind out like a land-finding crow to discover a peace beyond contrived formations.

When you have seen the defects of conditioned reality deeply enough, your mind will let go. This release may have the gentle quality of a sparkling bubble popping, the simplicity of a clenched fist unwrapping, or the power of a home-run swing in baseball. The feeling of release may vary, yet it will be release beyond anything that we can produce through effort.

Beyond Dependence, We Meditate

The Buddha taught meditation that was not fixated on objects, not entranced by form, and not dependent on the formless perceptions. He used sensory experiences, the four jhānas, mental states, and the four formless spheres as the means to cultivate the mind; however, he cautioned that meditation is not to be bound by these.

The Buddha described meditation as a negation of all possibilities where attention might become fixated:

> He does not dwell with a mind obsessed and oppressed by ill will . . . by dullness and drowsiness . . . by restlessness and remorse . . . by doubt, and he understands as it really is the escape from arisen doubt.
>
> He does not meditate (1) in dependence on earth, (2) in dependence on water, (3) in dependence on fire, (4) in dependence on air, (5) in dependence on the base of the infinity of space, (6) in dependence on the base of the infinity of consciousness, (7) in dependence on the base of nothingness, (8) in dependence on the base of neither-perception-nor-non-perception, (9) in dependence on this world, (10) in dependence on the other world, (11) in dependence on what is seen, heard, sensed, cognized,

reached, sought after, or examined by the mind, and yet he meditates.[130]

We are freed from attachment to both form and formless perceptions, yet we still meditate. What is this meditation that is not dependent upon a meditation object and that is not defined by a posture, a perception, or a technique? What is meditation that is not limited by perception of physical or mental objects, not defined by the cultivation of spiritual factors, and not bound by space and time?

To understand it, we must consider meditation beyond the confines of disciplined practices that cultivate certain factors of mind. The Buddha's teachings lead to an experience of emptiness and the realization of liberation from fixation, not bound to concepts and conventional perceptions. It is unborn, unchanging, unfabricated, and dimensionless. It cannot be characterized as a thing, a place, or a function. The experience of emptiness is revealed when grasping has ceased and when consciousness is not reaching toward perceptions to construct a sense of "I" in relationship to mental, physical, or environmental contacts. The cessation of these formations awakens such an unwavering state of pure rest, beyond all extremes and fabrications, that it may be referred to as abiding in voidness, resting in emptiness, or the realization of the deathless.

Contemplation of emptiness requires a mind open to the simplicity of what is. Glimpses beyond conventional reality will occur during meditation. Allow even simple and ordinary perceptions of emptiness to incline your mind toward letting go.

Each day allow the release of non-clinging in little and big ways. What can you know when you stop habitually seeing the world through familiar formations of *I*, *me*, and *mine*? When you observe the insubstantial nature of things or experience the emptiness of thoughts, you are recognizing the meditator's lack of substance.

An emptiness attributed only to the phenomenal world wrongly posits an observer who is viewing the emptiness. Emptiness then becomes conceptualized and the meditator is trapped again by this reference to spiritual success. Don't get stuck holding a dualistic vision of a quiet mind that looks out on objects and sees their emptiness.

A mind that is stable and concentrated can see the emptiness of thought without being seduced by the content of the thoughts. This is one of the important advantages of samādhi: it supports the release of *all* positions of fixation—subtle or gross, internal or external.

Conceiving Thins Out

When concentration is strong, perception commonly appears altered. You may emerge from formless spheres to meander about your day seeing things rather differently. After emerging from a formless state, you may see the world as brighter, clearer, more luminous, empty, and substance-less. The density of things may seem to have evaporated. Perceiving transparency is only a conditioned altered state when attributed to the corporeal objects of the world. Such perceptions come and go with meditation, and they may or may not be of any significant benefit. This shift in perception, however, can point to another way of relating to things—a knowledge that thins the conceiving out of experience.

The activity of clinging generally creates a subtle feeling of density in the mind. Attachment is the real burden, not perception. A tree does not need to be lighter. A building does not need to sparkle. There is no reason to reduce the corporeality of the world to spiritually desirable perceptions. The specific density of worldly things is not your concern. Leave that to nature.

Ceasing to insert self into phenomenal experiences is more useful than the altered perception of jhāna. When asked, "What is the deliverance of mind through voidness?" the Venerable Sāriputta

---

⤳ *Try This: Take a Wakeful Walk*

The next time you take a walk notice whether you are aware of present-moment experience.

Bring awareness to present-moment sounds, temperature, textures, and movement.

Anytime the mind gets lost in thoughts about things that are not here and now, let go of the seduction in thought, and reconnect to just walking.

See what you might notice about the sensations of movement.

Notice the contact with the earth.

Relax into a wakeful walk.

Feel the sensations where your skin contacts clothes.

Notice the sounds and activities in the environment.

Delight in seeing something you have never noticed before.

---

taught, "Here a bhikkhu, gone to the forest or to the root of a tree or to an empty hut, reflects thus: 'This is void of a self or of what belongs to a self.' This is called the deliverance of mind through voidness."[131] Experience is distorted by the delusion of self-interest whenever a concept of self creeps into perceptions. Rather than directly perceiving the nature of life, we conceive things in relation to "me." Conceiving of things as mine, or who I am, or relating through a position of me, is the primary problematic distortion of perception.

Most people find that much of the day they are not actually aware of their direct experience, but they are distanced by layers of judgement, analysis, comparison, and personal commentary. We conceive of our experience and view ourselves within the experience, but we rarely meet experience free of this chronic distortion of conceiving of self through contacts. Quietly drop into the flow of your actual sensory experience. You can do this while you work, while you eat lunch, while you talk on the telephone, while you stretch your body, while you sweep the floor or chop vegetables. You can try this right now. Become keenly aware of present-moment experience. Notice what is actually happening rather than believe a concept about the experience. You might hear sounds, feel sensations, or notice a mood that may be affecting your perception. Drop your personal interpretations about what is happening now, and intimately wake up to reality, here and now.

LIVING WITH UNWAVERING CLARITY

The spiritual journey may not come to final completion with a single glimpse into emptiness—or it may. Either way, the Buddha instructed his disciples to continue awareness practice. The Buddha instructs Sāriputta, in the wake of sublime attainments, not to dwell on the sublime qualities of emptiness but to diligently consider the state of his mind when he walks on the path to the village.

The Buddha brings the realization of voidness down to earth. He tells Sāriputta to consider whether any desire, lust, aversion, delusion, or hate arise with regard to things seen, heard, smelled, or cognized. He instructs him to review his mind to ascertain whether there are any activities or conditions in which attachment to sensory encounters or defilements in the mind remain unabandoned. And he instructs him to review his mind for positive qualities—mindfulness, effort, investigation, rapture, tranquility, concentration, equanimity, confidence, and wisdom—to determine whether any wholesome factors are as yet uncultivated. Should he find an unwholesome factor present, he should make an effort to abandon it—but "if by reviewing he knows there was no desire . . . then he can abide happy and glad training day and night in wholesome states."[132]

If you were hoping that the experience of emptiness would bring you to a quick spiritual retirement, these teachings might disappoint you. The Buddha encouraged his disciples to continue cultivating wholesome states long after hindering forces are abandoned.

This way the mind is emptied of all greed, hatred, and delusion. It is emptied of all suffering.

⤳ *Preferring the Peaceful*

Would you rather be right or be peaceful?

Would you rather fulfill that worldly desire or be free?

When you find your mind inclining toward something unwholesome—anger, ill will, envy, sensual desire—ask yourself those two questions. By reminding yourself that you value liberation and peace more than momentary personal pleasures, you will strengthen your intention to let go of the attachment that might otherwise draw you away from wholesome states.

You can ask yourself these questions in many situations throughout your day. But it can be particularly interesting to apply them to situations of subtle discomfort or conflict with your family or friends. When you feel irritated by someone, identify the desire, opinion, or expectation underneath the annoyance, and consider whether you want to strengthen your self-position or trust in peace.

EPILOGUE
Fearless and Awake

When a bhikkhu has heard: "Nothing is worth holding to" . . . he does
not cling to anything in the world. Not clinging, he is not agitated.
Being unagitated, he personally attains nibbāna.
—Aṅguttara Nikāya 7:61

THE PRIMARY PURPOSE of undertaking any spiritual discipline is to free the mind from suffering. Although concentration brings states of pervasive bliss, liberation lies beyond
concentration. Concentration alone, regardless of the level of jhāna
that you have attained, will not uproot attachment. On the path
of awakening, a wise practitioner develops a range of practices and
meditation skills, including renunciation, balanced effort, wisdom,
virtue, mindfulness, concentration, and investigation.

Awakening will manifest in a free engagement with complex daily
responsibilities as pervasively as it does during the sublime tranquility of formal sitting meditation. The mutually supportive practices
of concentration and insight support a profound capacity to let
go—the essence of liberation. Freed from the burden of habitual
attachments, consciousness encounters the ever-changing, sometimes challenging, and sometimes exhilarating experiences of life
with a stable clarity that ultimately frees the heart of all resistance.

From a conventional perspective, experiencing the sequentially distinct levels of jhāna might appear to be a significant personal attainment. However, the accomplishment that transforms consciousness manifests as the ending of self-interest, not as attachment to individual gain. Insights of genuine worth on the spiritual path generally amplify humility rather than attainments. The further we progress in the development of mind, the less we are inclined to claim success. Each attainment is an experience of release, and progress comes through deeper abandonment. As you explore the calm abidings available to the undistracted mind, consciousness is gloriously simplified—freed of its preoccupation with personal attainment.

Belief in the significance of personal progress depends upon the delusion of a self-centered orientation. When caught in the trap of gain and loss, success and failure, we feel happy when we attain absorption and disappointed when we are distracted.

In reality, however, there is no role for "self" in spiritual attainment. The paradox consists of this: a brief glimpse into the unfathomable depths of the concentrated mind shatters personal ambition and reveals the utter impossibility of the self succeeding in the spiritual arena. Attainment in a spiritual practice is "no attainment"—a fundamentally not-personal experience of reality.

Whatever level of individual accomplishment you master in this progressive training, don't stop short of complete awakening—the release of all attachment, the ending of conceit. The primary endeavor is to free the mind—beyond perfect equanimity, beyond form and formless, beyond the conceivable and the doable, beyond all constructs of self—and beyond the blissful states of jhāna.

Shortly after meeting H. W. L. Poonja in India, he told me: "You are just a half step from liberation." That was exciting! I had traveled to India, I was committed to the spiritual path and earnestly sought enlightenment. I assumed he meant I was on the right track and very close to awakening; I felt very inspired.

One day, as I was chopping cabbage in the kitchen, it suddenly became completely obvious—liberation was *always* only one half step away. A full step involves lifting the foot, moving it forward, and placing it down. A half step would be just lifting, moving—not landing.

A full step would imply fixation—seeing a pretty scarf and growing attached to it, touching a filthy rag and reacting with disgust, mulling over an opinion that solidifies a self-image, chopping onions or lighting a candle with a view that the task *should* be performed in one particular way. Fixation can form in the perception of sensory experiences, views and opinions, self-concepts, or ways of performing tasks.

Whether through the stylized form of ritual practices, the mundane routines we perform at work, or the mental patterns we reinforce, fixation—the attachment of the mind to its perception—can take root. The very activities that reinforce fixation can be simplified. When chopping carrots, just chop the carrots, without attachment to outcome. When seeing a beautiful sight, appreciate the pleasant sight, without triggering possessiveness. When performing a function, whether lighting a candle, cleaning the toilet, articulating a perception, or answering the telephone, let the action be simple: just the action without the addition of attachment.

When I came to understand about the half step, I realized that the mind does not need to land and fixate on objects, concepts, views, or perceptions. We do not need to perpetuate attachments in order to make daily-life decisions, to function at work, to socialize in our communities, and to live a full life.

Wisdom is a much more trustworthy guide than attachment. The metaphor of the half step describes a wise and unattached movement through life. Liberation is not discovered by traversing a distance; it cannot be measured in terms of "near" or "far." Awakening is always available when the mind is not attached to experiences.

≈

The practice of jhāna requires a steady cultivation of relinquishment. From the initial endeavor to focus a distracted mind to the clarity of insight, jhāna as a basis for insight is a practice of release. Reflect upon the expressions of letting go you have developed through these concentration exercises. You have practiced letting go of distracting sounds, repetitious thoughts, habitual judgments, hindrances, and harmful impulses. You have developed skills to rest at ease when difficult emotions and physical pain occur. As the mind purifies, letting go becomes more subtle.

By cultivating and then relinquishing the jhāna factors, you fortify consciousness before liberating the mind from fascination with these sublime pleasures. The fading away of attachment to diverse perceptions permits an exploration of formless dimensions. Insight into boundless perceptions and vast emptiness transforms consciousness, freeing it from bondage to coarse temporal delights. This is the basic progression developed through deep concentration.

As you abandon each attachment, a profound event is simultaneously occurring. Each experience of letting go teaches the mind to discern and remove the fundamental patterns of craving, clinging, and identification—not merely how to resolve a particular challenge. We discover that the problem is attachment. When you find yourself struggling at home or work, consider: Where does the problem lie? What am I attached to in this situation? Where can peace be found?

Not every challenge requires an external solution. By looking into the mind, we often discover that the problem lies in attachment to a view that does not correspond to the fact of things. Attached to opinion, preference, or fantasy, we suffer. Through sequentially refined experiences, the practitioner of jhāna as the basis for insight learns to identify states of subtle fixation, clinging, and attachment, and discovers that clarity frees the mind from attachment.

◈

More important than the step that takes you into jhāna is the step that takes you out again. How do you emerge to live your life? Can you engage at home and at work without the tension of grasping?

Ideally, jhāna practice will develop calmness, clarity, equanimity, joy, letting go, and wisdom that you can apply to the more chaotic activities of life: cooking, working, planning, cleaning the house, engaging in conversations, balancing your accounts, raising your children, living with pain or illness. The important skill to develop is not the capacity to attain deep absorption but rather the ability to abide undistracted and unattached in diverse fields of life.

The qualities developed during jhāna will enable you to encounter life with the confidence to open to the truth of things without attachment. You can let the world be as it is, active or still, quiet or noisy. A liberated mind is equally at rest in the dynamic interplay of perception, feeling, and thinking, in relationships, love, and work, as it is in the silent abiding of the jhānas. You will discover a quality of presence that is undisturbed by your daily responsibilities and social interactions.

◈

My grandmother was eighty-six years old when she had a heart attack and was admitted to a local hospital. In the intensive care unit her heart stopped several times, but she was resuscitated each time. She was dying; however, the attempts to keep her alive continued until we met in a family-doctor conference and made the decision to not resuscitate. With nothing left to do, nothing to accomplish, produce, or attain, others went home. I stayed by her bedside and sat with my Grammy for the remaining hour of her life. The struggle had ended. This was a time to be present, steady, and connected to the profundity of a life ending.

Concentration supports the capacity to remain present—a stability that is not blind to the painful moments of life. In fact, by remaining undistracted we are connected with the difficult truth of things. Undistracted attention does not require the secluded states of absorption. Open to the difficult and beautiful moments of life, we find peace in the fact of things. We are fearless and awake.

Although we may practice for some time in seclusion to develop our meditative skills, concentration brings forth a profoundly intimate connection with existence. Paradoxically, jhāna is cultivated in seclusion, yet this practice reveals intimacy and deep connection with life. Feelings of separation and alienation are impossible to sustain in the purity of undistracted presence.

Steadied by jhāna we know the profound peace of living free from all clinging.

Acknowledgments

T HIS BOOK EMERGED PRIMARILY from my personal experience during a ten-month meditation retreat in 2004 at the Forest Refuge at the Insight Meditation Society in Barre, Massachusetts. There is, however, little in this book that can be credited only to me. The lessons, stories, techniques, and teachings contained in this book are one reflection of a lineage of generosity that extends beyond my personal exploration. The contents reflect the influence of many teachers who have shared their wisdom and guided me through difficult lessons as I struggled to develop my mind and understand the nature of things. Most notably, Christopher Titmuss's unwavering encouragement over many years has challenged me to trust the liberating potential of the Buddha's teachings, even when it feels inefficient, inconvenient, and unpopular to do so. My guru, the late H. W. L. Poonja, revealed a depth of clarity, timeless and pure. Although nearly a decade has passed since his death, he continues to serve as my compass to truth. I have great appreciation for the dedication of the many teachers at the Forest Refuge who guided me during fourteen months of jhāna-based practice, especially Myoshin Kelley, Joseph Goldstein, Amita Amy Schmidt, Sarah Doering, Michelle McDonald, Venerable Pa Auk Sayadaw, and Venerable U Jagara. I am grateful to all my teachers, each of whom offered inspiration, insight, and encouragement that kept both my practice and this book developing during the years of its formation.

I am grateful to the many people whose generosity made it possible to spend a year in silence. The support of so many friends and students provided a wellspring of energy that carried me through the more demanding moments of retreat and sustained me through many drafts of this book.

I am grateful to the many friends and students who encouraged me to communicate my inner meditative experience in the form of this practical manual and then gave their time and talents to revise and refine each chapter. This book could not have taken shape without their thoughtful reflections, editorial contributions, and dedication.

I am especially grateful to the team at Wisdom Publications for their enthusiasm for this project and to the skilled editors, Josh Bartok, Barry Boyce, and Laura Cunningham, who shaped each edition of *Focused and Fearless*.

And finally, the truly essential and pervasive support may be the most difficult to distinguish. The love of my family is present as a backdrop to who I am and what I do in the world. My mother, Elizabeth, my sister, Lisa, and my brother, Philip, have given me the greatest of all forms of support—their unfaltering trust, interest, and love. Even when my explorations have drawn me to unfamiliar religions across the globe or separated me through prolonged periods of silent retreat, I have felt the presence of my family's unlimited love. This is a treasure and blessing that I cannot measure or repay.

Notes

Introduction: From Focused Concentration to Fearless Awakening

1. M. 36:31–37
2. Alara Kalama instructed the Buddha through the seventh level of absorption, and Uddaka Ramaputta instructed him through the eighth level (M. 26). Upon completing his studies, the Buddha realized that he had mastered all that his teachers could teach. Disappointed that these attainments did not bring his mind "to peace, to direct knowledge, to enlightenment, to Nibbāna" (M. 26:15) but only to a temporary

abiding, Siddhartha Gotama left the communities of these great teachers and undertook years of austerity practice.

3. A. 5:176
4. S. 35:118

Chapter 1: Cultivating the Focused Mind

5. A. 3:101
6. S. 48:10

Chapter 2: The Joy of Seclusion

7. This formulaic reference to jhāna is repeated in many discourses. See M. 66:19–21 as an example.
8. Dhp. verse 290
9. S. 1. note #525
10. M. 27:17; M. 39:12; M. 51:18; M. 107:8; M. 125:20
11. S. 22:88
12. S. 35:63
13. H.W.L. Poonja, *The Truth Is* (Lucknow, India, 1995).
14. S. 21:10
15. Ud. 1:10, from *The Island: An Anthology of the Buddha's Teachings on Nibbāna*, by Ajahn Pasanno and Ajahn Amaro.
16. Ud. 8:1, Bhikkhu Ñāṇamoli, *Life of the Buddha According to the Pāli Canon*, 3rd ed. (Kandy, Sri Lanka: Buddhist Publications Society, 1992).

Chapter 3: Happiness

17. A. 6:55
18. Vism. xii:60–66
19. Ud. 3:2
20. M. 89:12
21. S. 36:19
22. D. 21
23. S. 36:19
24. S. 36:19
25. Sn. verse 61
26. M. 10:32
27. The perceptions that occur in the fifth, sixth, seventh, and eighth levels of attainment are void of any attention to form and feelings of pleasure or pain. These states are so refined that the Buddha sometimes described them as "peaceful abidings" rather than "pleasant abidings." M. 8:2–9
28. M. 59:16

Chapter 4: Equanimity

29. Adapted from the translation of the Commentary to the Dhammapada verses 227–230 by E. W. Burlingame in *Buddhist Legends*, first
published 1921.

Chapter 5: The Wisdom of Letting Go

30. Joseph Goldstein
31. M. 37
32. M. 37:8
33. M. 66
34. M. 66:17
35. M. 66
36. M. 22:40
37. S. 36:12(2)
38. S. 36:6
39. S. 36:6

Chapter 6: Dynamics of Emotion

40. A. 4:117
41. A. 4:164
42. S. 35:95. The same progression is repeated regarding each of the six
senses (eye, ear, nose, tongue, body, and mind).
43. S. 36:6
44. S. 36:6
45. M. 36:32
46. M. 36:30
47. D. 2:75
48. M. 36:35–37
49. S. 36:14(4):

> Bhikkhus, suppose there is a guest house. People come from
> the east, west, north, and south and lodge there; khattiyas,
> brahmins, vessas, and suddas come and lodge there. So too,
> bhikkhus, various feelings arise in this body: pleasant feeling
> arises, painful feeling arises, neither-painful-nor-pleasant feel-
> ing arises; carnal pleasant feeling arises; carnal painful feeling
> arises; carnal neither-painful-nor-pleasant feeling arises; spiri-
> tual pleasant feeling arises; spiritual painful feeling arises; spiri-
> tual neither-painful-nor-pleasant feeling arises.

Chapter 7: Effort, Ease, and Intention

50. S. 6:15(5); D. 16
51. M. 19
52. M. 19
53. A. 6:55
54. S. 1:1
55. M. 78
56. A. 6:63
57. M. 19
58. M. 19
59. M. 53:19; M. 16:27
60. M. 4:32

Chapter 8: Calming the Restless Mind

61. A. 10:60
62. Vicki Mackenzie, *Cave in the Snow: Tenzin Palmo's Quest for Enlightenment* (New York: Bloomsbury Press, 1999), 170.
63. It. 94; M. 138
64. M. 138
65. M. 138
66. A. 3:100

Chapter 9: Happiness and the Five Factors of Absorption

67. Sn. verses 436–38. Traditionally Māra is said to be accompanied by ten armies. His ten primary obstructive forces include (1) sense desire, (2) discontent, (3) hunger and thirst, (4) craving, (5) lethargy and drowsiness, (6) cowardice, (7) uncertainty, (8) distraction and obstinacy, (9) gain, praise, honor, and undeserved fame, and (10) the extolling of oneself while disparaging others.
68. S. 5:5, verses 532–535
69. S. 4:22, verse 489
70. M. 151
71. Vism. viii:200
72. S. 4:20, verse 486–487:

> If there were a mountain made of gold,
> Made entirely of solid gold,
> Not double this would suffice for one:
> Having known this, fare evenly.

How could a person incline to sensual pleasures
Who has seen the source whence suffering springs?
Having known acquisitions as a tie in the world,
A person should train for its removal.

73. M. 111

Chapter 10: Access to Absorption: At the Threshold of Peace

74. D. 2:75

Chapter 11: Fearless Abidings—The First Jhāna

75. D. 9:9–10
76. D. 2:76
77. D. 2:75
78. M. 111; M. 43
79. Vism.
80. M. 52

Chapter 12: Drenched in Delight—The Second Jhāna

81. D. 2:77
82. D. 2:78
83. S. 28:2

Chapter 13: Absorbed in Joy—The Third Jhāna

84. D. 2:80

Chapter 14: Radiant Calm—The Fourth Jhāna

85. D. 2:82
86. S. 35:130
87. A. 3:101

Chapter 15: How Deep Is Deep Enough?

88. Leigh Braisington is an American Dharma teacher who has tirelessly brought jhāna into the mainstream of vipassanā practice. He generously shared numerous stories and examples that helped to clarify these states and offered a thoughtful reading of this manuscript.

89. A. 4:77:

> Bhikkhus, there are these four inconceivable matters that one
> should not try to conceive; one who tries to conceive them
> would reap either madness or frustration. What four? (1) The
> domain of the Buddhas.... (2) The domain of one in jhāna....
> (3) The result of kamma.... (4) Speculation about the world....

90. D. 16:4.27–33
91. Ud. 4:4
92. A. 9:35
93. M. 53:18

Chapter 17: Three Doorways to Insight

94. Idries Shah, *The Pleasantries of the Incredible Mulla Nasrudin* (New
    York: E.P. Dutton, 1971), 22.
95. S. 35:232; S. 35:233; S. 41:1
96. S 2:26
97. M. 102:25:

> This supreme state of sublime peace has been discovered by the
> Tathāgata, that is, liberation through not clinging, by under-
> standing as they actually are the origination, the disappearance,
> the gratification, the danger, and the escape in the case of the six
> bases of contact. Bhikkhus, that is the supreme state of sublime
> peace, discovered by the Tathāgata, that is, liberation through
> not clinging.

98. S. 35:99–100; S. 35:160–161; S. 22:5–6; S. 56:1–2
99. Vism. xii:14
100. Three discourses that use the analogy of purification of gold: A. 3:101;
     A. 3:102; S. 46:33.
101. D. 2:97
102. M. 106:11
103. M. 106:12
104. M. 66:26–34
105. S. 35:74
106. S. 35:162–164
107. S. 35:101

Chapter 18: A New Way of Seeing

108. A. 9:36
109. S. 48:9; S. 48:10, note #194

Chapter 19: Without Boundaries: Exploring the Infinite

110. D. 9:14
111. Vism. x:9
112. D. 9:15
113. D. 9:16
114. Vism. x:51
115. Vism. x:54
116. M. iii:19–20

Chapter 20: Realizing Emptiness

117. M. 113
118. A. 1:48
119. M. 102:24
120. A. 9:14
121. S. 28
122. M. 106:2; Sn. verse 61; S. 35:230
123. From author's personal notes.
124. M. 151
125. M. 121
126. Dilgo Khyentse Rinpoche, *Heart Treasure of the Enlightened Ones* (Boston: Shambhala Publications, 1992), 43.
127. Ibid.
128. A. 9:36; M. 64
129. Vism. xxi:65
130. A. 11:9
131. M. 43:33
132. M. 151

Bibliography

PRIMARY SOURCES

Bodhi, Bhikkhu, trans. *The Connected Discourses of the Buddha: A Translation of the Saṃyutta Nikāya*. Boston: Wisdom Publications, 2000.

Bodhi, Bhikkhu, trans. *The Numerical Discourses of the Buddha: A Translation of the Aṅguttara Nikāya*. Boston: Wisdom Publications, 2012.

Bodhi, Bhikkhu, trans. *The Suttanipāta: An Ancient Collection of the Buddha's Discourses, Together with Its Commentaries*. Boston: Wisdom Publications, 2017.

Fronsdal, Gil. *The Dhammapada: A New Translation of the Buddhist Classic*. Boston: Shambhala Publications, 2005.

Ireland, John D., trans. *The Udāna and the Itivuttaka: Inspired Utterances of the Buddha and The Buddha's Sayings*. Kandy, Sri Lanka: Buddhist Publication Society, 1997.

Ñāṇamoli, Bhikkhu, trans. *The Middle Length Discourses of the Buddha: A Translation of the Majjhima Nikāya*. Edited and revised by Bhikkhu Bodhi. Boston: Wisdom Publications, 1995.

Ñāṇamoli, Bhikkhu, trans. *Visuddhimagga: The Path of Purification: The Classic Manual of Buddhist Doctrine and Meditation*. Kandy, Sri Lanka: Buddhist Publications Society, 1991.

Walshe, Maurice, trans. *The Long Discourses of the Buddha: A Translation of the Dīgha Nikāya.* Boston: Wisdom Publications, 1995. (Originally published under the title *Thus Have I Heard*, 1987.)

OTHER WORKS

Bhikkhu, Buddhadasa. *Handbook for Mankind.* Bangplad, Thailand: Dhammasapa, 1998.
Khyentse Rinpoche, Dilgo. *Heart Treasure of the Enlightened Ones.* Boston: Shambhala Publications, 1992.
Lauck, Joanne Elizabeth. *The Voice of the Infinite in the Small.* Mill Spring, NC: Swan Raven and Co., 1998.
Mackenzie, Vicki. *Cave in the Snow: Tenzin Palmo's Quest for Enlightenment.* New York: Bloomsbury Press, 1999.
Ñāṇamoli, Bhikkhu. *Life of the Buddha According to the Pāli Canon.* 3rd ed. Kandy, Sri Lanka: Buddhist Publications Society, 1992.
Pasanno, Ajahn and Ajahn Amaro. *The Island: An Anthology of the Buddha's Teachings on Nibbāna.* Redwood Valley, CA: Abahyagiri Buddhist Monastery, 2008.
Poonja, H. W. L. *The Truth Is.* Lucknow, India, 1995.
Sayadaw, Pa-Auk Tawya. *Knowing and Seeing.* Revised ed. Kuala Lumpur: WAVE Publications, 2003.
Shah, Idries. *The Pleasantries of the Incredible Mulla Nasrudin.* New York: E.P. Dutton, 1971.

Index

Page locators in **bold** indicate information that appears in boxes in the text.

192, 200
exiting, 229, 234–35
foundation for, importance of, 199
four primary levels, 16–17
happiness in, distinct feelings of, 45–46
historical controversy about, 193–95
mastering, 226
methods, variances in, 4
mindfulness supporting, 88–89
as "near to happiness," 33
perception after emerging from, 196–97
pleasure in, sequential refinement, 41
prerequisites, 33
progression, sequential, 207
and psychedelic states, distinctions
    between, 6–7
reverse order, 188, 248
strengthening, 127–28, 208
sustaining, length of, 177, 199
technique, beginning, 206
uses of term, 2
See also individual jhānas
joy
in absence of hindrances, 32–33
apart from sensory pleasure, 37
Buddha's, 39
in concentration, 11
dwelling with, 40
limitless potential for, 46
lingering, 177
of release, 120
See also pīti

K
karma (kamma), 101
kindness, **144**

L
letting go, 109
benefits of, 79
fears about, 72
going beyond, 269
importance of, 65–66
reflecting on, **73**
skill of, 68
techniques for, 110–12

willingness in, 226
See also relinquishment
liberation
beyond definition, 269
examining, 225
as half step away, 284–86
as letting go, 283
positive knowledge of, 273
potential for, 224
through non-clinging, 4, 220, 296n97
See also enlightenment
love, 43
loving kindness, **152**
lust, 74, 126, 128, 130, 156, 224

M
Majjhima Nikāya, 109, 205, 263
Malunkyaputta, 38
Māra
blindfolded, 127
obstructive forces of, 125–26, 134, 294n67
working with, **129**
meditation
dependence on, moving beyond, 277–78
emotions in, 81
intention at beginning, **106**
intention during, **102**
maturation of, 108
meditation objects, **150**
and mind, unified, 16, 47, 169
traditional, 144–45
memories, 91, 92
mental brightness, 143, 145, 149, 153
mental objects. *See* nimittas
Migajāla, 29–30
mind
and body, and mind, relationship of, 13,
    42, 101
changing of, 265
five corruptions of, 222–23 (*see also*
    hindrances)
protecting, 55–56
purified, 105
reflecting on, **247**
releasing from fixation, 276–77
stabilizing, 11

state of, reflecting on, 281
unguarded, 82–84
mindfulness, 3, 216
within absorption, 141, 230
as antidote to Māra, 126–27
of breath, **19**, **20**, **50–51**
in daily life, **35**, **43**, **60**
emerging from absorption, 166–67
feelings associated with, **178**
of feeling-tones, 74–76
in formless absorptions, **260**
in fourth jhāna, 185, 190
momentary concentration and, 14
post-jhāna, 237
as protection, 82–84, 89
recognizing, **202**
sensation and, 81
thoughts and, 13, 70
"mine-making," 233, 235, **239**, **266–67**,
270
miraculous powers, 224
monastic sangha, cheerfulness of, 39

N
Nanda, 38
Nasrudin, Mullah, 213–14
nibbāna, 84, 275, 291n2
as absence of clinging, 226, 269, 283
preparing for, 257
nimittas
in access concentration, 148–49, 150,
151, 153
in first jhāna, 156, 158
length of stability of, 166
in third jhāna, 179
See also under breath
non-attachment, **50–51**, 232, 274
non-clinging, **239**, 267, 270, 278, 283
not-self. *See* anattā (not-self)

O
obstructive mental states, 32–33, **129**
one-pointed attention. *See* ekaggatā (one-
pointed attention)
ownership, 72

P
pain
in absorption, 16
author's experiences, 55–56
characteristics of, 224
feelings tones and, 76
investigating, 78
mindfulness of, 84–85
relating to, 86–87
Pāli Canon, 1, 230
Palmo, Tenzin, 112
Pasenadi, King, 39
people, four kinds, 71
perception, 120, 271
of abandoning, 110
after emerging from infinite consciousness sphere, 251
arrested, 255
in deep absorption, 196
deep seclusion and, 200
dynamics of, 81
feelings and, 74, 77
in first jhāna, 155, 156–57
formless absorptions and, 243, 260–61,
279–81
in fourth jhāna, 184–85
grasping, **50–51**
in jhānas, controversies about, 194
meeting, **88**
mindfulness and, 82
post-jhāna, 233
reflecting on, 273
sensory orientation and, 15
in third jhāna, 175
See also sensory perception
phenomena, empty nature of, 13, 235
physical sensations, qualities and characteristics of, 167
pīti
attachment to, 118
as distraction, 157, 172
fading, 174, 261
forms of, 136–37
function, 138, 170
hindrance overcome by, 128, 130

About the Author

SHAILA CATHERINE has been leading meditation retreats worldwide since 1996, emphasizing deep concentration, jhāna, and the path of liberating insight. Shaila is the founder of Bodhi Courses, an online Dhamma classroom, and Insight Meditation South Bay, a Buddhist meditation center in Silicon Valley in California. She has practiced meditation since 1980, studied with founders of Western insight meditation centers, and accumulated more than nine years of silent retreat experience. Shaila spent most of the 1990s studying with eminent masters in India, Thailand, and Nepal. From 2006 to 2014, she practiced under the guidance of Pa-Auk Sayadaw and twice completed his rigorous training in jhāna and vipassanā. Shaila loves deep meditation and appreciates a variety of approaches to exploring, developing, and liberating the mind. She is the author of *Wisdom Wide and Deep: A Practical Handbook for Mastering Jhāna and Vipassanā* and *Beyond Distraction: Five Practical Ways to Focus the Mind.*

Shaila Catherine (www.shailacatherine.com)
Bodhi Courses (www.bodhicourses.org)
Insight Meditation South Bay (www.imsb.org)

What to Read Next from Wisdom Publications

BEYOND DISTRACTION
Five Practical Ways to Focus the Mind
Shaila Catherine

"With clarity and heart, Shaila Catherine shows us many effective ways to be free of stressful, anxious, hurt, and resentful thoughts. Her book is deep and vast, grounded in science and illuminated by Buddhist wisdom, and useful for both specific issues and a lifetime of practice."
—Rick Hanson, author of *Neurodharma*

WISDOM WIDE AND DEEP
A Practical Handbook for Mastering Jhāna and Vipassanā
Shaila Catherine
Foreword by Pa-Auk Sayadaw

"If you are interested in Dharma study, then Shaila's book belongs in your library."
—Phillip Moffitt, author of *Emotional Chaos to Clarity*

MINDFULNESS, BLISS, AND BEYOND
A Meditator's Handbook
Ajahn Brahm
Foreword by Jack Kornfield

"Riveting, rollicking, and uncompromisingly real."
—Glenn Wallis, author of *Basic Teachings of the Buddha*

BEYOND MINDFULNESS IN PLAIN ENGLISH
An Introductory Guide to Deeper States of Meditation
Bhante Gunaratana

"This book is a joy to read and a great gift to us all."
—Joseph Goldstein, author of *Mindfulness*

SAMATHA, JHANA, AND VIPASSANA
Practice at the Pa-Auk Monastery
Hyunsoo Jeon

"This book is nothing short of extraordinary. With humility, clarity, and absolute fidelity to the original teachings, Dr. Jeon shares his direct experience of advanced states of absorption, along with technical details of practice, in a manner that makes the ancient texts come alive. This book will surely inspire meditators to practice more deeply and more sincerely for years to come."
—Christopher Germer, author of *The Mindful Path to Self-Compassion*

About Wisdom Publications

Wisdom Publications is the leading publisher of classic and contemporary Buddhist books and practical works on mindfulness. To learn more about us or to explore our other books, please visit our website at wisdomexperience.org or contact us as the address below.

Wisdom Publications
132 Perry Street
New York, NY 10014 USA

We are a 501(c)(3) organization, and donations in support of our mission are tax deductible.